TUGBOATS

ILLUSTRATED

TUGBOATS
ILLUSTRATED

HISTORY · TECHNOLOGY · SEAMANSHIP

WITH DRAWINGS BY THE AUTHOR

PAUL FARRELL

W. W. NORTON & COMPANY · NEW YORK · LONDON

Independent Publishers Since 1923

For Bob and Kay

Copyright © 2016 by Paul Farrell

Printed in China
First Edition

For information about permission to reproduce selections from
this book, write to Permissions, W. W. Norton & Company, Inc.,
500 Fifth Avenue, New York, NY 10110

For information about special discounts for bulk purchases,
please contact W. W. Norton Special Sales at
specialsales@wwnorton.com or 800-233-4830

Manufacturing by RR Donnelley
Book design by John Bernstein
Production manager: Louise Mattarelliano

Library of Congress Cataloging-in-Publication Data

Names: Farrell, Paul, 1946– author.
Title: Tugboats illustrated : history, technology, seamanship /
with drawings by the author, Paul Farrell.
Description: First edition. | New York : W.W. Norton & Company,
[2016]
Identifiers: LCCN 2016020981 | ISBN 9780393069310 (hardcover)
Subjects: LCSH: Tugboats—History. | Tugboats—Pictorial works.
Classification: LCC VM464 .F37 2016 | DDC 623.82/32—dc23 LC
record available at https://lccn.loc.gov/2016020981

W. W. Norton & Company, Inc.
500 Fifth Avenue, New York, N.Y. 10110
www.wwnorton.com

W. W. Norton & Company Ltd.
Castle House, 75/76 Wells Street, London W1T 3QT

1 2 3 4 5 6 7 8 9 0

Contents

Introduction | 7

What Is It About Tugs? | 8

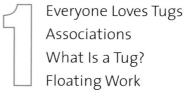

Everyone Loves Tugs
Associations
What Is a Tug?
Floating Work

Tugboat History | 18

Inventor of the Tugboat
The First Tug
Sternwheelers
Sidewheelers
From Paddlewheels to Screw Propellers
Classic American Steam Tugs
Compound Steam Engines

The Development of Modern Tugs | 32

From Steam to Diesel
The Diesel Tug
The Saga of Starting Air
Diesel-Electric Drive
Power Transmission

Tug Screws and Rudders | 42

Screw Propellers
Controllable-Pitch Propulsion
Rudders

Classic Shiphandling Methods | 50

5 Alongside: US-Style Shiphandling
On the Hook: European-Style Shiphandling

Tractor Tugs | 57

6 Invention of the Water Tractor
Cycloidal Propulsion
Azimuthing Propeller Drives, or Rudder Propellers
Shiphandling with Tractor Tugs

Tugs and Ships: Shape and Size | 70

7 Measuring Tugs
Measuring Ships
Ship Types
Reading the Ship

Who's Who | 79

8 Deckhands
Engineer
Cook
Mate
Captain
Harbor and Docking Pilots
The Dockyard
Port Captain and Dispatcher
Time on the Boats

Modern Tug Design and Construction | 90

9 Design of a Shipdocking Tug for Tight Quarters
Design of a Columbia River Tanker Escort Tug
Tug Hull Design: Chines
Newbuilding: Constructing a Tug

Tugs and Barges | 98

10 Barge Types
Mud Boats: Tugs for Construction Work
Canal Towing
River Towing

Coastal and Ocean Towing | 115

11 Going Outside: Coastal Towing on the Hawser
Cable and Chain
Ocean Towing
Sea Conditions: Pitching and Rolling
Articulated Tug-Barges

**Anchor-Handling Tug/Supply Vessels
for Offshore Oil Exploration** | 129

12 AHT/S Tasks at an Oil Rig
Origin of the Semi-Submersible Exploratory Drilling Rig
Anchor-Handling Decks and Winches
Anchors and Chains

Rescue and Salvage | 138

13 Salvaging a Ship on the Beach
Firefighting
Art of Salvage

Conclusion | 144

Acknowledgments | 146

The world is so full of a number of things,
I'm sure we should all be as happy as kings.

— Robert Louis Stevenson

To see is to forget the name of the thing one is looking at.

— Paul Valéry

Introduction

A ship traveling on a lonely sea is not as interesting to me as a tug, which is only useful when interacting with other vessels, most of the time in relationship to land. The edges of the sea, the ports people have made there, and the vessels that activate the shoreline are all fascinating. Buoyancy, the act of floating itself, puts people in motion, actively engaged with the elemental essence of water.

Most books on tugboats have pictures of tugboats. The books I have enjoyed the most described tugs in context, not as objects themselves but as shaped by their work, by tradition, and by the state of technology at a point in time.

I have been an architect for forty-five years (twenty years when I started this book!), and what interests me is the interplay between ideas, the things people build and the environment that shapes how they build them. In the case of tugs the environment is the sea, rivers and harbors, and the other vessels they engage as they work. I'm also interested in how we take advantage of being human at this unique point in evolutionary history. We live in consciousness, and in such a wonderful place to enjoy it: blue and cloudy skies, vast dramatic seas, and all the varieties of landscape. Consciousness also makes possible all that man has fashioned from intelligence applied to the raw materials of Earth.

I've never worked on tugs, only ridden them a few times, and don't do recreational boating or tinker with machinery. So much for my disqualifications. I do have the interest, and a skill set that seems to match the task: a compulsion to try to understand and explain the world, and a knack for constructing effective explanations in a grab bag of mediums. And no fear of doing it "wrong" if it gets the point across.

This book is, for better or worse, a product and a reflection of what goes on in my mind. It follows my literary predilections: from *Mad* magazine to *The New Yorker*, by way of Richard Scarry's *What Do People Do All Day?*

Even if tugs are not necessarily your thing, I hope this book will expand your appreciation for how madly interesting and amazing the world is, if there is this much to be known by expanding the picture in your head of a cute, stubby little tugboat.

Paul Farrell, Cambridge, Massachusetts

1 What Is It About Tugs?

Classic alongside tugs (built to work against the side of the ship) have the most beautiful curves in the machine world, without a flat spot in plan or elevation. The hull is curved to easily roll away from the sheer sides of ships. Follow the swooping gray line of the top of the bulwark on Great Lakes Towing's *Illinois*, meeting a bulk carrier entering the port of Cleveland, Ohio. From the tall bow, it curves out and down the sides, rising again to curve around the stern to keep waves off the aft working deck. The fat hull sits comfortably in the water. The broad working deck and low bulwarks all around allow deckhands to shift lines attached to the ship between bitts on the tug's bow and stern.

Great Lakes Towing has boats on all the lakes except Ontario. At 81 feet, *Illinois* is longer than she looks in this foreshortened view. Built in 1914, her steam engine was replaced by a 1,250 horsepower diesel in 1949. Great Lakes has a large fleet of these simple tugs, which are almost all hull, topped by a small pilothouse. The open hatch leads to stairs down to the engine room. On the stern, one horn of the towing bitts is canted to resist the upward pull the towline will impart when the tug is connected close under the bow of a ship. They are now building modern replacements, but still scaled down to suit the smaller ships that can fit through the canals leading to the lakes.

© Paul Csizmadia/Spec3Photography

The Classic Tugboat, Aesthetically Considered

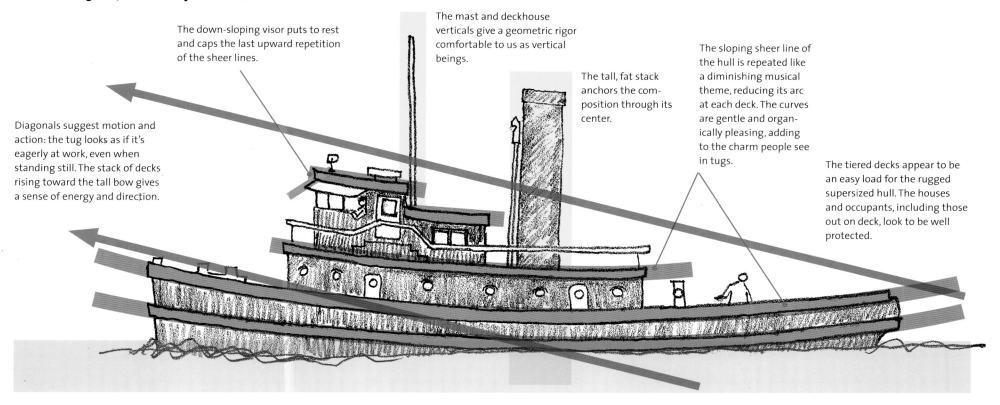

The down-sloping visor puts to rest and caps the last upward repetition of the sheer lines.

The mast and deckhouse verticals give a geometric rigor comfortable to us as vertical beings.

The tall, fat stack anchors the composition through its center.

The sloping sheer line of the hull is repeated like a diminishing musical theme, reducing its arc at each deck. The curves are gentle and organically pleasing, adding to the charm people see in tugs.

Diagonals suggest motion and action: the tug looks as if it's eagerly at work, even when standing still. The stack of decks rising toward the tall bow gives a sense of energy and direction.

The tiered decks appear to be an easy load for the rugged supersized hull. The houses and occupants, including those out on deck, look to be well protected.

EVERYONE LOVES TUGS

Stopped in traffic by a lift bridge on Chelsea Creek in Boston Harbor, I walked up to the guardrail to watch four tugs work a tanker through the narrow, difficult opening. A young jogger couple, halted by the open bridge, hopped in place as they waited. As she bounced, the woman said to her companion, "You know, I like tugboats!"

Why do we invest such interest and affection in these vessels, subjects of cartoons, storybooks, and salty nautical photos, adding character to waterfront movie scenes? Tugs give most of us a good feeling: to see one brings pleasure and awakens interest. (Even more so for "tug people." You know who you are!) How can an object, a machine, cause such pleasurable sensations? Why have so many people established positive associations with tugs, for example?

Contrast tugs with commercial fishing boats, which are certainly picturesque and take your mind to sea, but they're not engaging in the way tugs are. Fishermen are seen as a breed apart: fishing is rough, messy, hard work, something *they* do. We can

imagine a life at sea for weeks on a pitching, smelly boat, but we can't imagine ourselves doing it. A fishing boat looks thin-skinned and top-heavy with its tall hull and towering rigging. It doesn't give us the feeling of safety and security of a tug.

Most of us see harbor tugs at work, so they stand for all tugs: we think crews putter around the harbor all day, then head home to bed at night. Tugboating looks clean, quick, and helpful (but only because years of experience make it look easy). We can see ourselves handling rope hawsers, or driving the boat with an elbow casually hanging over the pilothouse windowsill. Tugs look stable and safe, riding on a massive black hull lined with cushioning rubber tires, easily supporting the small deckhouse. The tall bow looks protective, turning away waves (at least harbor waves). We like tugs. They look so secure and imperturbable, we can't imagine the reality of a tug at sea, closed up like a submarine as waves crash over the low bulkheads, or in harbor, trapped between a pier and a looming ship threatening to drive the tug under the surface.

ASSOCIATIONS

Tugs were never designed to appeal to us. They were, and are, utilitarian machines. Appearance is not neglected, but it doesn't drive form. It just happens that the requirements for a tug, and a tug's tasks, coalesce into an object onto which it is easy to project human characteristics. The most direct point of entry for seeing human characteristics in an object is a head with a face. Tug skippers need visibility, so the pilothouse is prominent, raised above the tug like a head on shoulders. The segmented glass windows can be seen as eyes, and the sun visor is hat-like. The jaunty rise of the hull to the prominent bow gives a sense of eagerness, energy, and direction. Tug tasks reinforce the sense of human qualities we admire. They're helpful, cooperative, bustling, with smooth multidirectional movements reminiscent of people's motions. Their relatively small size as they twirl around the ungainly ships they serve is similar to a purposeful group of people engaged in a large collective task.

Unlike imperious ocean-crossing giants, seemingly unmoved by the elements as they glide past harbor watchers, tugboats are accessible, lively in their fluid grace, with all the curves and fullness of ships compressed in a vessel almost house-like: lined with railings, punctuated by porthole windows and Dutch doors, and topped by a chimney-like smokestack behind the bay window of the pilothouse.

House-like tug

Little Toot, the book drawn by Hardie Gramatky in 1939, might have started the personification of tugs and set a standard that could never be equaled. His *Little Toot* is cheerful and eager in this drawing at the book's end, satisfied with his workaday tow (having just singlehandedly pulled the ocean liner off the rocky shore!). The rounded pilothouse with sun visor easily becomes a head with cap, and windows become eyes. The steam whistle is another smaller head, like a parrot on *Little Toot*'s shoulder. The giant smokestack expresses easy power, and everything sits in a fat, unsinkable-looking hull. Gramatky looked carefully at real tugs, and then interpreted and exaggerated what he saw, and added feeling.

Tug-like house

Five Whales and Five Tugs

Positive mental associations in this 1990 *New Yorker* cover by John O'Brien allow five whales to be tugs: big, slow and steady, friendly, rounded, powerful, effortlessly floating and moving through the water. A tug is not a shark!

Unlike ships that are usually singular places on the vast ocean, tugs are meant to be in association with other things: ships, barges, other tugs, harbors, docks, and piers.

John O'Brien

Five Moran tugs struggle to dock the *Queen Elizabeth* on the Hudson River in New York City. One reason we identify so strongly with tugs may be because they work the way people do. They're small in relation to their tasks (although not really small when you see them in person), agile, busily shifting from one leverage point to another as they cooperate in small groups. They even used to talk to each other, in whistle toots. Now they only toot to acknowledge the radio command from the docking pilot on the ship's bridge.

This photo captures an era of transition: four diesel tugs are joined by one steam tug at right, identifiable by her stack twice as tall as the others. Four of the tugs have lines up, ready to pull if ordered. The deckhand of each diesel boat stands at the stern, so the captain can see him out the windows across the back of the pilothouse, giving him one less thing to worry about.

Tugboat Photos + Research
Steven Lang Collection

WHAT IS A TUG?

Most oceangoing ships are made for cruising steadily through the open sea. When they reach their destination, they need help to get through congested harbors and into their berths. Tugs are like no other vessels in sturdiness of construction, power in relation to size, and the boat-handling ability of their crews.

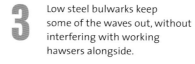

1 Tugs are in essence auxiliary engines available on call to nudge enormous ships and barges through tight spaces. Shiphandling tugs may have two diesel engines of over 2,000 horsepower each. This modern tug's engines drive independently controllable rudder-propellers encased in nozzles to direct the thrust in any direction through 360 degrees.

2 A sturdy hull floats the heavy engines, higher at the bow to deflect waves, sloping down to the low *counter* (raised bulwark) of the stern, which brings the working deck closer to the water for line handling and lowers the center of gravity from the towline.

Two auxiliary diesel engines make electricity for the boat and run the hydraulic pumps that turn winches and *capstans* (vertical rotating posts for pulling hawsers).

3 Low steel bulwarks keep some of the waves out, without interfering with working hawsers alongside.

A steel deck over the hull seals up the air inside, forming a buoyant cavity that allows the tug to bob like a cork in ocean storms.

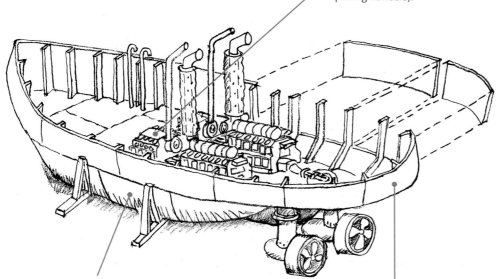

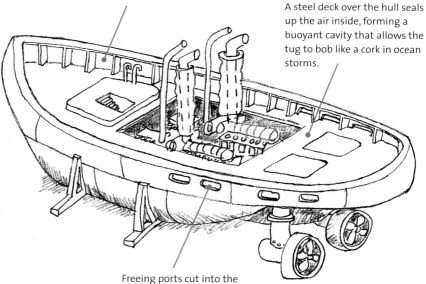

Enormous fuel tanks in the bottom allow the tug to stay at sea for weeks if necessary.

Steel plates are bent in only one direction over hull frames. It's too expensive to make hulls the old-fashioned way, from rounded plates bulged out in three dimensions.

Freeing ports cut into the bulwarks drain the water that sloshes in.

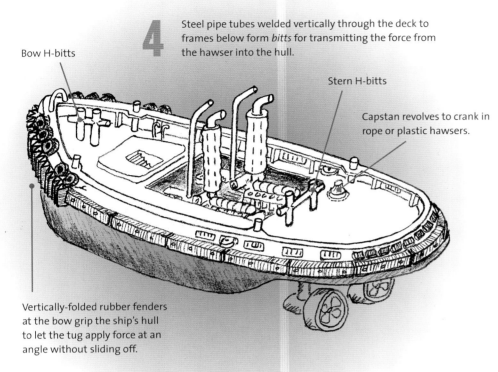

4 Steel pipe tubes welded vertically through the deck to frames below form *bitts* for transmitting the force from the hawser into the hull.

Bow H-bitts

Stern H-bitts

Capstan revolves to crank in rope or plastic hawsers.

Vertically-folded rubber fenders at the bow grip the ship's hull to let the tug apply force at an angle without sliding off.

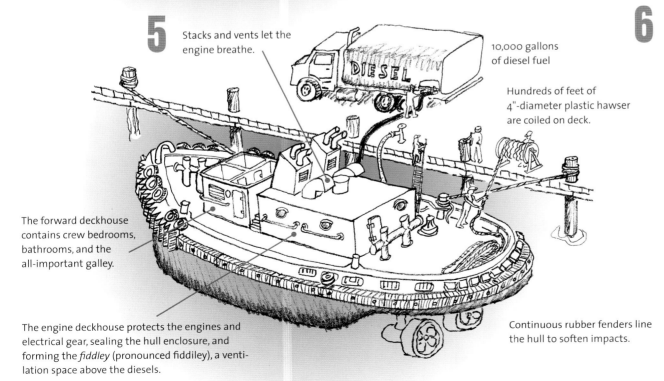

5 Stacks and vents let the engine breathe.

10,000 gallons of diesel fuel

Hundreds of feet of 4"-diameter plastic hawser are coiled on deck.

The forward deckhouse contains crew bedrooms, bathrooms, and the all-important galley.

The engine deckhouse protects the engines and electrical gear, sealing the hull enclosure, and forming the *fiddley* (pronounced fiddiley), a ventilation space above the diesels.

Continuous rubber fenders line the hull to soften impacts.

6 The pilothouse allows visibility all around and above and encloses engine and rudder controls and electronics. On top are a searchlight and radar dome. The hinged mast has been folded down between the stacks so it doesn't hit the flared-out bow of *Maunawili*, a container ship being floated out from the builder's dry dock at Aker Philadelphia Shipyard. The mast carries a vertical row of three lights to warn boaters away from the cable if there's a barge behind. The crew consists of the captain, mate, deckhand, engineer (and cook, if they're lucky), all skilled and adventurous enough to go out in any weather, pitting their skills and tough vessel against giant ships. Gladding-Hearn built the 2,400 hp *Lindsey* in 1989 for Wilmington Tug Company, after having built *Tina*, one of the earliest modern tractor tugs (see page 57) in the United States, for Delaware River tug master Hickman Rowland in 1977. The *Lindsey* is small enough to operate with only a captain and deckhand. The *Lindsey*'s deckhand stands at the stern, so he's in sight of the skipper looking out the back of the pilothouse window. The tug is pushing against the ship's bulbous bow, designed to lift water up and away, reducing the resistance of the bow wave. Underway with a full load, the bulbous shape would be below the surface (and a danger to tug skippers who forget it's there).

Aker Philadelphia Shipyard

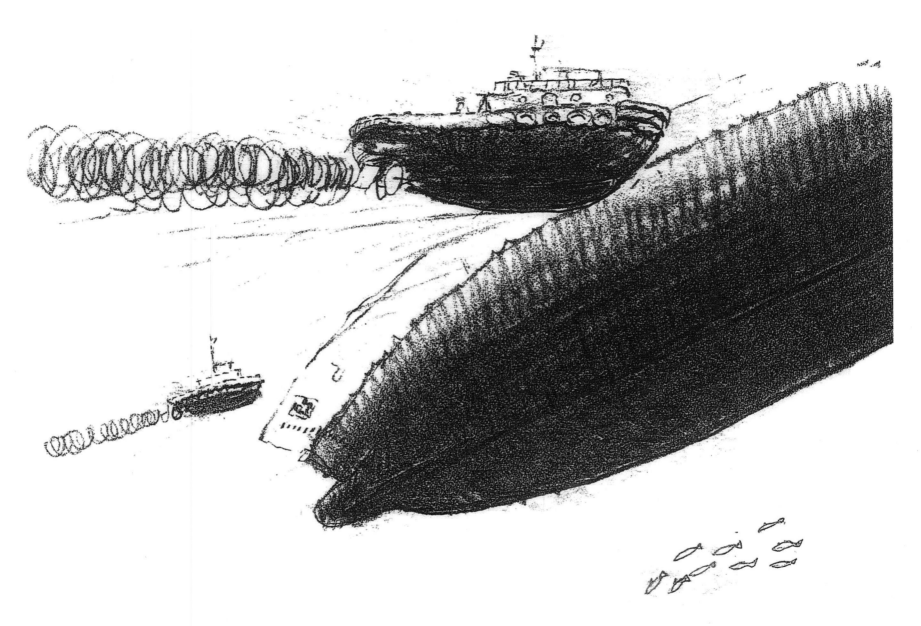

What makes it possible for tugs to pull ships thousands of times their mass? The vessels are suspended in a miraculous element, water. Uncountable vast numbers of tiny ball-bearing-like molecules, spread over three-quarters of the world's surface, jostle each other continuously, providing a globe-spanning low-friction advantage to floating vessels. A small tug of a few thousand horsepower can eventually overcome the inertia of a giant tanker and gradually get it underway. Moving a million pounds on land is enormously more complicated. And tugs look like they're working: when they pour on the power, diesels whine, smoke blasts from the stacks, water explodes into froth, hawsers sing as they stretch taut. The enormous forces become visible.

Thor spins alongside a wharf in Eureka, California, 1983. She was a small part of the giant Crowley "Red Stack" fleet that operates on both US coasts. (She was later sold, but sank during delivery to her new owners.) Looking at pictures of handsome tugs on printed pages, one can miss the closeness to the water inherent in tug work. They ride low, putting their props deep in the water. Deckhands work a few feet above the water surface, protected only by the knee-high bulwarks. Tug captain and harbor pilot John Powell, who took this picture, recalls the largest wave he ever took, which swept completely over *Thor* as she headed through the swells over the bar at the mouth of Humboldt Bay. The wheelhouse went dark as the tug bored through the wave, water pressure turning every pinhole in the window frames of the World War II–era tug into a spraying water jet.

Captain John Powell, Courtesy of Matt Lyons/Harbor Images

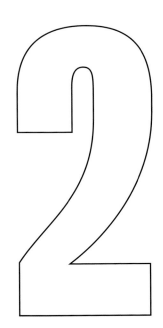

Tugboat History

Small ships such as this Cornwall "smack" could be pulled by rowboats, perhaps the ship's boat plus a local crew. This work was exhausting and only served for short distances and small vessels.

Basil Greenhill Collection, Maritime Historical Studies Centre, University of Hull, UK

Dragging the anchor: A ship could move upstream with the tide, but because it floated at the speed of the water, there was no flow past the rudder, and therefore it had no turning power. The ship's direction was uncontrolled. If the ship was over a muddy bottom, an anchor could be dragged to slow the boat and the rudder could be turned in the water flowing past, to give some steering force, albeit at loss of speed.

When his ministers showed him Robert Fulton's proposal for steam towboats, Napoleon told them it had come "too late to permit it to change the face of the world." He imagined using the towboats on a day of dead calm, when England's sail-powered domination of the sea would be neutralized, to pull a fleet of invasion barges to England. But he realized Fulton's steamboats would take years to perfect for travel on the open seas. (The entrepreneurial Fulton was at the time in secret negotiations to sell his attack submarine to England, France having turned down his offer to use it to attack the British.)

Nothing then existed to match the wind's power. Sailing vessels were the world's highest technology, wonderfully efficient at crossing the oceans, where vast areas allowed them to run before or cross the wind. However, the advantage disappeared when they approached land. Ships neared the shore cautiously, sometimes waiting days for the right conditions for crossing the bar (the sandbar that forms where the silt-laden flow slows outside a river mouth) to enter harbor. Difficulties of shiphandling in port limited the practical size of sailing ships. The giant five- and six-masted sailing schooners and full-rigged iron ships of the late nineteenth century would have been impossible to dock without the tugboats developed in the decades before.

Barges and small ships could be pulled by people or animals on towpaths alongside the waterway.

The most dangerous part of the voyage was entering port, with little room to maneuver and no means for assistance.

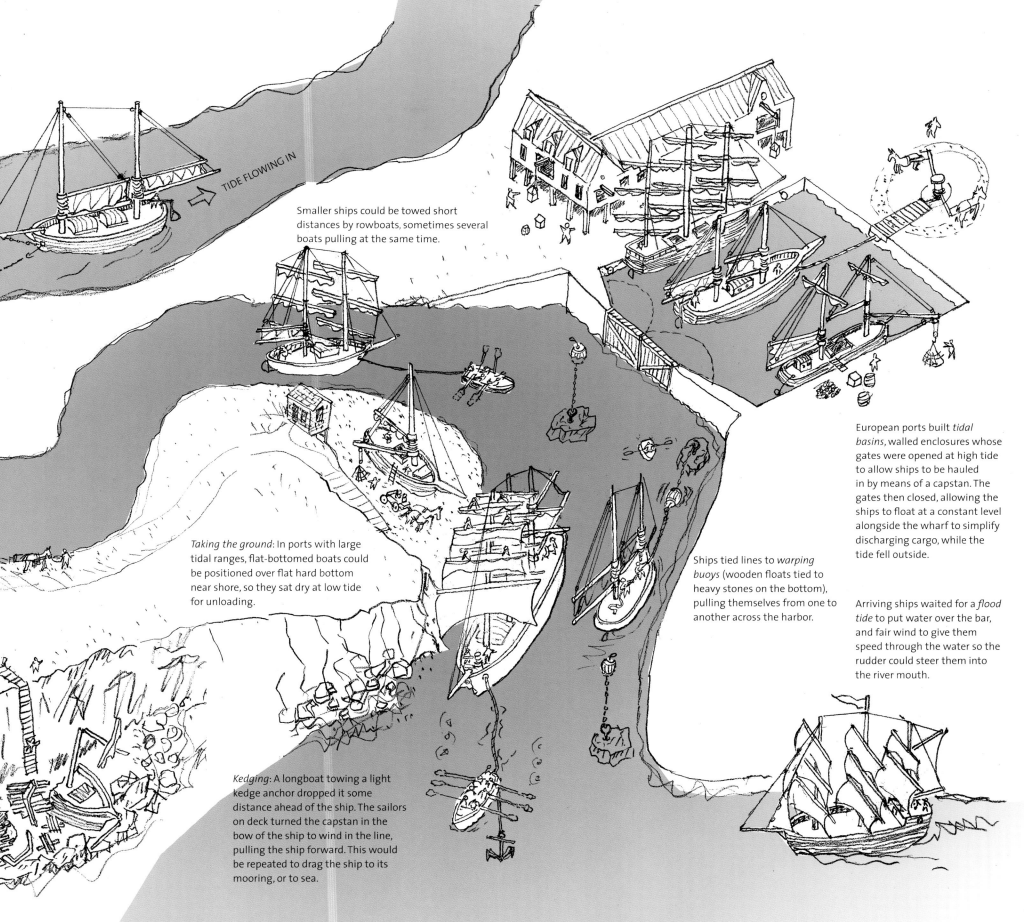

TIDE FLOWING IN

Smaller ships could be towed short distances by rowboats, sometimes several boats pulling at the same time.

Taking the ground: In ports with large tidal ranges, flat-bottomed boats could be positioned over flat hard bottom near shore, so they sat dry at low tide for unloading.

Kedging: A longboat towing a light kedge anchor dropped it some distance ahead of the ship. The sailors on deck turned the capstan in the bow of the ship to wind in the line, pulling the ship forward. This would be repeated to drag the ship to its mooring, or to sea.

Ships tied lines to *warping buoys* (wooden floats tied to heavy stones on the bottom), pulling themselves from one to another across the harbor.

European ports built *tidal basins*, walled enclosures whose gates were opened at high tide to allow ships to be hauled in by means of a capstan. The gates then closed, allowing the ships to float at a constant level alongside the wharf to simplify discharging cargo, while the tide fell outside.

Arriving ships waited for a *flood tide* to put water over the bar, and fair wind to give them speed through the water so the rudder could steer them into the river mouth.

INVENTOR OF THE TUGBOAT

In 1732, Jonathan Hulls, a well-educated farmer in Gloucestershire, England, applied for a patent for a steam tugboat (granted in 1736), and published a forty-eight-page pamphlet detailing the machinery and economics of his proposal. Crude pistons sitting over enormous masonry boilers (invented and built by John Newcomen starting in 1712) were then pumping out mines in the vicinity, and he may have seen one at work. He recognized the difficulty of bearing the weight of both the huge machine and a cargo, and therefore proposed to build his steamboat as a separate towing vessel that only had to accommodate the engine and boiler. Thus was born the *tugboat*, although the name was not applied until the nineteenth century. Hulls, a successful inventor of a slide rule and a method to identify counterfeit gold, may have started to build a vessel, but there is no record that he completed it. There were no boatbuilders who could have solved the double problem of building a steam engine in a boat hull and assembling a successful propelling mechanism.

Newcomen's engine was too big to be easily put in a boat. It was the world's first automated engine: a piston in an open-topped cylinder was pushed down by atmospheric pressure into a vacuum formed by squirting cold water into steam in the cylinder below the piston. This power stroke triggered a catch that opened the bottom of the cylinder, allowing steam at atmospheric pressure to enter, breaking the vacuum. This allowed the weighted pump rod on the other end of a seesaw beam to pull the piston up, filled the cylinder with steam again, and automatically sealed the chamber for another shot of cold water, starting the next power stroke. The machine made about twelve strokes per minute, somewhat irregularly since the cold water sprayed into the cylinder cooled the walls and condensed some of the steam before the power stroke. The rough motion and slow speed, and frequent manual intervention to keep the engine working, would have made it impractical and dangerous to use for meeting ships at the edge of the open sea.

Successful steamboats had to wait for James Watt's compact and efficient engine design, and the development of mechanics able to fabricate them. Steamboat inventors in Europe could buy a high-quality engine from Boulton & Watt or one of their licensees and concentrate on the drive train, propulsion, and steering, and fitting all this into a compact hull that would not shake itself to pieces. British protectionist policies forbade sale of the sophisticated engines to the United States.

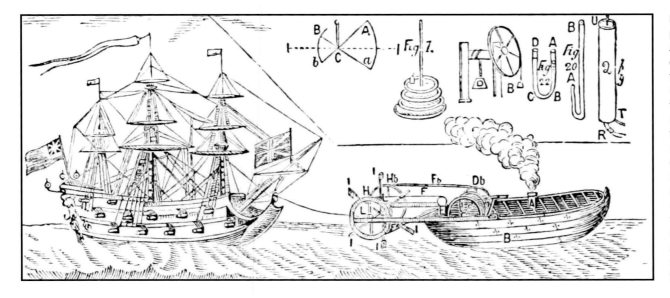

In "A New Invented Machine," published in about 1734, Jonathan Hulls wrote: "It is my opinion, it will not be found practical to place the machine here recommended in the vessel itself that is to be taken in or out of port etc., but rather in a separate vessel for these reasons: This machine may be thought too cumbersome and to take up too much room in a vessel laden with goods and provisions, etc. If this machine is put in a separate vessel this vessel may lie in port etc., to be ready on all occasions. A vessel of small burthen will be sufficient to carry the machine to take out a large one."

Charlotte Dundas retained the center paddlewheel from Symington's earlier boat, now recessed in the stern of a single hull, and cranked by a direct-connected double-acting engine. The boat was steered by cables from a steering wheel in the bow, turning rudders on either side of the paddle wheel. Barges were connected by twin towlines over cleats in the deck next to the paddlewheel cover. Recessing the paddlewheel reduced and focused the wake, reducing the erosion of the earth banks of the canal. The early history of steamboats is not well documented: after use the boats were abandoned or fell apart. Some engines were preserved, but the most careful, studied conjectures about early steamboats come from contemporary model makers, who are more like industrial archaeologists, combing through old sketches, paintings, and models to reverse-design the most likely layout that would have functioned properly given the technology of the time. B. E. G. Clark of East Sussex, England, researched and built this model as his projection of the poorly recorded actual vessel.

THE FIRST TUG

In 1788 Patrick Miller of Scotland, one of the newly invented "industrialists" created by the Industrial Revolution, experimented with man-powered paddlewheel boats, trying to interest the Royal Navy. He built a double-hulled skiff, locating the paddles between the hulls, where they would be protected from enemy cannons. His children's tutor, James Taylor, convinced Miller to allow him and inventor friend William Symington to install an engine of Symington's design in the skiff. They soon got the assembly to work, with the engine in one hull, the boiler in the other. Miller financed a larger boat for commercial service, which moved reliably at five miles per hour, the fastest steamboat ever. This didn't satisfy Miller, who abandoned Symington as incompetent, laid up the boat, and halfheartedly looked for a new designer. In 1803 Symington returned to steamboat design, financed by Lord Dundas of Scotland. The towboat Charlotte Dundas pulled two schooner barges almost twenty miles in six hours on the Forth and Clyde Canal.

Canal tugboats were an excellent use of existing technology: they didn't carry cargo, so the heavy boilers and engines were not a problem, and towing was done in developed areas where fuel could be replenished frequently. Charlotte Dundas ran perfectly, but was not enough of an improvement over animal power to win over traditionalists. The towboat's wake scoured the bank, so it had to travel slowly. It also threatened to put thousands of canal drovers out of their jobs. (In France, other early steamboats were torn apart by angry mobs of canal workers.) A better market would have been towing sailing ships into port, as Jonathan Hulls had suggested sixty years before. Shipowners and sailors would have been pleased to have their ships safely towed into harbor as soon as they arrived. However, the steamboat construction techniques of the time were not sturdy enough for the vessels to venture onto the edge of the ocean.

Logging on Mississippi River Davenport Iowa

Davenport, Ia.

80.

The homely *Harriet*, built as *Park Bluff* in 1884, rebuilt and renamed *Harriet* in 1906, is a good example of the simple, inexpensive river towboats of the nineteenth century. She's long and narrow, with two sets of hogging trusses: the taller trusses (including the pair with the decorative bracket between) support the bow and stern. The lower truss supports the paddlewheel: its chains run horizontal from the stern framing, then over short diagonal timbers and down to the deck near the engine-room doorway. The boiler is at the bow, where forward motion of the boat will supply air to the firebox. The jug at the front edge of the boat deck is an oil lamp with reflectors, for night work. On the boat deck amidships, the davits for the rowboat are empty and swung apart, *Harriet* having apparently launched her boat. *Push knees*—vertical bumpers to take the force when pushing—appear to be projecting from the bow, as indicated by the opening between the bow and the vertical post ahead of the bow.

Harriet is acting as the bow boat on a log tow, steering the tow from side to side by coming ahead or astern as needed. The larger *North Star* in the distance is pushing the load. The log raft is held together by a corduroy pattern of long logs spiked in rows over the mass of logs below.

Davenport Public Library

The canal sternwheeler *Charlotte Dundas* was the first effective tug of any sort. Sternwheelers would give way to sidewheelers, which put the paddles closer to the engine, shortening the drive train. Sternwheelers were also more prone to damage in high seas by waves from astern. They continued on the great inland Mississippi River system, and on the broad estuaries of the Pacific Northwest. The sternwheeler's great paddle width and large, shallow hull were ideal for rapids and shifting sandbars. The river currents were strong, and the power of the broad paddles was instantly effective. The shallow hulls could not be reinforced like the timber cross bracing of a deep hull, so

hogging trusses were developed: chains in tension between tall posts that ran down to the hull framing. The trusses kept the hull from hogging — lifting in the more buoyant middle of the hull and sagging at the ends, which were weighed down by the boiler at the bow and paddlewheel at the stern — a shape likened to a hog's back. Hogging trusses gave sternwheelers the appearance of floating bridges, as the hull supported the heavy loads of boilers in the bow and the paddlewheel at the stern. In fact they were the opposite of bridges, which use the ends to support the middle (the span).

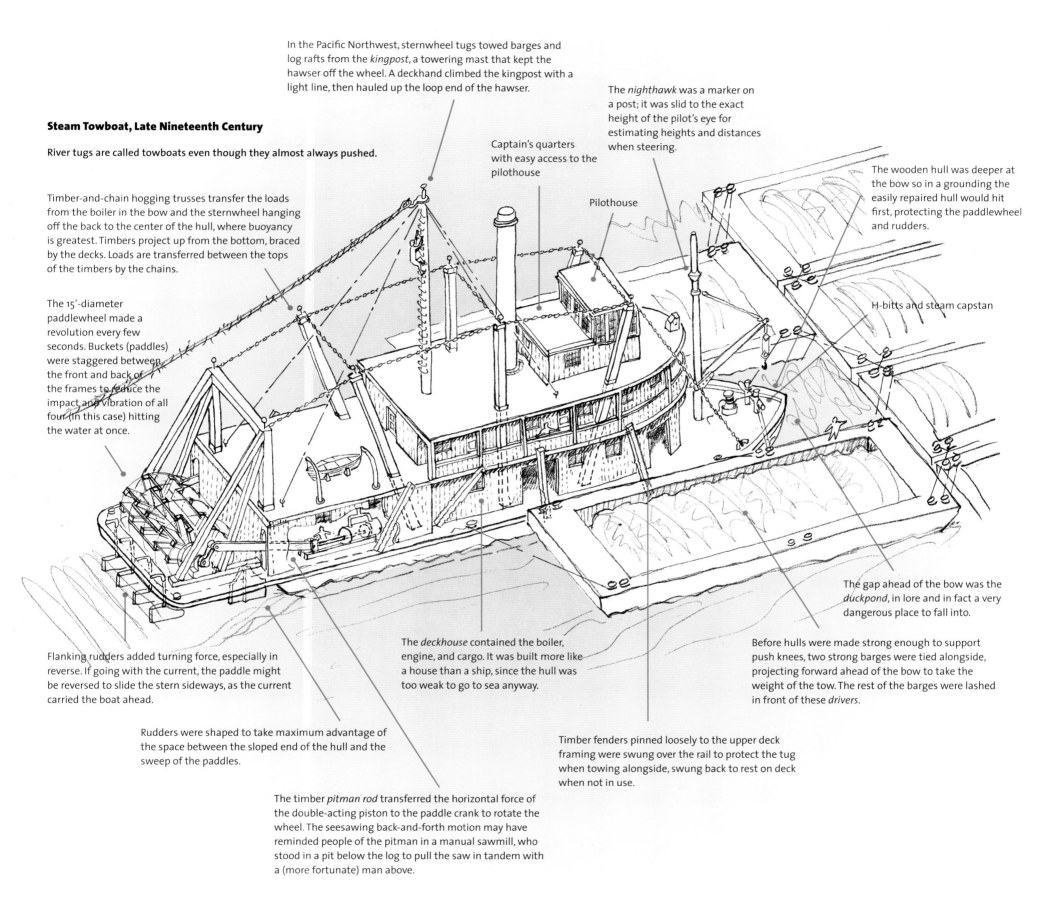

In the Pacific Northwest, sternwheel tugs towed barges and log rafts from the *kingpost*, a towering mast that kept the hawser off the wheel. A deckhand climbed the kingpost with a light line, then hauled up the loop end of the hawser.

The *nighthawk* was a marker on a post; it was slid to the exact height of the pilot's eye for estimating heights and distances when steering.

Steam Towboat, Late Nineteenth Century

River tugs are called towboats even though they almost always pushed.

Timber-and-chain hogging trusses transfer the loads from the boiler in the bow and the sternwheel hanging off the back to the center of the hull, where buoyancy is greatest. Timbers project up from the bottom, braced by the decks. Loads are transferred between the tops of the timbers by the chains.

The 15'-diameter paddlewheel made a revolution every few seconds. Buckets (paddles) were staggered between the front and back of the frames to reduce the impact and vibration of all four (in this case) hitting the water at once.

Captain's quarters with easy access to the pilothouse

Pilothouse

The wooden hull was deeper at the bow so in a grounding the easily repaired hull would hit first, protecting the paddlewheel and rudders.

H-bitts and steam capstan

The gap ahead of the bow was the *duckpond*, in lore and in fact a very dangerous place to fall into.

Flanking rudders added turning force, especially in reverse. If going with the current, the paddle might be reversed to slide the stern sideways, as the current carried the boat ahead.

The *deckhouse* contained the boiler, engine, and cargo. It was built more like a house than a ship, since the hull was too weak to go to sea anyway.

Before hulls were made strong enough to support push knees, two strong barges were tied alongside, projecting forward ahead of the bow to take the weight of the tow. The rest of the barges were lashed in front of these *drivers*.

Rudders were shaped to take maximum advantage of the space between the sloped end of the hull and the sweep of the paddles.

Timber fenders pinned loosely to the upper deck framing were swung over the rail to protect the tug when towing alongside, swung back to rest on deck when not in use.

The timber *pitman rod* transferred the horizontal force of the double-acting piston to the paddle crank to rotate the wheel. The seesawing back-and-forth motion may have reminded people of the pitman in a manual sawmill, who stood in a pit below the log to pull the saw in tandem with a (more fortunate) man above.

obert Fulton's sidewheeler, called simply *Steamboat*, won the race for the first practical steamboat in regular service, but side wheels presented inherent problems that caused them to be abandoned once screw-propeller drive was perfected. Tugs were almost the only exceptions. Sidewheel steam paddle tugs were used well into the twentieth century, when the only other sidewheel paddlers were steam excursion vessels on freshwater lakes and calm rivers. As Jonathan Hulls proposed in 1736, a large boiler, engine, and paddle mechanism in the center of a boat were not a problem for tugs, which carried no cargo. Ocean-going sidewheel ships were difficult to steer, because as the ships burned their coal and rose higher in the water, the paddles immersed less deeply.

A broadside wind would heel the ships over so the windward paddle was lifted higher and the leeward paddle forced deeper: the deeper paddle had more force and turned the ship off course. But tugs usually operated in harbors, where the wind was less of a factor, and where they could frequently replenish their small coal bunkers. Slow-turning steam engines were well suited to the rotational speed of paddles, and the end of steam power was essentially also the end of paddlewheelers.

Paddle tug *United Service* pulls a brigantine past the Yarmouth breakwater in England. Paddlewheelers were difficult to control in messy seas such as these. At this instant, the port wheel is barely in the water, not exerting much force, and the starboard wheel is deep in the water, pushing the tug's bow around. The next instant might be the opposite. The hawser is slack, disappearing into the water over the stern. In these conditions, it would be alternately slack and jerked taut. In addition to controlling the tug, the master (visible on the open bridge) had to manage the towline force by slowing if the strain became too great. An appreciative audience has gathered at the end of the pier to see how the dangerous passage turns out.

Basil Greenhill Collection,
Maritime Historical Studies Centre,
University of Hull, UK

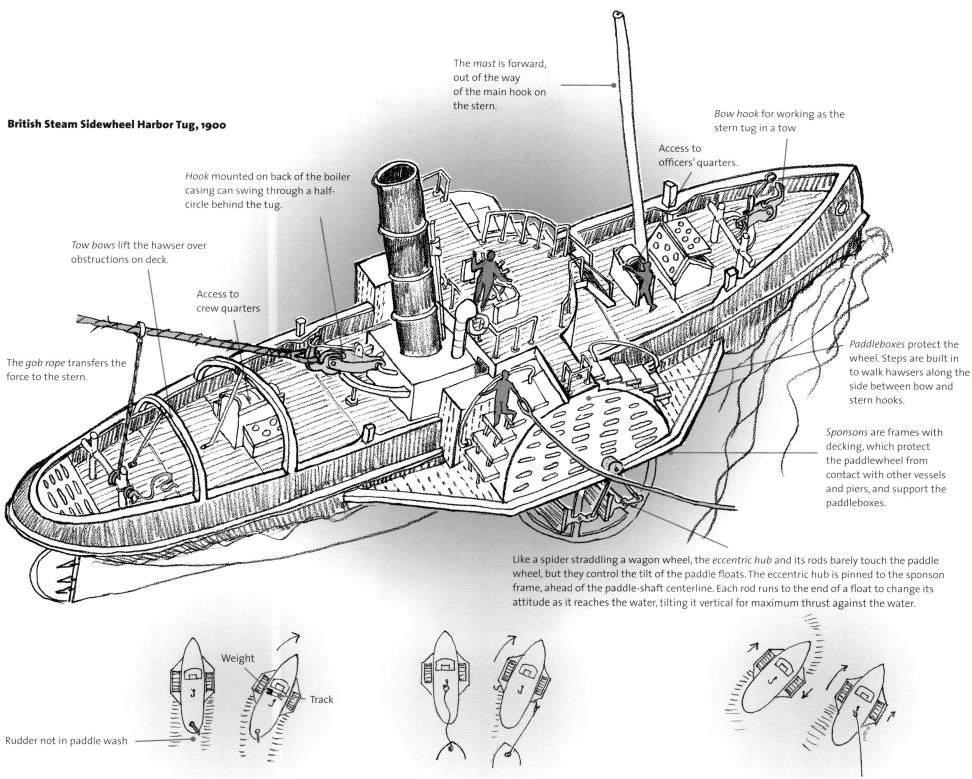

British Steam Sidewheel Harbor Tug, 1900

The *mast* is forward, out of the way of the main hook on the stern.

Bow hook for working as the stern tug in a tow

Access to officers' quarters.

Hook mounted on back of the boiler casing can swing through a half-circle behind the tug.

Tow bows lift the hawser over obstructions on deck.

Access to crew quarters

Paddleboxes protect the wheel. Steps are built in to walk hawsers along the side between bow and stern hooks.

The *gob rope* transfers the force to the stern.

Sponsons are frames with decking, which protect the paddlewheel from contact with other vessels and piers, and support the paddleboxes.

Like a spider straddling a wagon wheel, the *eccentric hub* and its rods barely touch the paddle wheel, but they control the tilt of the paddle floats. The eccentric hub is pinned to the sponson frame, ahead of the paddle-shaft centerline. Each rod runs to the end of a float to change its attitude as it reaches the water, tilting it vertical for maximum thrust against the water.

Weight

Track

Rudder not in paddle wash

With both paddles operating together and connected to one shaft, only the rudder can turn the tug, but at low speed not much water is hitting the rudder. (A screw propeller, which is mounted in front of the rudder, would push water past the rudder even when the tug was stopped, forcing the stern sideways if the rudder was turned.) One method of turning the tug was to push a box of scrap iron on a track to one side, dipping that paddle for more force.

Cant hooks were a crude turning method: the tug slowed to slack the towline, which was transferred from the towing hook to a cant hook on one sponson. The tug went ahead, the weight of the tow jerking the tug onto a new course. Then the hawser was moved back to the tow hook.

Steering problems were solved when each paddle got its own engine. They could be run in opposite directions to rotate the tug, or one slowed to turn. Sidewheelers became unmatched at slow-speed maneuvering until cycloidal propulsion (see page 61) gained popularity in the 1950s.

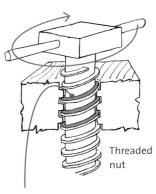

A *screw* is a continuous inclined plane wound around a cylinder. Before there were engines, a small, low-energy force continuously applied by one person, at an angle to the desired direction of force, gradually did the work, which would require many people or animals to do rapidly.

Threaded nut

The screw's continuous top surface slides against the underside of the nut's groove. Pressure is spread over the entire length of the screw blade inside the nut, reducing friction.

The screw advances a long distance diagonally for a short vertical displacement, but the horizontal power required to generate the vertical displacement is small.

FROM PADDLEWHEELS TO SCREW PROPELLERS

Paddlewheels generate power directly: boards push backward into the water, and water resists, so the boat has no choice but to move forward. This seems very straightforward and efficient, but there are drawbacks. The paddles can't push continuously: a canoe paddle pushes for the length of a person's stroke, then has to be lifted and moved ahead for another stroke. Likewise, a paddlewheel is only submerged for a small segment of its rotation. If it were submerged fully, it would act in all directions, producing no directional movement of the vessel. Paddles must be big to get sufficient surface in contact with the water. They are most efficient when hung outside the hull, where they are vulnerable to collision with piers and other vessels, especially problematic for tugs.

Screw propellers push indirectly: they don't push backward to generate forward motion. Just as a screw advances slowly down by moving mostly sideways, a screw propeller's canted blades push water away at an angle to the desired course. Because they are spinning around a shaft, the indirect force is applied all around the circle, generating a low-power linear force all around the shaft. The paddlewheel's float is very effective, but only over a third of its rotation. The screw propeller is less effective at any moment, but power is applied continuously. The propeller is also protected from contact with vessels and docks by the overhanging hull.

Windmills are an application of the screw to produce power from the wind passing a canted sail.

  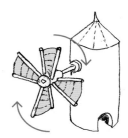

- If windmill blades were flat and perpendicular to the wind, they would receive a pushing force. The wind is slowed by the obstruction of the sail, losing energy, which is absorbed by the sail. Pressure is good for a sailboat going with the wind, but not for a windmill, where rotary motion turning a shaft can be used to grind, cut, lift, and drill.

- To produce rotary motion, the properties of a wedge are applied by warping the sail to create differential pressure across the sail. A warped blade runs from the front edge to the diagonal opposite corner.

- The wind is forced to detour around the sail in one direction, losing energy as it slows down. Since energy is never lost, but only transferred, the sail gains energy in the opposite direction, turning the shaft.

- Adding more sails increases power and balances the force on the shaft.

The elements of the windmill could be applied in reverse to use steam power to propel a vessel. Instead of the moving fluid (air) turning the vanes to generate power, power manufactured in a boiler would turn the vanes, which would push the fluid (water) astern. The water would be compressed, and as it tried to expand again it would press on the propeller, forcing the vessel forward. In about 1800, John Stevens of New Jersey built a small boat, engine and boiler, and screw propeller, all of his own design, and ran it on the Hudson River. Viewers marveled to see a vessel move with a boiler and engine but no visible paddles. Stevens had invented the practical screw-propelled vessel. He described his propeller as having "wings like those on the arms of a windmill."

Photo said to be of Stevens's original propellers (only one shown), made of sheet metal. He added the second propeller turning opposite to the other, possibly to counteract the tendency of a single propeller to build up pressure against one side of the hull, creating an unwanted turning force. (See page 44 for contemporary solutions.) Stevens's propeller was literally a windmill-blade design transferred to sheet metal, not accounting for the greater density of water and occasional contact with the bottom. Later propellers were thick metal castings, rounded at the tips.

The Mariners' Museum, Newport News, VA

CLASSIC AMERICAN STEAM TUGS

These timber-framed, wood-planked hulls were products of the same low-technology riverbank boatyards as the coastal schooners that would be replaced by the tugs towing barges, often the same schooners cut down into cargo hulks. The first vessels specifically designed for ship work, these screw-propeller steam tugs are ubiquitous in late-nineteenth-century port photos, pulling or tied alongside barges, pushing ships, or towing strings of fishing boats out of the harbor. Some steel-hulled diesel tugs today are still built following this style.

In this late-nineteenth-century photograph, at least one deckhand is visible on each of the three New York Harbor tugs in the foreground, with many tugs in the mist beyond. Deckhands spent their working lives outside, close to the water and inches from the towering sides of ships and barges.

These tugs are operating very close together, considering the complications of piloting *bell boats* (the captain can steer from the pilothouse, but speed and forward-reverse adjustments had to be anticipated by the captain and sent to the engineer by pulling cords that rang bell signals in the engine room below).

Each tug has the obligatory gilded eagle on the pilothouse, trying to belie their humble status in the harbor.

Tugboat Photos + Research
Steven Lang Collection

These old tugs were yacht-like, very long and narrow to accommodate the linear arrangement of boiler, steam engine, shaft, propeller, and giant rudder. They were usually 85 to 100 feet long, 20 to 25 feet wide, for a length-to-width ratio of 4 or 5 to 1. Modern twin-engine diesel tugs are more like 3 to 1, and tractor tugs with pairs of wide drives may be 2 to 1. Such long, narrow hulls were easily rocked by a crossing sea, making them very uncomfortable offshore unless their riding sails were set. Smaller tugs worked in harbors, while coal companies commissioned 150-foot multiengined coastal tugs with crews of fifteen or twenty, and beautifully appointed owners' suites.

Triple Expansion Steam Tug, 1880s

TYPICAL CREW:

- captain
- mate (assistant captain)
- engineer, assistant engineer
- firemen (2)
- deckhands (2 harbor, 4–6 coastal)
- cook

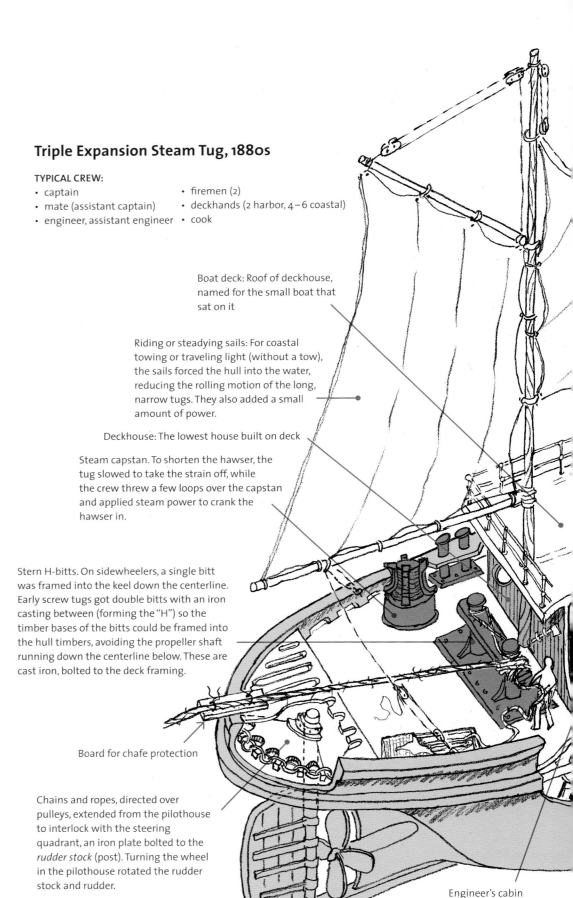

Boat deck: Roof of deckhouse, named for the small boat that sat on it

Riding or steadying sails: For coastal towing or traveling light (without a tow), the sails forced the hull into the water, reducing the rolling motion of the long, narrow tugs. They also added a small amount of power.

Deckhouse: The lowest house built on deck

Steam capstan. To shorten the hawser, the tug slowed to take the strain off, while the crew threw a few loops over the capstan and applied steam power to crank the hawser in.

Stern H-bitts. On sidewheelers, a single bitt was framed into the keel down the centerline. Early screw tugs got double bitts with an iron casting between (forming the "H") so the timber bases of the bitts could be framed into the hull timbers, avoiding the propeller shaft running down the centerline below. These are cast iron, bolted to the deck framing.

Board for chafe protection

Chains and ropes, directed over pulleys, extended from the pilothouse to interlock with the steering quadrant, an iron plate bolted to the *rudder stock* (post). Turning the wheel in the pilothouse rotated the rudder stock and rudder.

Engineer's cabin

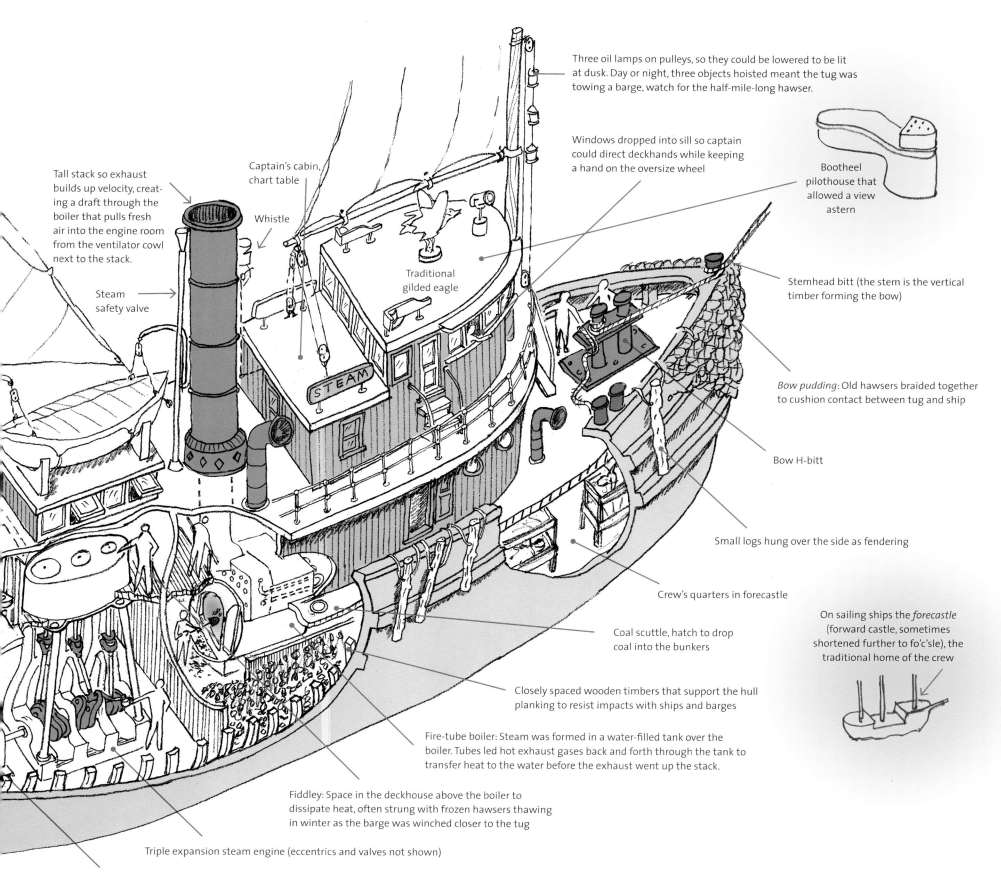

Three oil lamps on pulleys, so they could be lowered to be lit at dusk. Day or night, three objects hoisted meant the tug was towing a barge, watch for the half-mile-long hawser.

Windows dropped into sill so captain could direct deckhands while keeping a hand on the oversize wheel

Bootheel pilothouse that allowed a view astern

Captain's cabin, chart table

Tall stack so exhaust builds up velocity, creating a draft through the boiler that pulls fresh air into the engine room from the ventilator cowl next to the stack.

Whistle

Steam safety valve

Traditional gilded eagle

STEAM

Stemhead bitt (the stem is the vertical timber forming the bow)

Bow pudding: Old hawsers braided together to cushion contact between tug and ship

Bow H-bitt

Small logs hung over the side as fendering

Crew's quarters in forecastle

On sailing ships the *forecastle* (forward castle, sometimes shortened further to fo'c'sle), the traditional home of the crew

Coal scuttle, hatch to drop coal into the bunkers

Closely spaced wooden timbers that support the hull planking to resist impacts with ships and barges

Fire-tube boiler: Steam was formed in a water-filled tank over the boiler. Tubes led hot exhaust gases back and forth through the tank to transfer heat to the water before the exhaust went up the stack.

Fiddley: Space in the deckhouse above the boiler to dissipate heat, often strung with frozen hawsers thawing in winter as the barge was winched closer to the tug

Triple expansion steam engine (eccentrics and valves not shown)

Thrust block, which transfers propeller thrust to hull frame (see page 48)

COMPOUND STEAM ENGINES

Standing on the grating in the deckhouse, this engineer is at the top of his two-story compound steam engine. In front of him, at left, is the head of the large low-pressure cylinder, which receives the steam after it has been used in the high-pressure cylinder, at far right. In between are the covers for the valves that distribute the steam to and between the cylinders. The bottle-shaped objects are relief valves. In the foreground are levers for the throttle and for shifting the eccentric rods from forward to reverse. The controls are repeated in the engine room below, in case the engineer is below oiling or adjusting the mechanism. The cylinders and valves are insulated inside an oval metal enclosure. On tugs such as this, the captain ordered engine changes by pulling cords in the pilothouse to ring gongs and clusters of jingle bells in the engine room. One bell meant go ahead if stopped, or stop from either direction. Two bells meant to reverse if going forward, or start in reverse if not moving. Combinations of bells and jingles called for an increase or decrease in power. For a complete and evocative description of bell signaling between a tug's pilothouse and engine room, and steam whistle signaling between the ship's bridge and the tug, see photographer/writer David Plowden's 1976 book *Tugboat*.

*Tugboat Photos + Research
Steven Lang Collection*

The slow speed of revolution of paddlewheels was a good match for the big single-piston condensing steam engines of the early to mid-nineteenth century. However, screw propellers require much higher speeds of revolution. At first, giant wooden gears on the engine were keyed to small gears on the propeller shaft. As boilers and piping improved, power could be generated by high steam pressure itself, so the condensing of steam for the power stroke was abandoned. Engines could operate more quickly, but the high pressure of the steam was not used up in one cylinder. Steam continues to expand when released from the boiler, until it cools to below its boiling point.

The compound steam engine was developed to capture the expansion not used up by the single cylinder. The still-expanding steam from the first cylinder was directed to additional pistons in sequence, increasing the power of the engine. Smaller multiple pistons could also run faster than one big single piston.

Compound steam engines were installed in ships from the 1850s to the 1940s (when they powered the armada of Liberty ships in World War II). These complicated mechanisms are the best opportunity to see directly how things work. Except for the pistons and valves, all the workings are visible. (A trip on Mystic

Seaport's steamer *Seguin* puts you right next to one of these magical organisms.) Engine builders developed valves, valve gears, connecting rods, and crankshafts whose principles are in use today in gasoline and diesel engines. Compound engines hail from a time when work was tangible and visible, before it disappeared inside enclosures and computers. The rods and cranks pump in a purposeful (even mysterious, in the case of the aptly named eccentrics) amalgamation of motions.

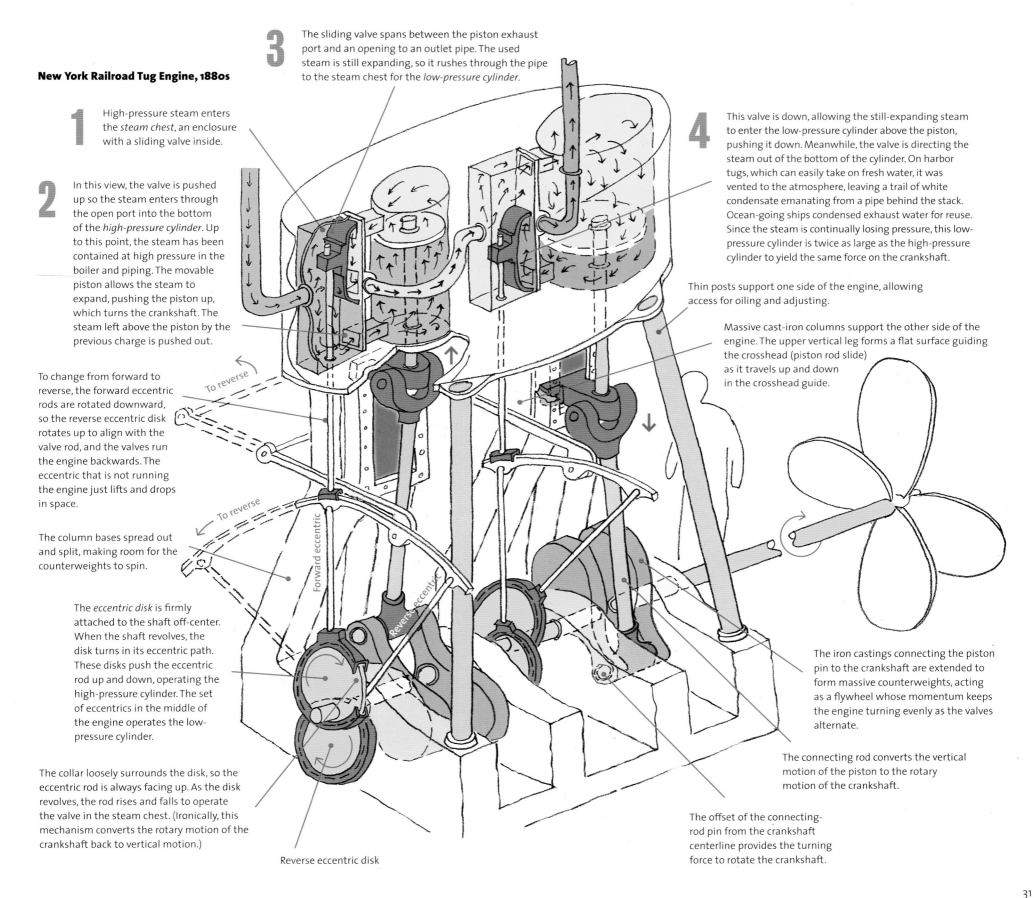

New York Railroad Tug Engine, 1880s

3 The sliding valve spans between the piston exhaust port and an opening to an outlet pipe. The used steam is still expanding, so it rushes through the pipe to the steam chest for the *low-pressure cylinder*.

1 High-pressure steam enters the *steam chest*, an enclosure with a sliding valve inside.

2 In this view, the valve is pushed up so the steam enters through the open port into the bottom of the *high-pressure cylinder*. Up to this point, the steam has been contained at high pressure in the boiler and piping. The movable piston allows the steam to expand, pushing the piston up, which turns the crankshaft. The steam left above the piston by the previous charge is pushed out.

4 This valve is down, allowing the still-expanding steam to enter the low-pressure cylinder above the piston, pushing it down. Meanwhile, the valve is directing the steam out of the bottom of the cylinder. On harbor tugs, which can easily take on fresh water, it was vented to the atmosphere, leaving a trail of white condensate emanating from a pipe behind the stack. Ocean-going ships condensed exhaust water for reuse. Since the steam is continually losing pressure, this low-pressure cylinder is twice as large as the high-pressure cylinder to yield the same force on the crankshaft.

To change from forward to reverse, the forward eccentric rods are rotated downward, so the reverse eccentric disk rotates up to align with the valve rod, and the valves run the engine backwards. The eccentric that is not running the engine just lifts and drops in space.

The column bases spread out and split, making room for the counterweights to spin.

Thin posts support one side of the engine, allowing access for oiling and adjusting.

Massive cast-iron columns support the other side of the engine. The upper vertical leg forms a flat surface guiding the crosshead (piston rod slide) as it travels up and down in the crosshead guide.

To reverse

To reverse

Forward eccentric

Reverse eccentric

The *eccentric disk* is firmly attached to the shaft off-center. When the shaft revolves, the disk turns in its eccentric path. These disks push the eccentric rod up and down, operating the high-pressure cylinder. The set of eccentrics in the middle of the engine operates the low-pressure cylinder.

The collar loosely surrounds the disk, so the eccentric rod is always facing up. As the disk revolves, the rod rises and falls to operate the valve in the steam chest. (Ironically, this mechanism converts the rotary motion of the crankshaft back to vertical motion.)

Reverse eccentric disk

The iron castings connecting the piston pin to the crankshaft are extended to form massive counterweights, acting as a flywheel whose momentum keeps the engine turning evenly as the valves alternate.

The connecting rod converts the vertical motion of the piston to the rotary motion of the crankshaft.

The offset of the connecting-rod pin from the crankshaft centerline provides the turning force to rotate the crankshaft.

The Development of Modern Tugs

In this 1946 photograph, the fireman is using a bar to loosen clinkers (unburnt residue left by burning coal) so they drop through the grate to the ash pit, allowing air to rise through the grates and the burning coal. The hot exhaust passes through tubes immersed in a tank of water on its way to the stack, transferring heat to the water. Diesel engines eliminated the fireman, coal, clinkers, and water for steam.

Tugboat Photos + Research
Steven Lang Collection

FROM STEAM TO DIESEL

As a power source, steam was well suited to the maneuvering demands of ship-handling tugs, which were the last class of vessels to give it up, in the early 1950s. Steam pressure in the engine could be turned on or off instantly through a valve from the boiler (external combustion). However, the process of generating the steam was not ideal. In addition to an engineer who maintained the engine and responded to the captain's signals, it required a fireman, who shoveled coal into the boiler, stoked the fire, and poked soot out of the fire tubes that transferred the fire's heat to the water. Coal was a bulky, dirty fuel, but even when oil replaced it, the boiler was still a very large, demanding machine requiring a dedicated engineer. Water tanks for replenishing steam took up space. Boilers had to be tended overnight so steam was available next morning. If the boiler went out, it could take four or five hours to raise steam pressure again.

Diesel Ignition by Compression

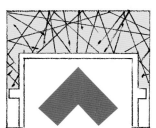

In a gas such as air, the molecules are in rapid, wide motion, only occasionally colliding.

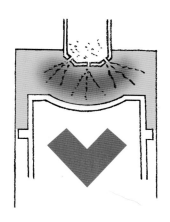

Compressing the air causes the molecules to collide more frequently, raising heat by friction.

When the air has been compressed by the rising piston, diesel fuel is sprayed into the cylinder and burns explosively, forcing the piston down.

Diesel Engine Operation

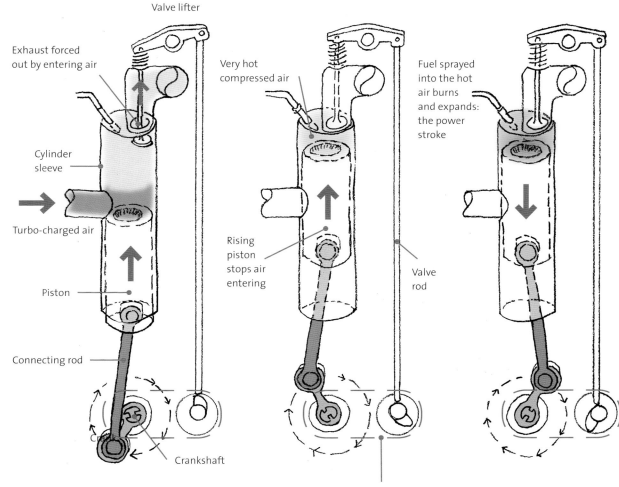

Valve lifter

Exhaust forced out by entering air

Very hot compressed air

Fuel sprayed into the hot air burns and expands: the power stroke

Cylinder sleeve

Turbo-charged air

Rising piston stops air entering

Piston

Valve rod

Connecting rod

Crankshaft

Belt from crankshaft turns camshaft to operate valves

Internal combustion engines, so named because they moved combustion into the cylinder, allowed the elimination of the boiler. Gasoline engines were in wide use in the early twentieth century, but were not a good replacement for steam in ships and tugs. Gasoline engines run on oil that has been refined so that it is easily exploded by a single spark. Storage tanks of the highly refined fuel give off vapors that can build up in a closed hull.

Rudolph Diesel invented his efficient engine in 1894, and diesel was a better match than gasoline for vessels, because diesel engines use a less volatile distillation of oil, without explosive fumes. Diesel fuel is ignited when a rising piston compresses air, raising the air temperature. Cylinders can be much larger because the heat from compression is spread across the cylinder head, not concentrated at one point like the spark in a gasoline engine. However, the instantaneous availability of power from a steam

boiler was lost. Diesel engines large enough for tug work were too big for electric starters, and required compressed air to force the pistons up to initiate the firing sequence. This shot of compressed air, called *starting air* (see page 36), added a level of complication and time to reversing the engine's direction, and thus the tug's direction.

THE DIESEL TUG

The first US diesel tug was built in 1914, and by the 1940s most tugs were diesel powered. Some big World War II salvage tugs were still steam powered, as with the Liberty ships, to make use of available compound-engine manufacturing capacity in the wartime rush to produce vessels. Diesels run at 500 to 2,000 rpm, which is too fast for the big propellers needed by tugs. Many engineering methods were used over the years to convert the engine speed to the 100 or so revolutions required at the propeller, until reliable clutches and transmissions were perfected. Engines had four cylinders, then eight, and were standardized at sixteen cylinders in a "V" configuration in the 1950s. Tugs usually have several small four-cylinder auxiliary diesels producing electricity and running fire pumps, winches, and capstans.

Dropping a diesel engine into a steam tug was easy, since the diesels were smaller than the steam engine and boiler they replaced, and the tugs had a removable hatch/skylight directly over the engine room. However, noise and vibration were worse in diesels than in steam engines. The engines took in combustion air from the engine room, so fans connected to air vents on the boat deck added to the din. Flexible isolation pads reduced vibration, but engineers suffered until effective ear protection was developed (and accepted by conservative tugmen). On tugs converted from steam, the now-empty fiddley provided lots of space over the engine to dissipate heat.

As the increasing size of ships and barges called for more powerful tugs, new boats kept the classic steam tug design, widened from 25 to 35 feet to fit two engines side by side, each with its propeller, or geared to a single wheel as was common on Coast Guard tugs. (Two engines spinning a single propeller increased power and redundancy but maintained the simplicity of a single prop, which also was less likely to be damaged by ice than twin wheels because it was centered under the wide hull.)

Engineer Chris Stradiotti stands in the compact engine room, between Shuswap's twin 1,600 hp engines. The auxiliary generator is mounted in the center, with its day tank mounted directly on top holding enough fuel to get the generator started immediately, while the pump delivers fuel from the main tanks. The exhaust pipes are wrapped in quilted insulation. The photograph was taken from the fiddley, which provides access to the engine room as well as space to dissipate heat. Because the engine is automated, the engineer can also act as deckhand, handling the hawser for ship docking, then climbing to the wheelhouse to operate a winch control station next to the skipper's steering station. Note handrails around engines for rough weather.

Alan Haig-Brown

Forty-Cylinder Diesel Tug

The drawing is loosely based on *Crusader*, purpose-built in 1967 to tow oil barges along the US East Coast. She is still at the same task, now named *Ivory Coast*. Her forty cylinders consist of two sixteen-cylinder main engines plus two four-cylinder auxiliary engines for power generation, compressing air, and running winches.

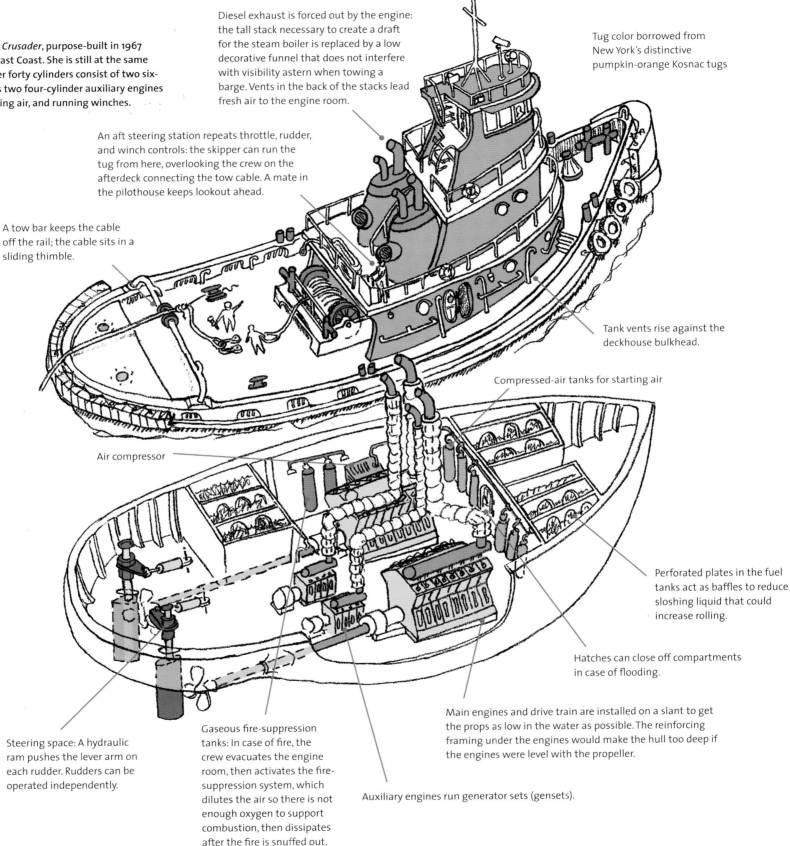

Diesel exhaust is forced out by the engine: the tall stack necessary to create a draft for the steam boiler is replaced by a low decorative funnel that does not interfere with visibility astern when towing a barge. Vents in the back of the stacks lead fresh air to the engine room.

Tug color borrowed from New York's distinctive pumpkin-orange Kosnac tugs

An aft steering station repeats throttle, rudder, and winch controls: the skipper can run the tug from here, overlooking the crew on the afterdeck connecting the tow cable. A mate in the pilothouse keeps lookout ahead.

A tow bar keeps the cable off the rail; the cable sits in a sliding thimble.

Tank vents rise against the deckhouse bulkhead.

Compressed-air tanks for starting air

Air compressor

Perforated plates in the fuel tanks act as baffles to reduce sloshing liquid that could increase rolling.

Hatches can close off compartments in case of flooding.

Steering space: A hydraulic ram pushes the lever arm on each rudder. Rudders can be operated independently.

Gaseous fire-suppression tanks: In case of fire, the crew evacuates the engine room, then activates the fire-suppression system, which dilutes the air so there is not enough oxygen to support combustion, then dissipates after the fire is snuffed out.

Main engines and drive train are installed on a slant to get the props as low in the water as possible. The reinforcing framing under the engines would make the hull too deep if the engines were level with the propeller.

Auxiliary engines run generator sets (gensets).

The *Patricia Moran* sailing (commonly used on ship-assist tugs as the opposite of "docking") the *Statendam* in late-1970s New York. In spite of their new power source, or on purpose to reassure conservative shipowners, US diesel tugs retained the lines of the classic steam tug: rounded hull, long house for engine and accommodations, and bootheel pilothouse. The funnel contains a few small diesel exhaust pipes, but the primary purpose of all that sheet metal is to make the boat look like a powerful steam tug, and serve as a billboard for the Moran "M." Harbor water to cool the engine is pumped through a heat exchanger and back out the side of the hull. When she was built, *Patricia* had a diesel-electric drive system. Round-topped air vents on the boat deck ventilate the engine room. Here the *Patricia* is in a typical dangerous position, out of sight of the docking pilot on the ship's bridge, squeezed between the ship and pier, and under the port anchor, which might be dropped in an emergency. (With familiarity, tugs as well as people come to be called by their first names). A ship's officer is keeping watch from over the *Statendam*'s rail, probably as worried about damage the tug might do to the ship's paint as about the danger the tug is in. The tug's mast is *tabernacled*: folded back out of the way. The wooden ladder is for the docking pilot, usually the captain of one of the tugs working the ship, to return to the tug. The hawser across the ship's bow is holding the tug in place so she can push the ship out into the stream and quickly shift to the other side of the

bow if necessary. (The wrinkle in the bow may be from a tug less careful about how to push at the bow.) A deckhand in plaid at the back corner of the deckhouse may be heading to the traditional location at the fantail, in sight of the captain from the windows in the back of the pilothouse, but away from hawsers that might snap under strain.

Tugs are built to take punishment, and *Patricia*'s eventful history is not unique. When launched in 1962 she was the most powerful tug ever built for New York Harbor service. On January 12, 1966, as she was backing out of the Moran yard on Staten Island, she was

hit broadside by the bow of a small tanker and capsized and sank immediately. The accident occurred at 6:20 a.m., as the shifts were changing, so everyone was awake. But four crewmen died, including the chief and assistant engineers, who were likely down in the engine room with no way out. The tug was soon raised and back in service, and now works in Hampton Roads, Virginia, with Z-drives (see page 64) in place of her propellers.

©*John McGrail/MaritimePhotos.com*

THE SAGA OF STARTING AIR

Heavy diesel engines are too large for battery-operated starters, so ships are cranked up by blowing *starting air* into the cylinders: compressed air from storage tanks sets the pistons in motion so the diesel firing cycle can begin. After starting, most ship engines are not stopped again until the end of the voyage. Until transmission advances at mid-century, diesel engines were too large for shifting transmissions that could incorporate a reverse gear. To reverse, the engine had to be stopped, and the camshaft pushed ahead so a set of reverse cams would line up with the valves. Starting air was injected to restart the engine in the opposite rotation: the pistons

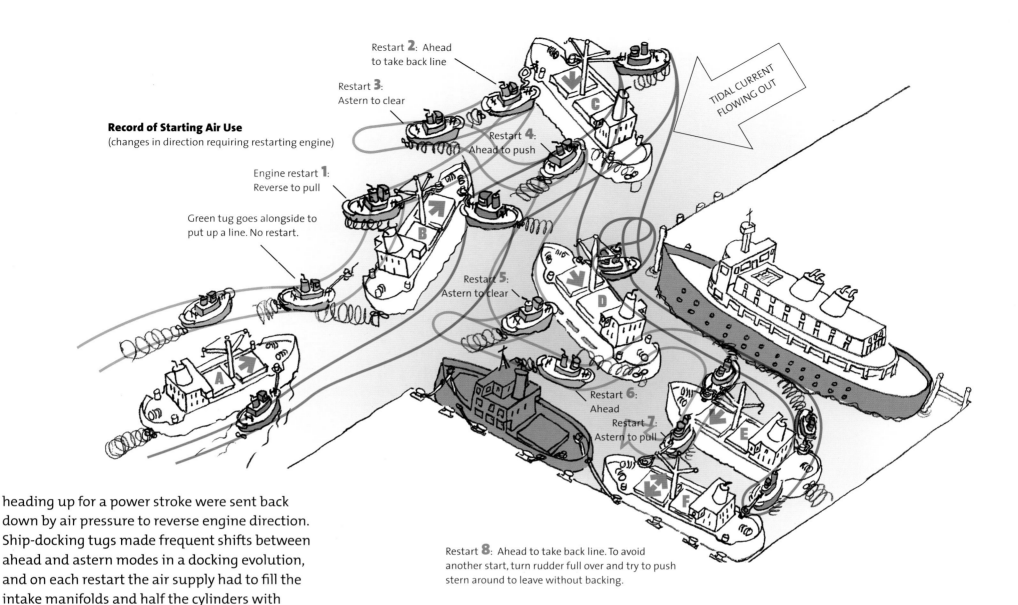

Record of Starting Air Use
(changes in direction requiring restarting engine)

Restart **2**: Ahead to take back line

Restart **3**: Astern to clear

Restart **4**: Ahead to push

Engine restart **1**: Reverse to pull

Green tug goes alongside to put up a line. No restart.

Restart **5**: Astern to clear

TIDAL CURRENT FLOWING OUT

Restart **6**: Ahead

Restart **7**: Astern to pull

Restart **8**: Ahead to take back line. To avoid another start, turn rudder full over and try to push stern around to leave without backing.

heading up for a power stroke were sent back down by air pressure to reverse engine direction. Ship-docking tugs made frequent shifts between ahead and astern modes in a docking evolution, and on each restart the air supply had to fill the intake manifolds and half the cylinders with enough air pressure to turn over the engine (and the propeller, since there was no clutch to disengage it from the engine). Too many restarts in shifting between ahead and astern depleted the compressed air in the tanks faster than the compressor could replenish it, leaving a tug unable to restart its engine in the middle of a critical docking maneuver. Currents, winds, and the momentum of giant ships are relentless, so losing a tug while she waits for the compressor to refill the tanks by battery power could be catastrophic. Ship docking is stressful, and the number of starts remaining in the tanks was just another complication that the team had to keep in mind.

Ship and Tug Movements

A Ship approaches the slip (waterway between piers), facing into tidal current going out. Red tug is connected as they transit the harbor, in case of emergency.

B Ship starts a turn to be parallel to the slip. Green tug puts up a line to pull the bow around. Red tug takes in some line but stays connected to push bow around. Ship couldn't make such a tight turn itself. Ship's momentum carries it ahead into the current.

C Ship is turned parallel to the slip but upstream. If the tugs turned her next to the slip, the current would carry her downstream before they finished.

D As the current carries them past the opening, ship backs. Tugs hold her perpendicular. While ship's stern enters the slack water of the slip, green tug bumps her as she passes, so the ship's bow is not pushed sideways by the current.

E Red tug disconnects and enters the slip. After ship passes, green tug crosses to starboard side. Tugs put up headlines, but then go ahead to push to start ship's momentum toward the berth.

F Tugs reverse against the headlines to slow ship's momentum so it touches gently. Tugs go ahead to take in their lines. Green tug leaves, red tug presses at the center to hold ship while mooring lines are set.

New York was a railroad tug, pushing barges of railroad cars between Manhattan Island and mainland ports across the Hudson and East Rivers. Many railroads did not have access to bridges and tunnels, so they built fleets of tugs and barges to cross rivers and harbors. Railroad barges are seldom used now, but many harbor tug fleets have collected a few old railroad tugs, recognizable by the tall pilothouse for visibility over the boxcars, without a captain's cabin behind. General Motors' Electro-Motive Division (EMD) supplied most of the railroads with diesel-electric power units for their locomotives, so the railroads often put the familiar systems into their tugs as well. As a bonus, they got tugs with excellent slow-speed maneuvering for the river railheads.

© John McGrail /
MaritimePhotos.com

DIESEL-ELECTRIC DRIVE

Designers of tugs and ferries, which maneuver intensively, looked for an alternative to solve the starting-air problem and reduce the time required to switch from ahead to astern propulsion. One answer was to couple a diesel engine to a generator to make electricity, and use the electric power directly or from batteries to turn an electric motor attached to the prop shaft. The engine could run at a constant, efficient speed, and the skipper had infinitely adjustable control of propeller speed and direction from the pilothouse without worrying about starting air or needing the engineer to be in the engine room. The engine was not required to be on axis with the shaft, and could be located for the best weight distribution in the hull. Giant tug/supply vessels are built with diesel-electric drive so the underdeck storage areas are free of propeller shafts. The engines sit under the pilothouse, and the propeller motors are under the stern. However, diesel-electric drive is not common, because in addition to the engine, the owner pays for a generator, batteries, big switchgear, and an electric motor, all susceptible to corrosion in the saltwater environment.

Some benefits of diesel-electric drive have been overtaken by more recent technologies. Controllable-pitch propellers (page 46) offer propeller control independent of engine speed and direction, and directional propeller systems such as rudder-propellers can control speed and direction by their orientation.

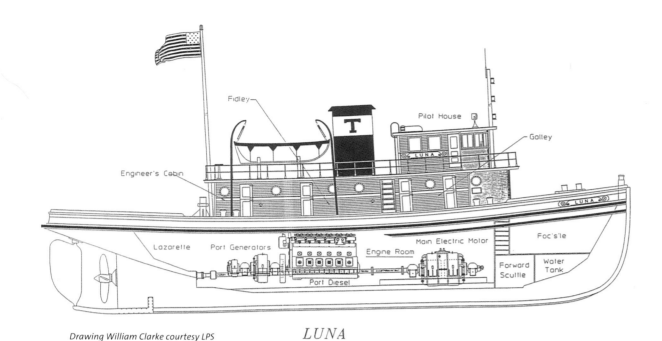

LUNA is a hybrid: a traditional nineteenth-century wooden boat in an age of steel hulls, designed by renowned yacht architect John Alden, but also the first tugboat powered by diesel-electric propulsion. Her two diesel engines generate electrical power for the motor that spins the propeller. *Luna* was built for the Boston Towboat Company for ship work and barge towing in Boston Harbor. The "T" on her stack refers to the T-shaped wharf where the tugs were berthed. Abandoned, she was rescued by a crew of tug enthusiasts (her twin *Venus*, sinking beside her in the Charles River, was too far gone to save). The *Luna* Preservation Society has almost completed a twenty-five-year process of restoration, which was aided at a critical point by a federal transportation grant for the preservation of historic transit artifacts. The diesel-electric system is being cleaned up for display; returning it to service would be too expensive. As with other restored tugs, a smaller propulsion engine powerful enough to move her around the harbor will be installed in a location that will allow restoration of the original drive system in place for display.

Drawing William Clarke courtesy LPS   *LUNA*

Luna: Diesel-Electric Tug Arrangement

The skipper has direct control of the electric motor from a rheostat in the pilothouse and is able to select any speed of rotation and quickly switch from ahead to astern, limited only by how fast the shaft and prop can be stopped (reversing while the prop is still spinning ahead would put damaging torque into the shaft). Diesel-electric power was a clever way to get two engines running one propeller in a short hull. If the gearing and thrust block were mounted behind the engines, as in a conventional arrangement, the drive train would require more length than is desirable for a harbor tug.

Power from the generators is carried by bus duct (solid metal bars with more capacity than cable, not shown) to the switchgear on the main deck in the fiddley.

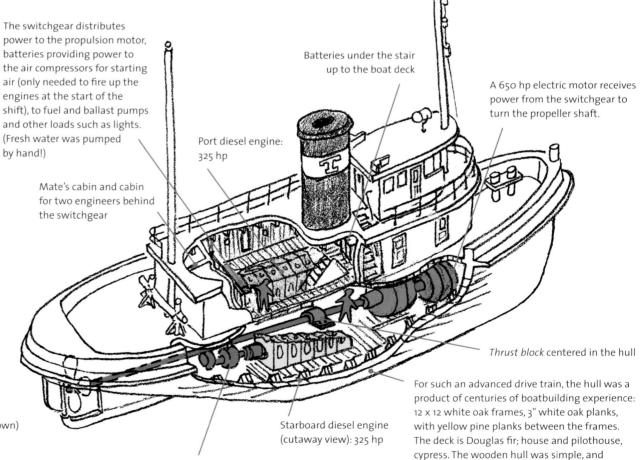

The switchgear distributes power to the propulsion motor, batteries providing power to the air compressors for starting air (only needed to fire up the engines at the start of the shift), to fuel and ballast pumps and other loads such as lights. (Fresh water was pumped by hand!)

Mate's cabin and cabin for two engineers behind the switchgear

Port diesel engine: 325 hp

Batteries under the stair up to the boat deck

A 650 hp electric motor receives power from the switchgear to turn the propeller shaft.

Thrust block centered in the hull

Starboard diesel engine (cutaway view): 325 hp

Each diesel engine spins a generator, producing electricity.

For such an advanced drive train, the hull was a product of centuries of boatbuilding experience: 12 x 12 white oak frames, 3" white oak planks, with yellow pine planks between the frames. The deck is Douglas fir; house and pilothouse, cypress. The wooden hull was simple, and flexible when crushed by contact.

A heavy drum was connected to the engine drive shaft, open toward the transmission. The drum also acted as a flywheel, maintaining engine momentum. The transmission shaft extended forward into the drum, ending in a disk smaller than the drum. The disk had a rubber tube around the edge connected to a compressed air supply valve. When the tube was inflated, it pressed against the drum, and the rotation of the drum was forwarded to the transmission, putting the tug in drive. When the tube was deflated and the transmission was not receiving power, the tug was in neutral, with the engine still running, turning the drum.

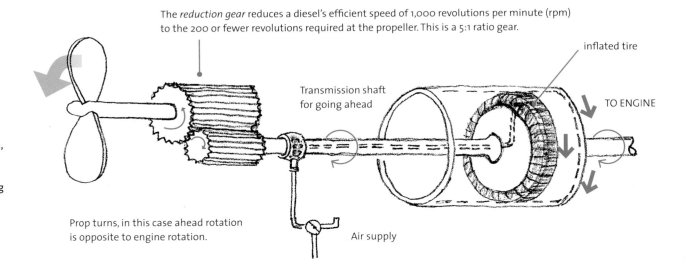

The *reduction gear* reduces a diesel's efficient speed of 1,000 revolutions per minute (rpm) to the 200 or fewer revolutions required at the propeller. This is a 5:1 ratio gear.

inflated tire

Transmission shaft for going ahead

TO ENGINE

Prop turns, in this case ahead rotation is opposite to engine rotation.

Air supply

Now add a disk that turns a reverse gear sequence. Air was bled from the forward gear disk, leaving the tug in neutral. After the propeller stopped turning, or was stopped by a shaft brake, the rubber tube on the reverse disk was inflated, sending power to a set of gears that turned the propeller shaft in the opposite direction. The gear not selected was still engaged, so it spun the disk inside the drum, but had no effect.

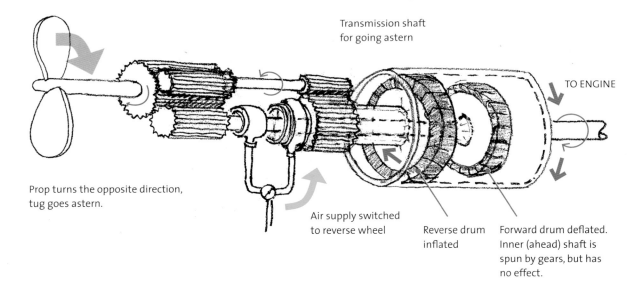

Transmission shaft for going astern

TO ENGINE

Prop turns the opposite direction, tug goes astern.

Air supply switched to reverse wheel

Reverse drum inflated

Forward drum deflated. Inner (ahead) shaft is spun by gears, but has no effect.

Pneumatic Clutches

Diesel-electric drive solved the problem of reversing the propeller's rotation, but at the cost of expensive and high-maintenance equipment. Pneumatic clutches and later fluid coupling transmissions developed in the 1930s were lower-cost options than diesel-electric drive; fluid coupling became the standard, allowing the skipper in the pilot-house to switch between ahead and astern gears without stopping the engine or reversing its direction.

Fluid Coupling

Most tug engines now are connected to fluid couplings as a means of controlling the connection between the engine's power and the propeller. Two wheels, each with a ring of cells, face one another. The wheels are free to rotate independently. The hollow formed by the opposing cells is filled with a fluid, usually oil. The wheel spun by the engine acts as a pump, forcing the oil across the gap to press on the opposite wheel, which acts as a turbine, forwarding power to the propeller. By draining oil into a reservoir, the power being transmitted can be reduced, without having to slow the engine. By pumping out all the oil, the propeller can be stopped, and the transmission switched to reverse or changed to a different gear. The engine is more efficient when running at a steady rate, letting the skipper use the fluid coupling to adjust the propeller speed. The slip inherent in fluids allows the wheels to spin at different speeds, so the engine wheel can build speed without being bogged down as the propeller wheel spins slower while the propeller overcomes water resistance. The slip also isolates the engine from the drive train in case either one has a failure that brings it to a sudden stop. (The fluid temperature will rise to damaging levels in a short time, unless power is cut or the fluid is pumped out.)

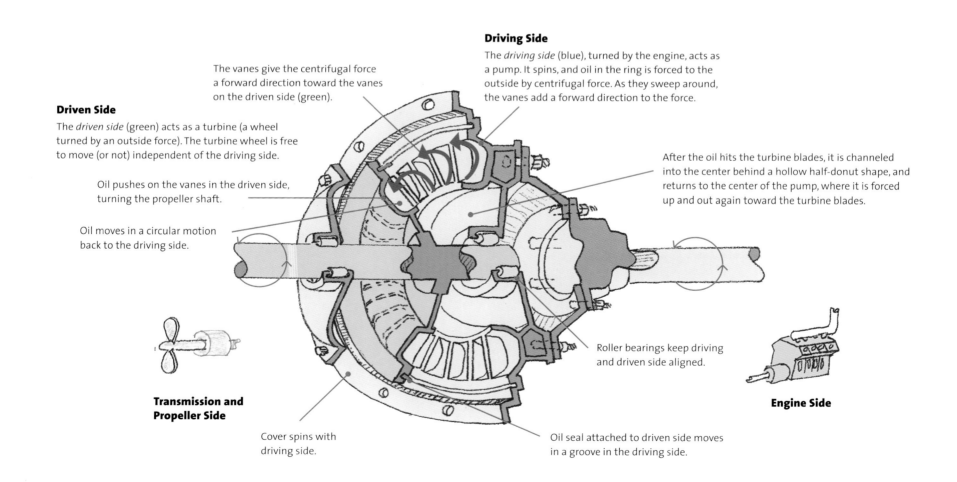

Driving Side

The *driving side* (blue), turned by the engine, acts as a pump. It spins, and oil in the ring is forced to the outside by centrifugal force. As they sweep around, the vanes add a forward direction to the force.

The vanes give the centrifugal force a forward direction toward the vanes on the driven side (green).

Driven Side

The *driven side* (green) acts as a turbine (a wheel turned by an outside force). The turbine wheel is free to move (or not) independent of the driving side.

Oil pushes on the vanes in the driven side, turning the propeller shaft.

Oil moves in a circular motion back to the driving side.

After the oil hits the turbine blades, it is channeled into the center behind a hollow half-donut shape, and returns to the center of the pump, where it is forced up and out again toward the turbine blades.

Roller bearings keep driving and driven side aligned.

Transmission and Propeller Side

Engine Side

Cover spins with driving side.

Oil seal attached to driven side moves in a groove in the driving side.

The *Captain Bill* on a marine railway in Gloucester, Massachusetts. She is an old single-screw tug built in 1950, 100 by 27 feet, 1,800 hp. This is a five-blade, right-hand-turning wheel. Turning direction is identified looking from astern at the top, as the prop will rotate to drive the boat forward. In action, the top of this propeller would be moving away from us. Picture the wide canted blades pressing on the water behind the tug as the propeller spins, forcing the tug forward. In reverse, the top of the blade would move toward us, slicing into the water to pull the tug backwards. Note the draft marks on the left in the photo: the top of the propeller is about eight feet below the waterline, where there is plenty of water surrounding it to form the column of compressed water that forces the hull forward. A few inches of the shaft show, extending out of the stern tube (which is painted the same color as the hull). The stern tube contains a set of interlocking seals between the tube and the spinning shaft, to stop water from entering the hull or channel it to a pump. Bolts connect the propeller boss to a flange on the propeller shaft.

Joey Ciaramitaro

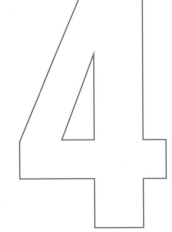

Tug Screws and Rudders

A tug's propeller is the "wheel." The demands on a tug wheel are particular and contradictory. Barge towing takes place at a steady 7 to 8 knots, loading the prop heavily for days, or even weeks on ocean crossings. In contrast, a tug assigned to ship work runs without load for much of the time, transiting to and from docking assignments. Such a big, slow-turning wheel burns up fuel just to spin itself when the tug is traveling light. When working a ship, the tug is pushing and pulling against enormous inertia, so the prop is churning up vast amounts of water but hardly moving as it incrementally builds momentum. A prop selected to slice through a lot of water for barge towing may bog the engine down during low-speed ship work, stalling or overheating it. Before controllable-pitch propellers (see page 46), a tug wheel was a compromise between all these conflicting requirements.

By definition, a tug is over-powered: it carries enough engine for two vessels in as small a hull as possible. One big propeller that turned slowly, pushing a lot of water, was a good match for the slow revolutions of a big steam engine. With the advent of faster-turning, compact diesel engines, it is costly to gear down the propeller rotation to the slow speeds most effective for a large propeller. The requirement for a small hull and minimum draft for working in shallow water means that adding power cannot be achieved with a bigger wheel. Twin-screw tugs add horsepower with two smaller engines and propellers side by side. Tugs that need to work in very shallow water add a third screw to increase power without adding depth.

SCREW PROPELLERS

A *screw propeller* is a set of very short fins "cut" from (imaginary) multiple helical screw blades. In this case three helices are wrapped around one shaft, resulting in a three-bladed propeller.

Three screw threads wound around a shaft

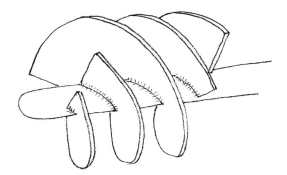

Each propeller blade is a segment "cut" from one of the threads.

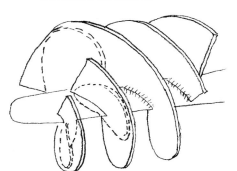

Three-bladed propeller

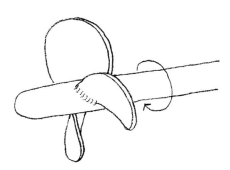

Direction of force is diagonal to the line of the shaft, perpendicular to the surface of the blade. Looking from astern (end of shaft), imagine the shaft turning clockwise. As the blade comes down and toward you, it will be pushing water away at an angle toward the stern.

Pitch

Pitch defines the angle the blade makes with the shaft. It measures how far one blade tip would advance in turning one revolution if it were turning in a solid such as wood. Propellers are described by both the diameter between the blade tips and the pitch. Bigger wheels have higher pitch numbers. A typical tug has a diameter of 100 inches and pitch that is a compromise, a number between 80 inches (good for low-speed towing) and 95 inches (good for speed when running light between assignments). A tug with a pitch of 85 inches would actually only advance about 70 inches on one rotation when running in the water due to slip (the inefficiency of water as a medium to screw into).

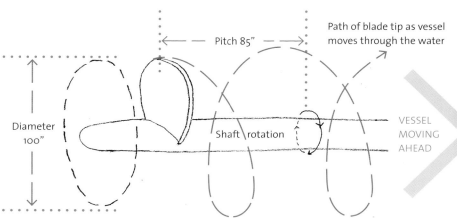

Path of blade tip as vessel moves through the water

Pitch 85"

Diameter 100"

Shaft rotation

VESSEL MOVING AHEAD

Propeller Blade Shape

The first blades were metal sheets. Later, airfoil shapes cast in bronze or brass were introduced to ship propellers. The forward face of the blade bulged out so that when the blade cut through the water molecules, those traveling along the bulging front side took a longer path than those passing the flatter, aft side of the blade. The longer path on the front side spreads the water out, lowering the water pressure on that side. The blade is pulled ahead by suction into the lower pressure, adding to the pushing pressure force from the aft side.

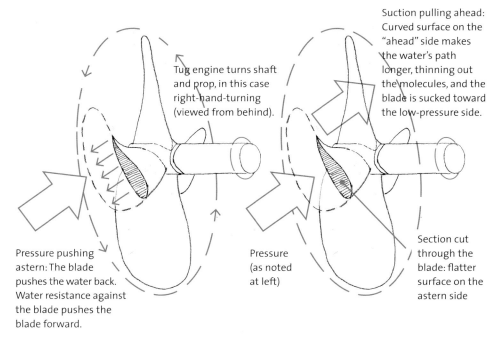

Tug engine turns shaft and prop, in this case right-hand-turning (viewed from behind).

Suction pulling ahead: Curved surface on the "ahead" side makes the water's path longer, thinning out the molecules, and the blade is sucked toward the low-pressure side.

Pressure pushing astern: The blade pushes the water back. Water resistance against the blade pushes the blade forward.

Pressure (as noted at left)

Section cut through the blade: flatter surface on the astern side

Single-Screw Tug

Ship work with a single-screw tug is often a process of outsmarting the propeller. The direction of rotation of the shaft has a major impact on the handling of the tug at extremely low speeds, when the giant propeller blades generate large thrust forces in all directions.

2 High pressure on the tug's port side pushes the stern to the right (to starboard) when the tug is cranking against a ship's side. This is "stern walking." If the tug is moving ahead, the effect would be less pronounced, but the stern would still shift slightly but persistently. When moving ahead, the net effect would be a continuous slight turn to port. Some rudders had wedges attached to the side opposite to the propeller turning direction, to keep the tug on course without continually turning the wheel.

3 In ship work, the rudder can be held over slightly so some prop thrust is forced to the right, counteracting the tendency of the stern to "walk" to starboard. Alternatively, a stern line can hold the tug in shape, but it takes time to put one up and to haul it back if ordered to shift position on the ship.

1 As the propeller blades rise toward the overhang of the stern, they push water up into the hull, creating an area of high pressure. In the right-turning propeller shown here, the blades rise toward the left side.

Twin Screws

Twin-screw tugs eliminate the problem of stern walking because the propellers are opposed in rotation. An added advantage is that one wheel can be put astern, the other ahead, and the tug can rotate 180 degrees without changing location. Dividing the power between two smaller wheels and engines allows a shallower hull. Inward-turning propellers (rising on the outside) increase pressure away from the centerline, rather than building up double the pressure in the center.

This is *Elsbeth II,* one of Smith Maritime's triple-screw boats, in dry dock. All propellers are left-turning. Captain Latham Smith built *Rhea* and *Elsbeth III* with one propeller opposed in direction to help hold course, but all the boats have performed equally well. Each propeller is independently controlled, and each prop is backed by twin rudders for maximum maneuverability. To turn the boat sharply, the outer prop in the turning direction can be reversed as the other two power ahead. The skipper can engage only the outer wheels in opposition, to turn in place.

The propellers are inside nozzles that focus and augment the propellers' thrust, as well as protecting the propellers from debris and hitting bottom.

Captain Latham Smith built *Elsbeth II* and *Rhea,* at left, plus *Elsbeth III,* to please his own unique conception of an ocean tug. They have triple screws connected to triple diesel engines, to get the most power in the shallowest hull, plus redundancy for months-long voyages from Captain Smith's Florida base to remote destinations in Latin America. The steep Viking bow is a signature of his boats, as are the squared-off pilothouse and wood-paneled wings reminiscent of English tugs from the early twentieth century. In fact he built his first boat, beside a canal in Miami, from classic portholes and cabin fittings scavenged from an old Scottish steam tug and a New York Central railroad tug. He sold the brass and bronze he didn't reuse to pay for new materials. His boats are well-appointed homes away from home, finished with wood paneling and rich fabrics.

Both photos Smith Maritime, Inc.

CONTROLLABLE-PITCH PROPULSION

Controllable-pitch propulsion (CPP) is a relatively recent innovation that changes the orientation of the blades as they are spinning, to adjust the level of thrust for different loads (especially important for tugs), or to change vessel speed or direction. The blade orientation can also be set to just spin without exerting any force on the water, a way to put the vessel in "neutral" without shutting off the engine or disengaging a clutch. Besides being too complicated for early propeller builders, this ability was less necessary. Steam engines could be easily stopped, and then reversed if desired. Power to the engine could be cut

immediately simply by shutting the steam valve. To reverse, the engine was stopped, and levers thrown to start the crankshaft in the opposite direction when steam was reapplied. But faster-running diesels are difficult to stop and to reverse. Adjusting engine speed to change vessel speed, and to respond to load conditions, burns a lot of fuel. Each diesel engine model has a most economical rpm (revolutions per minute) setting, and ideally it will be run as much as possible at that speed. CPP offers a solution to both stopping/reversing, and running the engine at a constant speed. Any amount of thrust can be selected, so the

engine can run at its ideal speed while the prop changes characteristics. To avoid suddenly loading the blade, which might cause it to shear off, the system used on tugs is designed to take at least half a minute to go from forward to reverse, and for a large ship it takes several minutes. Another reason for the delay is that, if the engine is running at full load and the pitch is increased suddenly, the engine could stall or overheat. Controllable-pitch propellers are too complicated and expensive for most vessels, but are useful for tugs, ferries, and cruise ships that require careful maneuvering ahead and astern in frequent dockings.

Typical Fixed-Blade Propeller

The root of each blade rises behind the next (see photo page 42). The direction of rotation of the shaft has to be stopped and reversed to change from going ahead to going astern.

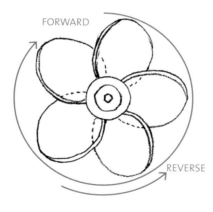

FORWARD

REVERSE

Controllable-Pitch Propeller

Blade orientation can be altered to go from making way ahead to astern, as the shaft keeps turning in the same direction. The blade roots cannot overlap if the blades are to move past each other. The blade base is intentionally the weakest point: if a blade hits something, it shears off, leaving the CPP controls and other blades working. Blades are bolted to the collar that is turned by the CPP linkage, so a new blade can be bolted on without removing the propeller.

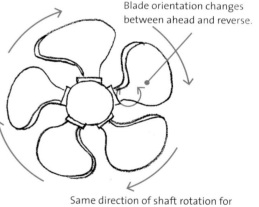

Blade orientation changes between ahead and reverse.

Same direction of shaft rotation for forward and reverse

Tug Going Ahead

Blades tilt to push on the water behind the tug, forcing it forward.

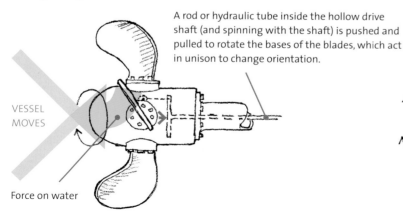

A rod or hydraulic tube inside the hollow drive shaft (and spinning with the shaft) is pushed and pulled to rotate the bases of the blades, which act in unison to change orientation.

VESSEL MOVES

Force on water

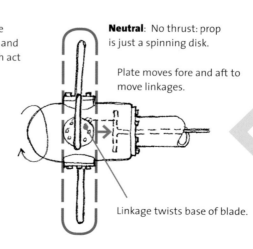

Neutral: No thrust: prop is just a spinning disk.

Plate moves fore and aft to move linkages.

Linkage twists base of blade.

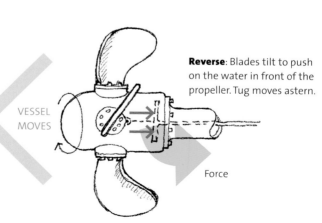

Reverse: Blades tilt to push on the water in front of the propeller. Tug moves astern.

VESSEL MOVES

Force

The propellers on this new tug are inside *Kort nozzles*, thrust-increasing shrouds that surround the propellers, adding thrust to vessels at low speed. The increase is canceled out by increased drag at speeds higher than 10 knots, so they are usually fitted only to tugs and trawlers, which require high thrust at low speeds. The nozzle ring has the section of an airplane wing: the front edge is rounded, and the inside of the ring is curved, tapering toward the stern. The outside of the ring is flat, so water passing inside the ring is spread out, creating a low-pressure vacuum relative to the outside of the ring, which augments the propeller's thrust. The nozzle also focuses the propeller's thrust and increases the force on the rudders mounted behind the ring.

Crowley Maritime Corporation

The "wheels" on Crowley Maritime's *Ocean Wave,* the first of a series of long-distance ocean towing vessels, which is replacing the Invader class that has been the Crowley heavy tow mainstay since the 1960s, are controllable-pitch propellers, distinguished by the individual petal-like blades bolted to the hub. In this prelaunch view, lines are up to hold the tug in place as the floating dry dock is submerged, which will float the tug for the first time. Earlier tug hulls were a long oval under the water, narrow at the bow and narrowing again toward the stern to allow water to flow to a centered propeller or one on each side of the hull. The

Ocean class design is more like a Mississippi River towboat: the entire hull is wide and deep in front of the propellers, then rises to make room for the big wheels and fixed nozzles. The hull is dotted with zincs, a metal that corrodes easily, reducing the corrosion on the hull itself. They must be replaced when they have sacrificed themselves by dissolving in salt water. The stern roller that would ease the friction of towing gear being winched over the stern is not installed yet in the circular recess across the stern (behind a rusty steel construction frame not yet removed).

Drive Train

The force generated by the spinning propeller doesn't just magically move the boat forward. (If this book has a theme, it's that *nothing* is as simple as it seems.) The propeller is generating thrust, which has to be channeled to the hull to force the vessel through the water. The *thrust block* intercepts the force that is pressing the propeller shaft forward. If the forward thrust were not intercepted, it would continue to the engine, pushing the crankshaft out of its alignment with the pistons, causing the engine to seize up from internal friction.

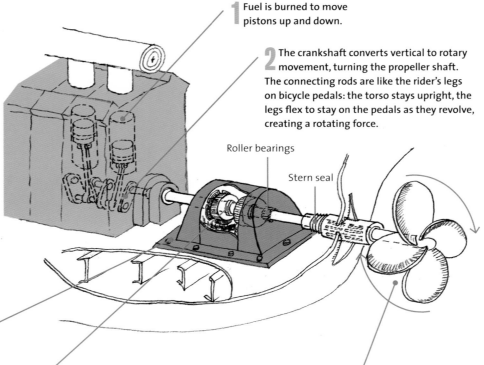

1 Fuel is burned to move pistons up and down.

2 The crankshaft converts vertical to rotary movement, turning the propeller shaft. The connecting rods are like the rider's legs on bicycle pedals: the torso stays upright, the legs flex to stay on the pedals as they revolve, creating a rotating force.

Roller bearings

Stern seal

The propeller shaft

passes into the hull through the stern tube which was the most serious obstacle to the screw propeller, because it was difficult to seal the hull against the spinning shaft underwater. The metal stern tube was lined with a replaceable bearing surface to support the weight of the shaft. The bearing surface stopped short of the inner end of the stern tube, leaving a space between the spinning shaft and the stern tube, filled with a rope-like packing that allowed the shaft to turn, but kept water from coming in. The stern tube was lined on the inside with white metal, a tin alloy, or strips of live oak, a very slow-growing, durable wood. Seawater was allowed into the tube from the water side to lubricate the shaft as it rotated against the wood. Liners are now often rubber or plastic, with lubricating fluid pumped throughout the tube.

5 The thrust block is firmly bolted or welded to the hull framing so the force is transmitted to the hull, driving the vessel forward. Between the thrust block and the crankshaft the shaft is in torsion only, allowing the crankshaft to spin freely.

4 A disc that spins with the prop shaft presses on a set of fixed pads in the thrust block. Oil is continually pumped over the pads. The thrust is transferred through the layer of oil, from the spinning disc to the fixed thrust block that is attached to the hull, thus propelling the hull forward. An identical set of pads on the stern side of the thrust block picks up the thrust when reversing.

3 The propeller screws itself forward, sending thrust along the propeller shaft, toward the engine. Between the propeller and the thrust block, the shaft is in compression from thrust, in addition to torsion from the resistance of the water to the turning screw.

RUDDERS

As tugs maneuver around the ship they are working, rudders and propellers are used in combination more than on any other vessel. This interaction of two force-makers is complicated: tug skippers are continually playing off the throttle against the rudder as a docking evolution unfolds. (*Evolution* is the ship-docking term for the purposeful improvisation between tugs and ship that brings a ship to shore or sends it off.) This was even more complicated in the days of bell boats, when the captain controlled the rudder with the wheel but the steam engine was controlled by the engineer below. The captain needed to watch the ship, the pier, and his deckhands working with hawsers, turn the wheel, and reach for bell cords that he had to pull just before he needed an engine change, to allow time for the engineer to respond and for the engine to adjust or reverse. When rudder-propeller and cycloidal drive systems that combined thrust and steering in one mechanism were perfected, tugs were the first to make use of them, as did ferries, which also maneuver frequently.

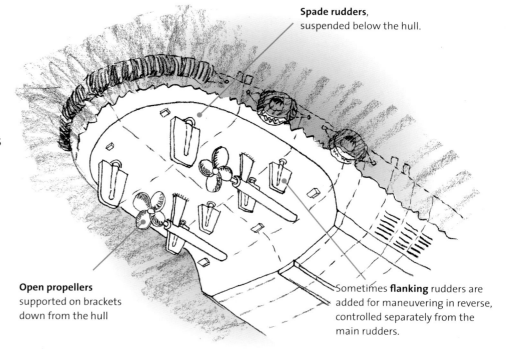

Spade rudders, suspended below the hull.

Open propellers supported on brackets down from the hull

Sometimes **flanking** rudders are added for maneuvering in reverse, controlled separately from the main rudders.

East Coast Steam Tug *William M. Mills*, 1925. Built in Baltimore in 1919 for the Ontario and Western Railroad, presumably for service on Lake Ontario, the *William M. Mills* was soon sold to McAllister Brothers of New York. Since she was built to withstand the wild storms of the ocean-like Great Lakes, she was well suited to work coastwise between North Atlantic ports. As the Roman numerals on her rudder attest, these tugs sat very deep in the water, in this case XII (twelve) feet from the typical waterline to the keel. The depth was necessary to set the weight of the tall steam engine low for stability, and so the propeller was deep in the water where it could be effective even at the top of its rotation. The gentleman in the center is pointing to the business side of the iron propeller: it will rise when turning to the right to push water back and thrust the tug forward. The propeller shaft emerges from the *deadwood*, where the hull narrows to lead water to the propeller and rudder. The bottom of the deadwood ends in a "deadwood stack," massive timbers set crosswise to carry the weight of the tug in dry dock (next to the workman's hand).

The massive rudder is assembled from heavy timbers also, spiked together and capped by an iron bracket topped by the cylindrical rudder stock (only a few inches are visible) disappearing up into the fantail. The rudder stock passes up through a vertical tube set in the hull framing, which acts as a bearing transferring the turning force to the hull. Ahead of the rudder, a massive timber hung from the hull framing supports the extension of the keel that the base of the rudder bears on. Iron straps at the base of this timber, and the end of the deadwood, tie the assembly together.

Collection of Brent Dibner

Alongside Lines

All lines are shown up for illustrative purposes. In reality, any tug would only have one or two of these lines up at one time.

A *head line* leads forward from the bow bitts to the ship. The tug can reverse on it to slow the ship.

A *spring line* leads forward from the bow bitts on the tug's foredeck, then doubles back around the bullnose to lead aft to the ship. The double-back moves the line out so it doesn't rub on the tug's deckhouse. The tug uses the spring line to pull ahead on the ship.

Manila lines connect the tug to the ship's bitts. (Manila refers to the Philippines, where fiber stripped from the giant leaves of the abaca plant was cleaned and shipped to ropewalks around the world.) The hairy fibers "grow" whiskers as the fibers split with hard use on a tug. When thrown over the bits in multiple wraps, the fibers lock overlapping coils together, holding the load by friction rather than knots.

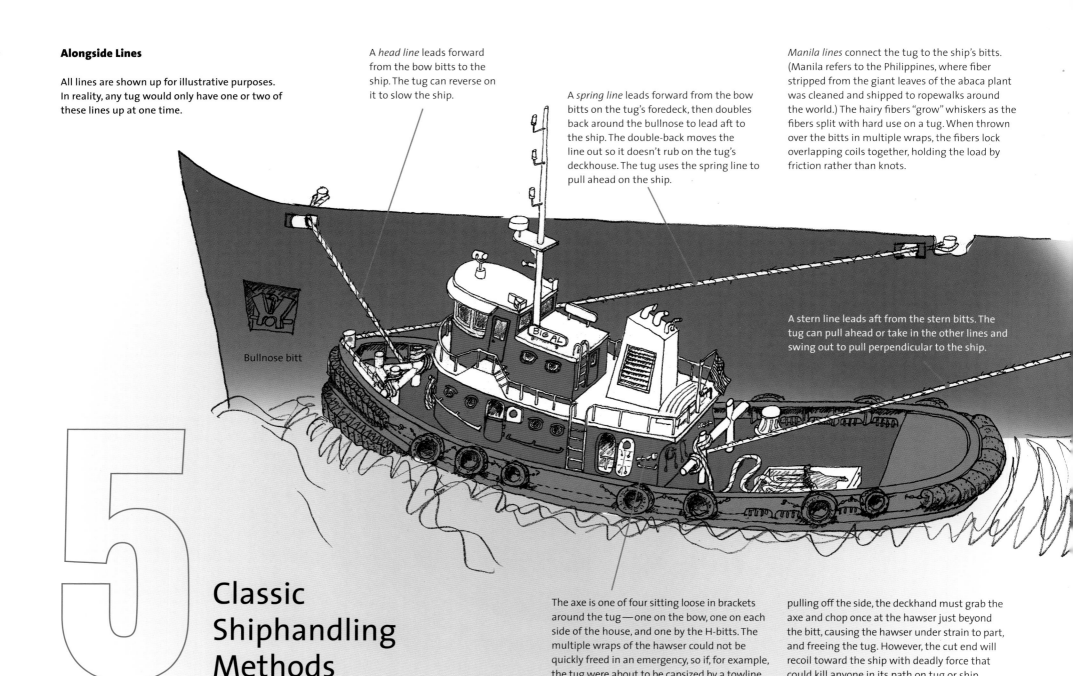

Bullnose bitt

A stern line leads aft from the stern bitts. The tug can pull ahead or take in the other lines and swing out to pull perpendicular to the ship.

The axe is one of four sitting loose in brackets around the tug—one on the bow, one on each side of the house, and one by the H-bitts. The multiple wraps of the hawser could not be quickly freed in an emergency, so if, for example, the tug were about to be capsized by a towline pulling off the side, the deckhand must grab the axe and chop once at the hawser just beyond the bitt, causing the hawser under strain to part, and freeing the tug. However, the cut end will recoil toward the ship with deadly force that could kill anyone in its path on tug or ship.

5

Classic Shiphandling Methods

ALONGSIDE: US-STYLE SHIPHANDLING

In the United States, and in many ports around the world, ships are handled "alongside": the tugs are tied tight to the side of the ship. Because they spend all their time banging into huge ships, tugs are the sturdiest vessels afloat, so strongly built that many fifty-year-old tugs are still in service. (The average age of US tugs in 2015 was forty-one years!) The most dangerous maneuver is getting alongside, which means cutting into the ship's bow wave. Once inside the bow wave, the tug runs parallel to the ship and then turns in to contact the hull. The skipper sets the tug's throttle to match the ship's speed, with the bow turned in slightly to stay in position until a line can be connected. Alongside ship work is safer than any other method because any unexpected movement of the ship due to error or mechanical malfunction simply pulls the tug along like a barnacle. Alongside shiphandling developed in the burgeoning nineteenth-century ports of North America, which were large enough for ships to transit under power, with the tugs alongside only as a precaution, until the final berthing maneuvers. Older, more compact European harbors didn't have the space to put tugs alongside.

Hull Shape

Tug hulls built for alongside towing are a distinctive peapod shape: sharp forward, then curving continuously to the wide, round stern. Having no straight lines makes it possible for the tug to come alongside a moving ship with minimum contact and roll toward the hull while a line is put up. When a tug comes near a ship's hull, a *Venturi effect* is produced: water speeds up in the narrow channel between the two hulls, with lower pressure than the water on the outer side of the tug. The tug is forced toward the ship's hull. Having a rounded hull allows the tug to rotate its bow outward when departing, biting into the slack water to tear itself away. A tug with a straight hull is harder to pull away from the suction between the two hulls. Many tugs from the 1970s were built with minimal curves, and became infamous "pigs" among shiphandling skippers, clinging to the ship's hull when it was time to leave.

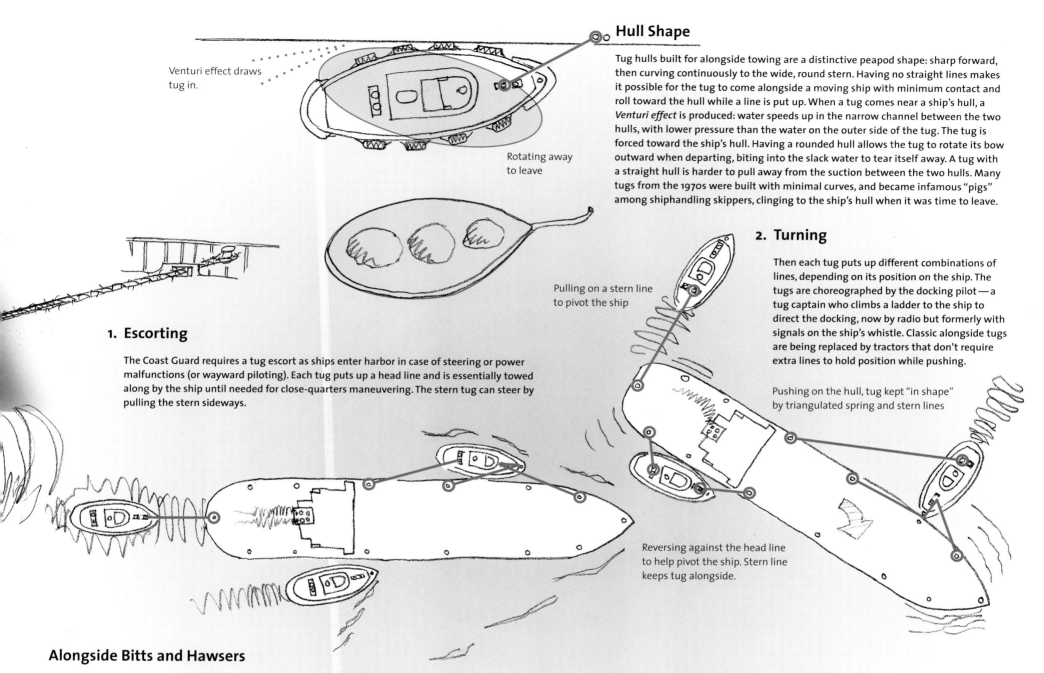

Venturi effect draws tug in.

Rotating away to leave

1. Escorting

The Coast Guard requires a tug escort as ships enter harbor in case of steering or power malfunctions (or wayward piloting). Each tug puts up a head line and is essentially towed along by the ship until needed for close-quarters maneuvering. The stern tug can steer by pulling the stern sideways.

Pulling on a stern line to pivot the ship

2. Turning

Then each tug puts up different combinations of lines, depending on its position on the ship. The tugs are choreographed by the docking pilot—a tug captain who climbs a ladder to the ship to direct the docking, now by radio but formerly with signals on the ship's whistle. Classic alongside tugs are being replaced by tractors that don't require extra lines to hold position while pushing.

Pushing on the hull, tug kept "in shape" by triangulated spring and stern lines

Reversing against the head line to help pivot the ship. Stern line keeps tug alongside.

Alongside Bitts and Hawsers

Putting up a line (technically, a *hawser* if it's a large-diameter rope for towing and mooring, but called a line for most purposes) is what tugs are all about. From the ship's bitts, several hundred thousand pounds of force are transmitted through the hawser to the fittings built into the tug's deck framing. Traditional lines were manila: coarse hemp fibers twisted into strings, which were twisted into ropes, several of which were twisted into hawsers as big around as a fire hose. Wire cable is too stiff for ship work. A cable would go taut instantly, suddenly exerting all the force on the bitts, and jerking the tug. Manila hawsers have give—they stretch out over a few seconds as tension is put on them, either as the tug captain applies power, or as the tug powers down to be towed alongside a ship passing through the harbor, ready to assist.

Winches big enough for the fat hawsers were too expensive and bulky for a harbor tug. European tug hawsers with an eye at each end don't allow any adjustment in the length of the line, so the relationship of tug to ship is fixed, whatever the evolution. The American practice was to splice an eye only on the ship end of a long hawser. The connection on the tug's deck was made by twisting the hawser in coils around the deck bitts. The connection was not tight until the tug and ship pulled apart, squeezing the coils together, and gripping the bitt. The tug could connect with any desired length of line out, depending on the situation.

In traditional American ship work, the tugs met the ship at the entrance to the harbor, and one or two put up lines to the ship's bow. They then let up on the throttle, so the ship towed them, and they would be ready if the ship suddenly needed assistance. (This is reminiscent of a "Nantucket sleighride," meaning a whaleboat towed madly by a harpooned whale until it exhausted itself.) Being pulled by the ship put enormous force into the hawser wraps on the H-bitt, locking them together. The hawser is stretched as taut as an iron bar ("bar tight"). If the deckhand looped the hawser carelessly, with gaps between the coils, when tension was put on the connection an outer wrap

could become jammed between inner wraps. Then when it was time to loosen the wraps and reposition the ship for final docking, the hawser might jam. Precious seconds during a critical maneuver could be lost while deckhands struggled to lever the jammed loop out of the pile. A craftsman-like connection would have each loop neatly set tight to the next, with no spaces between for outer wraps to burrow into. It is possible, but risky, to throw off a few outer loops while under tow, releasing enough friction that the hawser would start to slip, and the tug could let itself slide back along the hull to a new position, where the loosened wraps would be tossed back on the bitt.

This velvety photo of the steam tug *Ned Moran* being pulled by the tanker *Pan Virginian* in New York Harbor captures the roughness of the water surface that is a tug's natural environment, although the immaculately white-suited cook might be at the back door of a restaurant, not in a terrifying and dangerous maneuver on a tug. Note the wheel at the back of the boat deck, for steering when pulling a barge, and the three lamps strung up the after mast, lit if the tug was towing a barge.

Photo by Jeff Blinn, Moran, Collection of Brent Dibner

This unusual 1970s view shows the bow of one Moran tug and the stern of another, both made up alongside a dead ship being shifted to a repair yard, in New York Harbor. The far tug is connected alongside the ship, from bow and stern bitts, to move the ship around the harbor. The near tug may be connected perpendicular to the barge's bow to push or pull for steering.

At the far right edge of the picture is the white top of the capstan. When towing astern on a long hawser, the capstan would be used to pull the hawser in to shorten the distance between the tug and barge—for example, when entering port. The tug would slow enough to take the strain off the line leading from the barge to the H-bitt (in the center, also wrapped in hawsers). The deckhands would wrap the loosened hawser a few times around the capstan, and turn it on. Slowly rotating, it would pull in the hawser as the deckhands stacked the loose end in the square pile in the stern. When setting out the hawser upon leaving port, the tug would pull ahead of the barge as the hawser slipped neatly off the pile. When the barge was at the desired distance for towing, the deckhands put wraps on the H-bitt as the tug slowed, gradually putting tension on the hawser to avoid snapping it.

One hawser is connected to the far tug's stern bitt, in the center of the tug. The hawser rises from under the crossbar up to the ship, so the force is pulling up on the bitt, instead of pulling the connection apart.

The profile of the far tug illustrates *tumblehome* as it applies to tugs. On sailing vessels, this describes the inward curve of the hull between the waterline and the rail. On tugs, tumblehome is the stack of progressively smaller decks, so the tug can be rocked against the ship's hull without contact (in reality, bent pilothouse visors are a common feature of experienced tugs). This tug has a small, one-person pilothouse added at the top to give visibility when the tug is pushing barges from behind.

On the bow of the near tug, a deckhand is building up the multiple overlapping loops on the H-bitt that will firmly connect the tug to the barge. On tugs there are few knots because they would be pulled so tight they could not easily be opened. When the tug pulls away from the ship, the force on the hawser will pull all the loops tight to the bitt and each other. The hairy fibers of manila thread provide friction, holding the connection together. It may be that the turn around the stem post (built into the bulwark at the bow) and the loop around its cleat are temporary, and will be released before the tug backs, so all the force will be on the main H-bitt. Hawsers degrade in sunlight and when wet, so when not in use the ship docking lines are stored in boxes with hinged lids. Sitting on the near box is the *messenger* line with a metal link on one end. The weighted end of the messenger is thrown to the ship's deck crew, who use it to pull up the ship end of the hawser.

© John McGrail / MaritimePhotos.com

ON THE HOOK: EUROPEAN-STYLE SHIPHANDLING

British tug *Alfred Lamey* towing the *Belgulf Enterprise* toward the dock on a hook mounted to the back of the engine housing. The captain is operating from the flying bridge on top of the pilot-house, common in Europe. Many Pacific Northwest and Canadian tugs have flying bridges, as well as some US construction tugs, but they are seldom installed on US ship-docking tugs.

In the European shiphandling method, the ship's propeller would be idled when near the berth, so the bow tug could control the ship. Docking with only tug power became impossible as ships grew exponentially in the last years of the twentieth century. The tug traveling stern first behind this ship is steering the stern: it can only pull the stern from side to side, not add any towing force. This arrangement presages modern tractor-tug operations, in which a bow tractor ahead, traveling backward, pulls the ship, and a stern tractor steers, with the advantage that the stern tractor can come ahead to nudge the ship's hull.

Tugboat Photos + Research Steven Lang Collection

In Europe, and in European-influenced ports around the world, the traditional shiphandling method was *on the hook*: tugs pulled with a hawser looped over a hook mounted to the back of the engine casing. A second tug trailed behind to steer the ship side to side. Until nearly alongside its berth, the ship was also under power. The connections were simple and quick. Since the tugs didn't come in contact with the ship's hull, their hulls were not as heavy as hulls built for alongside towing. The stern hook was mounted as far forward as possible, so the hull formed a lever between the load on the hook and the propeller. Such towline work is the quickest but most dangerous way to move ships. The biggest danger is that, as the ship maneuvers with the tugs, it may move unexpectedly, "girding" the tug — pulling her sideways, plunging the bulwark into the water, and scooping a deck-full of water that could sink the tug. To avoid this, the eye in the tug end of the hawser is looped over a quick-release hook that can be tripped by a cord from the pilothouse to disconnect the hawser immediately.

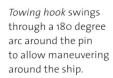

Towing hook swings through a 180 degree arc around the pin to allow maneuvering around the ship.

For quick release in an emergency, a lanyard is pulled, freeing the heavy hook to drop so the eye of the hawser slips off.

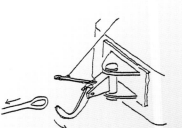

British River and Dock Tug, Early Twentieth Century

Traditional European tug design revolved around the hook, mounted as low as possible to reduce overturning forces from sideways pulls, and as far forward as possible so half the length of the hull becomes a lever arm between the forces at the prop and rudder and the load on the hook.

Everything aft of the hook (engine room and crew's quarters) was squashed to allow the hawser to swing over, lifted off the deckhouse by the arching tow bar.

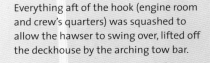

Towing hawser

Tow bow

Captain's cabin, skylit officers' mess, and bunks for junior officers

The boiler casing on a steam tug (equivalent to the US fiddley) had to be tall to ventilate the fire so it was pushed forward to allow the hook mounted on the back wall to be as far away from the stern as possible.

The stoker, cramped between the coal bunker and the firebox, spent his watch shoveling coal and tending the fire.

The crew got the space left between the engine room and the propeller, over the shaft. Some have said the throbbing of the shaft and the frothing of the prop were an aid to sleep in old steam tugs, with their gently swooshing piston engines.

Line boat

Docking on the Hook

1 Tugs approach the stopped ship stern first. The ship drops her hawsers to the tugs. The line boat comes out to begin ferrying mooring lines to the pier.

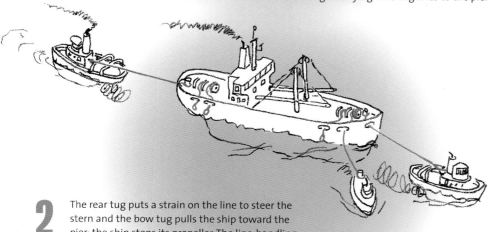

2 The rear tug puts a strain on the line to steer the stern and the bow tug pulls the ship toward the pier; the ship stops its propeller. The line-handling boat begins trips from ship to shore, bringing the ends of the mooring lines to dockworkers.

3 The tugs put tension on the lines to ease the ship towards the pier. The ship's deck winches begin to pull her toward the pier.

4 Tugs shift to put a strain away from the pier, so the ship touches gently as the winches pull the ship in.

Tractor Tugs

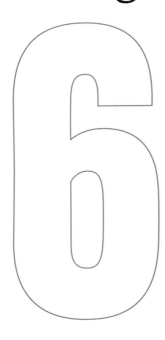

INVENTION OF THE WATER TRACTOR

In the 1920s the Voith Company, an international manufacturer of turbines for power generation and paper production equipment, based in Germany, was looking for smaller, more easily sold products within their area of expertise in spinning rotors. Inventor Ernest Schneider went to them with his design for a spinning propeller mounted vertically under the hull, which became the Voith Schneider Propeller (VSP). VSPs were promoted for passenger vessels, minesweepers, and other vessels that operated at speed most of the time, but also required close maneuvering on demand. When it began rebuilding its war-decimated business in the early 1950s, Voith Schneider concentrated on vessels requiring slow, careful, responsive maneuvering, such as tugs, ferries, crane barges, and buoy tenders. The company also developed a naval architecture department to design hulls that took maximum advantage of the unique characteristics of their drives.

Naval architect Wolfgang Baer used Voith's new design capabilities to develop a novel tug concept that has revolutionized shiphandling around the world. He put the VSPs at the bow and the tow hook at the stern, and called the tug a water tractor. (Ernest Schneider had a similar idea, and the same name, in 1926 for a shallow, disk-shaped hull with diagonally opposite VSPs. But at the time all his attention went to perfecting the drives themselves, and the concept was not developed.)

Until the Voith Water Tractors patent expired in 1976, VWTs were the world standard for tractor tugs. Then water tractors began to be built with less expensive, less responsive rudder propellers in place of the VSP drives, but still mounted forward of center and working ships over the stern. The next step was mounting rudder propellers under the stern, a design called azimuthing stern drive (ASD), multipurpose tugs that could also tow barges over the stern. (Tugs with the propulsion mounted forward are thought to be less effective at maintaining a course in long-haul towing.) To the extent that ASD tugs do shiphandling while traveling backward with the towline on the bow, they follow the water tractor method of having propulsion and load at opposite ends of the hull.

Tractor tugs turn the nuclear-powered aircraft carrier USS *George Washington* in Busan, Korea. The circles painted on the deck at the stern of the orange tug indicate the locations of the rudder-propeller drives. Although slowly being replaced with world-standard tractor tug designs, Asian tugs have had a distinctive bow: the stem (vertical line of the bow) is sharp, like a traditional boat, with the deck overhanging beyond to form a horizontal semi-circle hung with truck tires. American tugs had fuller bows, with rubber tendering attached directly to the rounded bow. The sturdy mast carries electronics and fire monitors. Exhausts are led out ports in the stern, similar to classic inboard speedboats. A tow bow protects engine room vents when the tug has a hawser or towing cable over the stern The tug is pulling with the rudder propellers at an angle, as can be seen by the direction of the roiling water. Conventional screw-propeller tugs could pull in reverse (with less power than going ahead), but the thrust could not be directed at an angle to maneuver the tug sideways.

Erin Devenberg, U.S. Navy

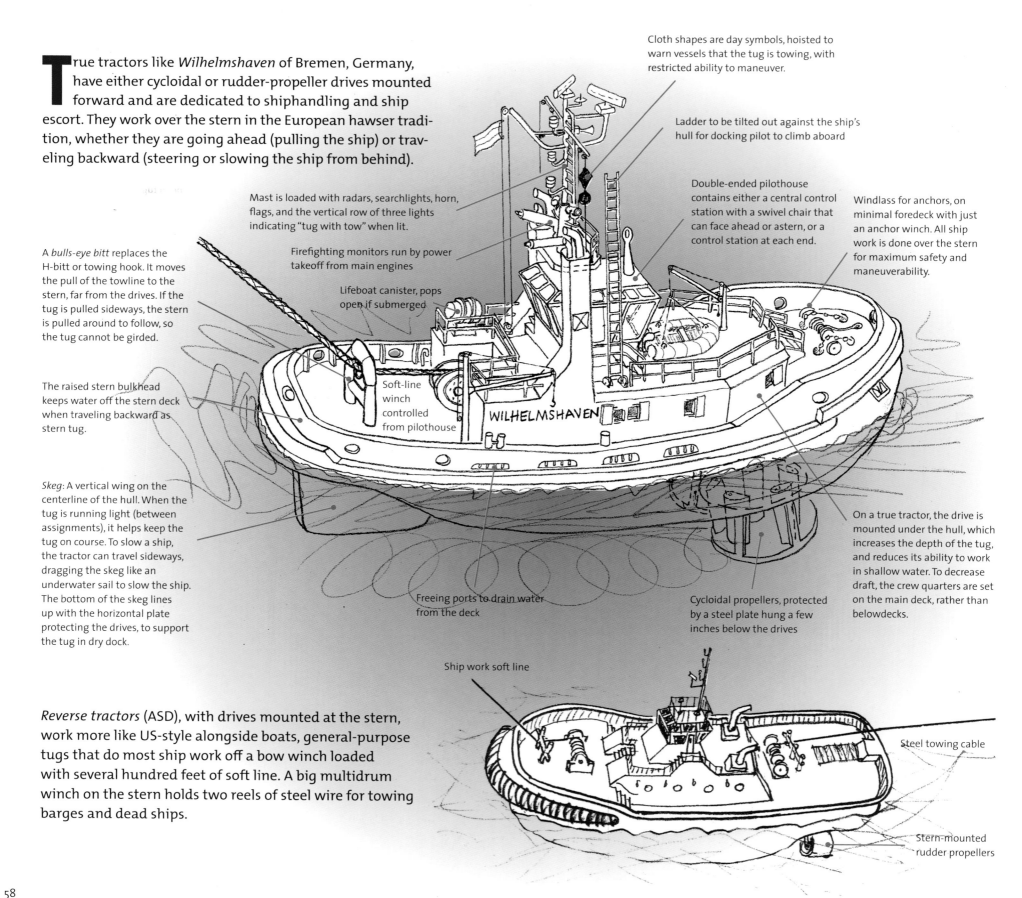

True tractors like *Wilhelmshaven* of Bremen, Germany, have either cycloidal or rudder-propeller drives mounted forward and are dedicated to shiphandling and ship escort. They work over the stern in the European hawser tradition, whether they are going ahead (pulling the ship) or traveling backward (steering or slowing the ship from behind).

A *bulls-eye bitt* replaces the H-bitt or towing hook. It moves the pull of the towline to the stern, far from the drives. If the tug is pulled sideways, the stern is pulled around to follow, so the tug cannot be girded.

The raised stern bulkhead keeps water off the stern deck when traveling backward as stern tug.

Skeg: A vertical wing on the centerline of the hull. When the tug is running light (between assignments), it helps keep the tug on course. To slow a ship, the tractor can travel sideways, dragging the skeg like an underwater sail to slow the ship. The bottom of the skeg lines up with the horizontal plate protecting the drives, to support the tug in dry dock.

Mast is loaded with radars, searchlights, horn, flags, and the vertical row of three lights indicating "tug with tow" when lit.

Firefighting monitors run by power takeoff from main engines

Lifeboat canister, pops open if submerged

Soft-line winch controlled from pilothouse

Cloth shapes are day symbols, hoisted to warn vessels that the tug is towing, with restricted ability to maneuver.

Ladder to be tilted out against the ship's hull for docking pilot to climb aboard

Double-ended pilothouse contains either a central control station with a swivel chair that can face ahead or astern, or a control station at each end.

Windlass for anchors, on minimal foredeck with just an anchor winch. All ship work is done over the stern for maximum safety and maneuverability.

On a true tractor, the drive is mounted under the hull, which increases the depth of the tug, and reduces its ability to work in shallow water. To decrease draft, the crew quarters are set on the main deck, rather than belowdecks.

Freeing ports to drain water from the deck

Cycloidal propellers, protected by a steel plate hung a few inches below the drives

WILHELMSHAVEN

Reverse tractors (ASD), with drives mounted at the stern, work more like US-style alongside boats, general-purpose tugs that do most ship work off a bow winch loaded with several hundred feet of soft line. A big multidrum winch on the stern holds two reels of steel wire for towing barges and dead ships.

Ship work soft line

Steel towing cable

Stern-mounted rudder propellers

Arrangement of a Screw-Propeller Tug

1 When powered ships were being developed, the screw propeller proved to be the most effective ship propulsion mode. The propeller was placed at the stern for several reasons:

- The bow is already complicated enough without adding a propeller there.
- A propeller at the stern has a free area of water far behind the vessel to push against.
- The propeller at the stern is protected by the hull, which will hit any obstruction first.

2 The rudder went behind the propeller so that if the rudder was turned at slow speed, the prop wash would push the stern sideways, aiding in steering. (The practicality of mounting the rudder at the stern had also been demonstrated on centuries of sailing ships.) Ships and tugs were long and narrow to accommodate the linear sequence of boiler–engine–drive train–propeller.

However, tugs are unique in that they add another force: a ship or barge on a towline. Mounting the towline on the stern seemed logical and simple, but the towing force is directly over the propeller and rudder. This arrangement made turning the tug at low speed less effective.

It was as if the tug were pinned through the stern, which should be free to pivot sideways to make the bow move in the opposite direction.

3 For this reason, the towing bits on American tugs were moved forward to just behind the deckhouse. The load of the hawser was moved forward to create distance between the load and the force of the propeller pushing on the water.

4 Similarly, the tow hook on European tugs was moved to the center of the tug, so a moment arm was created between the prop/rudder and the load on the hook. The tug stern could pivot around the load in the center.

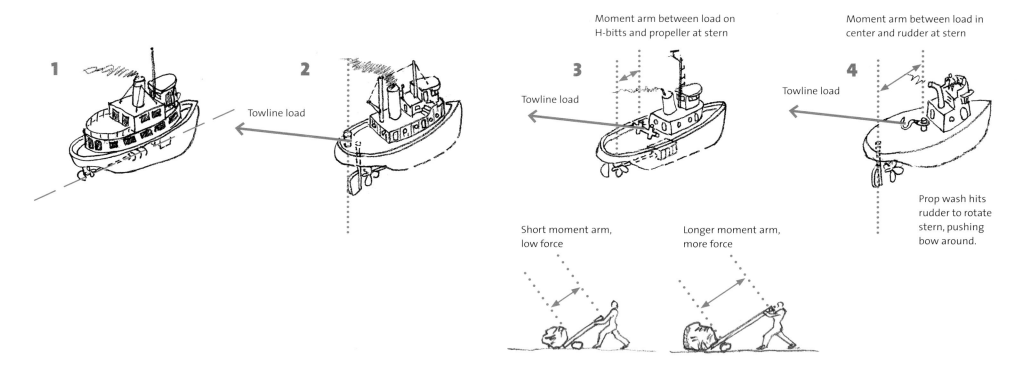

Moment arm between load on H-bits and propeller at stern

Moment arm between load in center and rudder at stern

Towline load

Towline load

Short moment arm, low force

Longer moment arm, more force

Prop wash hits rudder to rotate stern, pushing bow around.

Arrangement of a Cycloidal Tug

Since the cycloidal propeller projects vertically down under the hull, it could be located anywhere along the bottom. It also eliminated the rudder and the need for water flow in turning the hull. If the drive is mounted away from the center point, it can pivot the hull in the water.

The double-ended ferries and crane barges Voith built may have given Walter Baer the idea to move the VSP to the bow, and he moved the tow hook to the stern so that the two forces could be opposed. This eliminated the complicated arrangement of having the hawser pass over the prop/rudder on the way to the hook in the center (the arrangement shown in 3 & 4 above). Tractor tugs no longer needed to be linear, and hulls became wider to accommodate multiple drives, adding horsepower without adding length that would interfere with ship work. Increasing the hull width relative to length also formed a rounded hull that gave better water flow when the tractor moved sideways.

Dangers of Conventional Tug Ship Work

Tug operating backward to control the stern of the ship under way

The centered hook of traditional European tugs was good for maneuverability, but not for safety. If the tug working on the stern got turned sideways and lost power, or the ship suddenly powered ahead, the tug could be *girded*: capsized by the sideways pull of the hawser connected at the center of the tug.

A tug is traveling at the ship's bow to receive the towline. Transferring the towline between the ship and tug is done at speed, so the ship doesn't lose time as it enters or leaves the harbor, and also to keep water flowing past the rudder so the ship can maneuver.

But when a tug comes close alongside a moving ship the Venturi effect tries to pull the tug against the ship. If the tug's bow is pinned to the ship by suction, the rudder at the stern can't push the stern toward the ship to rotate the bow away. For example, if the ship slows and the tug doesn't get the message, it can jump ahead under the concave form of the ship's bow and be rolled over.

Safer Ship Work with a Water Tractor

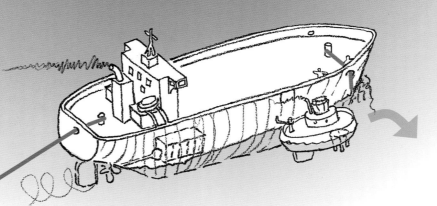

If the drive fails when towing astern on a Voith Water Tractor, the tug is just pulled along stern first since the hook is at the stern.

At the bow, the VWT drive can pull the tug away from the ship so it does not get pinned against the hull. It is like front-wheel drive on a car, pulling and steering, versus rear-wheel drive trying to push from the back to get the front to change direction. If the tug's power fails after the tug is connected, since the hook is at the stern instead of in the center, the tug is just pulled around by the towline and dragged through the water stern first.

This is a prelaunch view of Crowley Maritime's *Leader* intended for West Coast ship-handling. The stern is sitting on concrete and wood blocks to match the bow, supported on the guard plate under the drives. The boat is on a marine railway trolley for moving her around the shipyard. As with most cycloidal tug installations, there are two drives, side by side under the bow. (Double-ended ferries had one drive at each end, interlocked to work together.) The blades are the vertical metallic fins: each set of five is canted away from the centerline, following the hull chines. The guard plate (painted to match the hull) protects them in case of a grounding, or as here in dry dock, and focuses the water thrust at the low speeds customary for ship work. The guard plate and supporting struts create drag at higher speeds, so CP is not used much in higher-speed vessels.

At the stern, visible between the concrete dry-dock supports, a big fixed skeg projects down from the hull to keep the tug on course when going ahead and to act like a sail when the tug turns sideways, creating drag to slow a ship down in an emergency. The deep double-chine hull (see Tug Chines, page 93) serves the same purpose. The hull is designed to be as shallow as possible to make up for the added depth of the drives installed underneath.

Crowley Maritime Corporation

CYCLOIDAL PROPULSION

Cycloidal propulsion (CP) is complicated to explain, but it is an elegant and minimal mode of operation in which one mechanism imparts both propulsion and direction. As illustrated on the next pages, four or five vertical fins mounted around the perimeter of a spinning disk follow a circular track under a vessel's hull. A linkage from the steering station in the wheelhouse transmits directional commands, and the fins are toed out or in as they circle, pushing on the water at the point that will create thrust in the selected direction. The elegant engineering on simpler units can be directed by mechanical rods from the pilot-house, without electronics. CP creates the most instantaneous and finely focused change in steering direction of any drive. For this reason it is often installed in ferries, oceanographic research vessels, minesweepers, floating cranes, and of course tugs, which must change direction quickly and accurately. It was popularized for tugs in Europe first, in the 1950s, because it reduced the danger of ships pulling the tug over sideways. (In the US, most ship work at the time was done by tugs tied alongside instead of at the end of a hawser, so there was less need for a new method.)

Five-Bladed Cycloidal Propeller

Hydraulic pumps controlled from the pilothouse collectively direct servomotors to steer the tug by pushing the control rod.

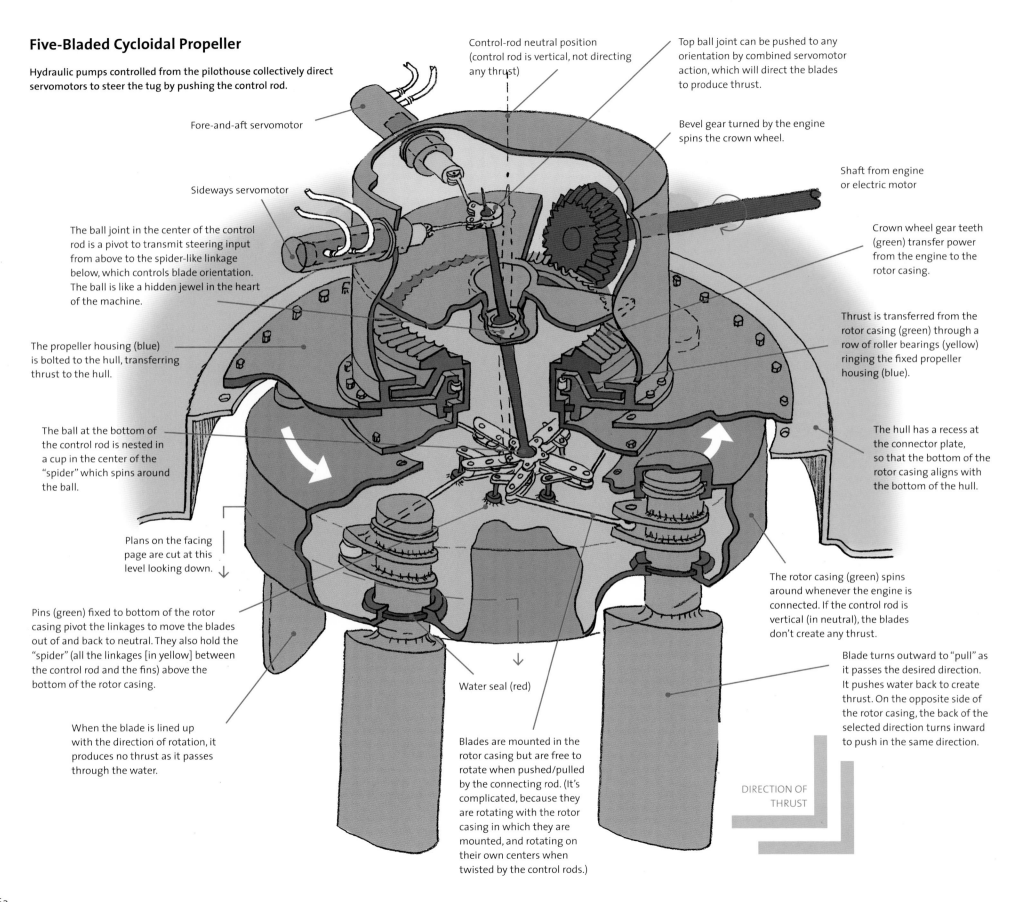

Fore-and-aft servomotor

Control-rod neutral position (control rod is vertical, not directing any thrust)

Top ball joint can be pushed to any orientation by combined servomotor action, which will direct the blades to produce thrust.

Bevel gear turned by the engine spins the crown wheel.

Shaft from engine or electric motor

Sideways servomotor

The ball joint in the center of the control rod is a pivot to transmit steering input from above to the spider-like linkage below, which controls blade orientation. The ball is like a hidden jewel in the heart of the machine.

Crown wheel gear teeth (green) transfer power from the engine to the rotor casing.

The propeller housing (blue) is bolted to the hull, transferring thrust to the hull.

Thrust is transferred from the rotor casing (green) through a row of roller bearings (yellow) ringing the fixed propeller housing (blue).

The ball at the bottom of the control rod is nested in a cup in the center of the "spider" which spins around the ball.

The hull has a recess at the connector plate, so that the bottom of the rotor casing aligns with the bottom of the hull.

Plans on the facing page are cut at this level looking down.

The rotor casing (green) spins around whenever the engine is connected. If the control rod is vertical (in neutral), the blades don't create any thrust.

Pins (green) fixed to bottom of the rotor casing pivot the linkages to move the blades out of and back to neutral. They also hold the "spider" (all the linkages [in yellow] between the control rod and the fins) above the bottom of the rotor casing.

Water seal (red)

Blade turns outward to "pull" as it passes the desired direction. It pushes water back to create thrust. On the opposite side of the rotor casing, the back of the selected direction turns inward to push in the same direction.

When the blade is lined up with the direction of rotation, it produces no thrust as it passes through the water.

Blades are mounted in the rotor casing but are free to rotate when pushed/pulled by the connecting rod. (It's complicated, because they are rotating with the rotor casing in which they are mounted, and rotating on their own centers when twisted by the control rods.)

DIRECTION OF THRUST

Four-Bladed Cycloidal Propeller, Plan View in Neutral

These sketches are cut through the rotor casing, looking down. A four-bladed example is shown for simplicity.

When the control rod is in the center (neutral), the blades simply follow each other around, not creating thrust. Since the blades are in motion all the time, they can instantly provide thrust when the control rod is pushed over.

The control rod (red), suspended from above, is the only item here not connected to the rotor casing below. It does not spin as the hub of the spider spins around it.

The blade pin is attached to the rotor casing.

The blade is suspended on the blade pin below the rotor casing. The top of the blade is shaded in this view because it is under the casing, hanging off the end of the pin that passes through the casing.

The rods and linkages (yellow), referred to here as the spider, are suspended inside the rotor casing, free to move in a horizontal plane to twist the blade pin when a direction is chosen.

The pins (green) attached to the rotor casing will be the pivot point for the linkages once a direction is chosen.

Rotor casing (green) is spun by the gears above. It spins everything in this drawing except the control rod.

Plan View in Drive

As each blade passes around the circle, the linkage twists it to push on the water as it passes the desired direction, then back to neutral at the "side" for that direction, then to push the water as it passes the back for that direction. Any direction can be selected. The linkages are similar to the cyclic controls that adjust helicopter blades to set direction.

Water that is pushed back creates thrust ahead.

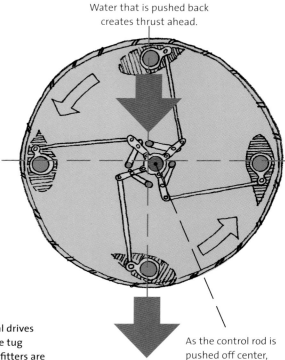

As the control rod is pushed off center, it pushes or pulls the linkages, which pivot around the fixed pins (the small green dots). In this geometry, the offset of the control rod is 90 degrees to the desired direction.

One of two cycloidal drives in the Foss Maritime tug *Garth Foss*. The shipfitters are standing on the fixed plate (suspended by tubular struts) that protects the cycloidal drives, supports the tug in dry dock, and at low speeds directs the thrust horizontally. The fins hang down to within a few inches of the top of the plate. Above the workmen is the disk that spins to move the plates, set in the vast flat hull that allows thrust from the drives to move uninterrupted in any horizontal direction. The men seem safe and protected on their perch, but that location is a maelstrom when the tug is in the water with the fins roaring around at several hundred revolutions per minute.

Foss Maritime

AZIMUTHING PROPELLER DRIVES, OR RUDDER PROPELLERS

Azimuthing drives, also called Z-pellers for the path of the drive train, or rudder propellers, mount the propeller on a rotating arm extending down from the hull. The tug can move in any horizontal direction, but unlike tugs with cycloidal propulsion, can't change direction instantly. To go from ahead to astern, the assembly of the propeller and supporting arm (often referred to as a pod) swings through 180 degrees, which takes seconds and transmits force in each direction it turns through. It also can't idle: as with a conventional tug, if the engine is turning, so is the prop. (Some rudder propellers are now built with controllable-pitch props that can feather so they don't produce thrust as the arm swings around to the new direction.) Tugs with two pods can turn them to face away from each other, so the tug stays stationary.

Nevertheless, Z-pellers are ordered ten to one over cycloidal propulsion: they're cheaper, and apply slightly more of the available engine power to the water. For most shiphandling tasks they are effective enough. (Cruise ships are also increasingly driven by pod-mounted props, in part to reduce dependence on tugs as they island-hop daily to small ports.)

Twin rudder propellers installed in *Bulldog*, a 6,700 hp 98-foot tug built for Crescent Towing of New Orleans to dock liquefied natural gas tankers at Elba Island, Georgia. Washburn & Doughty's small shipyard in East Boothbay, Maine, specializes in Z-drive tugs. Tugs are not "little boats," as can be seen by comparison to the people waiting for the ceremony in this prelaunch photo. The Z-drives are turned sideways to avoid damage when the boat splashes into the river. The silver-colored cubes on the nozzles are *zincs*: the plates that sacrifice themselves to the seawater so the bronze-alloy prop doesn't corrode. The cable over the stern will be connected to a tug which will pull *Bulldog* into the water along the greased timbers.

The shop in this photo burned in a spectacular fire with two tugs inside in 2008. A big barge-pushing tug was towed from the pier by a lobster boat while the fire raged. Washburn & Doughty immediately started building replacement hulls outside. For their first five years they had built fishing boats outside in Maine, preheating steel before welding in subzero temperatures, so they knew how to survive while a new shed was being constructed.

Washburn & Doughty Associates, Inc.

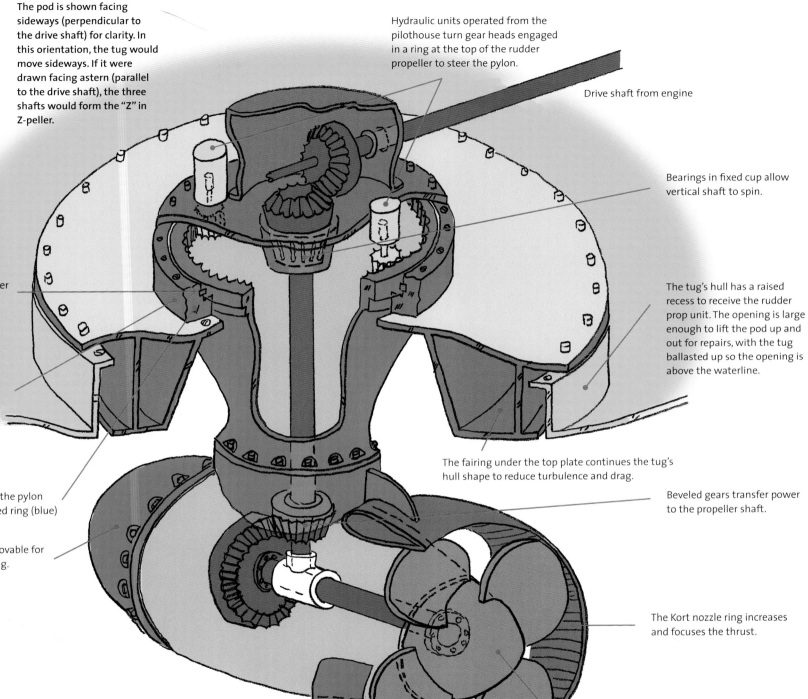

Azimuthing drives use two different motions.

For *propulsion* the engine spins a driveshaft (orange), which turns down through the center of the pylon, then turns again inside the pod, to spin the props and move the tug.

For *direction*, pilothouse controls turn geared units (yellow) to adjust the direction the pod faces, and the tug is pushed in that direction.

The pod is shown facing sideways (perpendicular to the drive shaft) for clarity. In this orientation, the tug would move sideways. If it were drawn facing astern (parallel to the drive shaft), the three shafts would form the "Z" in Z-peller.

Hydraulic units operated from the pilothouse turn gear heads engaged in a ring at the top of the rudder propeller to steer the pylon.

Drive shaft from engine

Bearings in fixed cup allow vertical shaft to spin.

A sliding water seal (red)

The tug's hull has a raised recess to receive the rudder prop unit. The opening is large enough to lift the pod up and out for repairs, with the tug ballasted up so the opening is above the waterline.

A fixed ring (blue) is bolted to the tug and supports the pylon, which rotates to steer the tug. The pylon also transfers the thrust from the propeller to the fixed ring and thus to the tug's hull.

Bearing surface, where the pylon (green) rides on the fixed ring (blue)

The fairing under the top plate continues the tug's hull shape to reduce turbulence and drag.

Beveled gears transfer power to the propeller shaft.

The nose is removable for access to gearing.

The Kort nozzle ring increases and focuses the thrust.

The pod assembly (green) can revolve through 360 degrees horizontally. The bevel gear at the bottom of the shaft is free to "walk" against the propeller-shaft gear while they both continue to spin, transmitting power to the propeller. The pylon and its vertical drive shaft can face any direction and still receive power from the fixed engine drive shaft.

The prop boss (hub) spins the blades through the water. Some rudder props also incorporate controllable-pitch blades.

Essentials of the Azimuthing Tug

"Invented" in Florida, the Ship Docking Module (SDM) designed and built by Erik Hvide put the drives in the diagonal opposite corners of a flat, wide hull, so prop wash from one drive is not hitting the other when the tug goes sideways. SDMs are operated by a captain and deckhand, and only for harbor ship work. Unknown to Hvide, British Columbia barge-handling tugs had been designed the same way in the 1970s. SDM *St. Johns*, now owned by Seabulk Towing, is shown sailing the tanker *Sunshine State* from Port Everglades, Florida. This is a tug stripped to its essentials. A winch sits in the shade of the small pilothouse, otherwise the deck is as bare as a barge. The vast empty deck (90 by 50 feet) is merely covering a hull that has been stretched to put the two azimuthing drives as far from each other as possible. The hull is rounded so the tug can work sideways in small spaces such as this (note the side of another ship at top left), as well as fore and aft. SDMs are too shallow to take to sea with a barge, because waves would wash over the flat deck. In this photo, the deckhand has just thrown the messenger line up to the crew on the ship.

Brian Gauvin

Courtesy of Harbormaster Marine Livonia, MI

In 1940 the US Army requested that Boston marine engine-builders Murray and Tregurtha, Inc. produce a self-contained barge drive based on the outboard motor. Marketed under the name "Harbormaster," the unit consists of an engine and fuel tank mounted on a plate that is welded to the barge deck. A synchronous belt drive (under the elongated rounded cover in red beside the engine) sends power to a transfer at the top of the propeller, which turns down to the propeller shaft at the bottom of a long pylon. A steering control on a stand on deck rotates a gear at the head of the propeller pylon through 360 degrees of horizontal motion. The pylon is shown here partly lifted to avoid damage in transit.

In the early 1950s Josef Becker of Germany invented the rudder propeller. He founded the Schottel Group, now one of the prime manufacturers of azimuthing rudder propellers for tugs and an increasing range of other vessel types.

SDM Viewed from Below

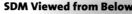
Skeg

Skegs protect drive units and aid directional control when transiting between assignments.

SHIPHANDLING WITH TRACTOR TUGS

Tugs that could move immediately in any direction were quickly adopted in harbors in which towing was done on the hook, especially European ports rebuilding their fleets after World War II. The chances of being girded or overrun when shiphandling "on the hook" are significantly reduced by the tractor's ability to quickly move sideways or astern to escape danger. An added benefit was that the tug could push with the side of its hull also, a benefit in Europe's tight docks. In the US, operators had plenty of prewar and surplus conventional tugs available, and their alongside-towing methods were not as susceptible to mishap during shiphandling, so they were decades behind Europe and Asia in building tractors. Eventually, the exponential increase in ship size caused a gradual worldwide shift to tractors, one of whose benefits was that the compact drives accommodate more horsepower without exceeding the 100 feet that is a practical maximum for a handy ship-docking tug.

On azimuthing stern drive tugs, the helmsman sits between two control modules, one for each drive. The seat can be reversed, usually facing the shiphandling winch on the tug's bow that is connected through the hawser to the ship. The tug might be operating bow-forward following the ship, or stern-forward ("backwards") pulling the ship from ahead. In this picture, the white synthetic hawser rising to the ship passes through a bow bitt lined with stainless steel, to protect the expensive line from chafing. The chart on the screen shows the Mystic River between the Boston neighborhood of Charlestown and the cities of Everett and Chelsea. The line across the water on the right is the Tobin Bridge. The Island End River empties into the harbor near the top of the screen, and the ship shows as a shape in the center, as the tugs turn it to dock next to the river mouth.

One of the losses in the conversion to tractors is that the skipper sits in the center of the pilothouse, away from the windows, in one-way communication with the deck by loudspeaker. On the old boats the captain stood at a drop-down window next to the wheel, able to steer, push the throttle, and lean out the window to casually converse with the deckhands. The windows on the new boats don't even open. In this photo, the deck speaker microphone hangs off the overhead console. It and the VHF radio are operated by foot pedals. The red button overhead is the emergency engine shutoff, surrounded by engine controls, alarms, and radios. Overhead at the front is a rear-view mirror to show what's going on behind, especially when the tug is operating backwards, towing the bow of the ship. The winch control is the lever in the lower left corner of the photo.

Brian Gauvin

Connecting Tractors

As tug horsepower and ship size increased, manila hawsers became the weak link, in strength and susceptibility to damage and degradation in salt water. Plastic lines replaced them, each type with a different set of characteristics and therefore uses. Nylon was used for barge towing, because it stretches under strain. It could break catastrophically when it reached its limit: this was not dangerous underwater, between the tug and barge, but would kill deckhands if it happened during ship work. Dacron was used for ship work and alongside barge towing, since it had less give. Recently, composite fibers (developed to replace steel wires in tires, and for flexible body armor) have been twisted into ropes, then braided into 3-inch-diameter "soft lines" many times stronger than the traditional 6-inch hemp or plastic hawser. Because it is thinner and less springy, the soft line can be wound onto a powerful winch that carries the load to the deck, eliminating the craftsman-like figure-8 overlays of hemp hawsers on bow H-bitts, as well as the H-bitts themselves. Composites, or soft lines, are not cheap: they may be ten times the cost of wire cable. Since they are light, they don't droop under the water as cable does (see page 118). Soft lines tend to break when stretched sharply between the tug and barge, whereas cable droops down under tons of water that acts as a shock absorber. Therefore most barge towing is still done with wire rope.

To match the increased power required by ever-larger ships, tractor tugs carry a winch loaded with ultra-high-molecular-weight polyethylene, a molecule of which consists of a chain of millions of carbon atoms, each with two hydrogen atoms attached. When two of these long molecules lie side by side, atoms in each chain form a weak bond with atoms of the other; so many points of bonding produce enormous strength in tension. Fibers built by spinning out these molecules from a liquid solution are built up into strands that can be twisted into rope, which is braided to form hawsers fifteen times stronger than steel cable, weight for weight. Since the ropes are braided, they don't twist when tension is applied. (Conventional cables and rope hawsers are built by twisting strands and ropes together, but when tension is put on the line, they start to untwist. When the tension is taken off, they return to their original twist, sometimes violently when the load is suddenly released.) The polyethylene is extremely slippery and difficult to grip. The orange color of this hawser by Samson Rope is a urethane coating on the strands, which gives it a surface texture that can grip on a tug's bitts and protect it from heat buildup that occurs when lines pass around bitts or cleats. These lines also float, don't absorb water, and are self-lubricating, which avoids the pollution that occurs when wire cable is dipped in oil occasionally to lubricate between the strands. On the other hand, polyethylene is made from oil, which is nonrenewable.

On the left side of the winch, a *gypsy drum* (an auxiliary for occasional use, like a horizontal capstan) is available to take up an additional line, for example to make up to a barge. The large wheel on the right of the winch is a hand brake. The bitt that the hawser is passing through (called a *fairlead* in this configuration), has horns on the sides to wrap a hawser in the old figure-8 style if necessary. The big pipe radius eases the line's turn up to the ship, with no damage from sharp bends.

Courtesy Samson Rope Technologies

Tanker Escort

If a ship loses its steering, a tug can control its direction for the mile or so it will take to stop the ship's momentum. Crowley Maritime's cycloidal tug *Master* is performing a test of the indirect mode of steering a ship that has lost steering ability, in this case a *ro-ro* (roll-on roll-off) car-delivery vehicle in the Port of Los Angeles. She has sheered off from behind the ship, to put herself at an angle. Her wake shows the direction of travel, parallel to the tanker. The tug skipper gives almost enough power to keep up, so the ship is pulling the tug's deep hull at an angle to the ship's course. The towline pulls the ship's stern to the side, changing its course. The tug can quickly swing across the stern and steer in the opposite direction.

Crowley Maritime Corporation

A series of devastating and well-publicized oil tanker groundings and founderings (breaking apart at sea) has led to much higher standards for tug and petroleum-barge operations, including gradual elimination of single-screw tugs towing petroleum barges in favor of the redundancy and increased maneuverability of twin-screw tugs. In some ports, environmental standards require near-shore escorts of tankers by tugs of the Best Available Technology, determined to be large, seaworthy, firefighting tractor tugs of at least 4,000 hp. Escort tugs must be large enough to meet tankers in the open ocean outside the port, and fast enough to keep up for a transit that may be fifty miles, in some cases, before they get to the dock. The tug crews train to respond to emergencies that could result in oil spills: loss of power, loss of control over power, steering loss, a ship overwhelmed by currents or weather conditions, or human error.

Transverse Arrest

Stopping a tanker in an emergency requires quick and powerful response from the tug. Rudder-propeller tugs can turn their Z-drives to face away from each other at full power, projecting a column of water out each side that acts like a solid mass being dragged through the water. This can be twice as effective in slowing the tanker as just reversing the thrust. Here the tug is being dragged by the ship, slowing the ship down.

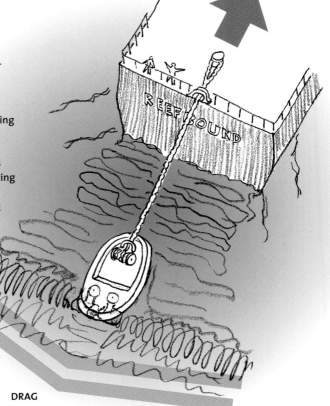

DRAG

Tugs and Ships: Shape and Size

Courtesy Smit Maritime

Largest Tugs

Among the largest true tugs are ocean salvage vessels such as *Smit Amandla*, one of a pair built in 1975 for rescue and salvage around South Africa's wild Cape of Good Hope. (Tankers too large for the Suez Canal had to pass the Cape from the Middle East to Europe and the US.) She's almost as big as the bulker she's heading to assist: the *Nena J* passing Cape Town en route between India and Chile. At 26,000 hp, she's more powerful than most ships, but she's clearly recognizable as a tug by the clear afterdeck with steel bows to lift the cable off the deck, and by the hook mounted amidships. The winches are inside the deckhouse, near the center of the boat. Her top speed of 20 knots gets her to a casualty quickly. With the construction of hundreds of oil patch anchor-handling tugs that can do many of the same tasks, these dedicated salvage/rescue tugs are becoming obsolete. A similar sleek German salvage tug, Bugsier's *Arctic*, was converted to an ocean cruising yacht in 1993, with staterooms filling the open stern deck. *Smit Amandla* is 296 by 50 feet, powered by two engines running one controllable-pitch propeller.

MEASURING TUGS

Tugs were traditionally paid by horsepower, but due to frequently optimistic horsepower claims by owners, classification societies that rate the capacity of tugs and other vessels have set the standard measurement for tugs as *bollard pull*. The tug is tethered to a bollard on a pier by a 1,000-foot cable ending with a strain gauge. Being that far from shore allows a smooth column of water to be compressed behind the prop over several minutes. This simulates the load on a towline at sea. A bollard pull test measures the performance of the tug as a system: engines, drive train, propeller, and hull shape, which is critical for water flow to the props. Other factors besides

power come into play. Cycloidal tugs produce 22 pounds of pull per horsepower, compared to 27 for screw propellers inside nozzles, but cycloidals are more effective in complicated docking maneuvers. Escort tugs may have props which sacrifice power in favor of speed to follow tankers from the sea in case of trouble. Usually the speed of a tug is not crucial, and in any case speed is limited by the deep, heavy hulls that give the vessel mass to stand up to heavy ships. After about 15 knots, applying more power just causes the giant propellers to pull water from under amidships, leaving the tug's center sitting in a hole in the water, with no gain in speed.

Smallest Tugs

Small tugs called *boom boats* are used to corral logs into booms: masses of logs surrounded by a string of large logs chained together. The booms are towed downriver to sawmills or to be loaded on ships or barges. These Foss Maritime boom boats are gathering logs from the boom for the grapple on the barge to load on deck. A few sections of boom are at right. The barges are unloaded at the sawmill or shipping point by flooding one side to tip them over, dumping the logs back into the water to be processed. The boom boats are powered by four-cylinder, 100 hp diesels and steered by a swiveling steel nozzle around the fixed propeller that directs the thrust as well as protecting the propeller.

Mike Stork, Courtesy of Foss Maritime

Invader was the first of her class of twenty-five large all-purpose tugs built by Crowley Maritime in the mid-1970s, as the Alaska oil rush began to demand delivery of equipment barges to the North Slope. Their twin 20-cylinder engines give a total of 7,200 hp, and recent bollard pull tests to requalify them for tanker escort service yielded 145,000 pounds of bollard pull, even after thirty years of hard service. Naval architect Philip Spaulding made sure these handsome boats measured just under 200 gross tons, avoiding stricter manning and inspection requirements by the Coast Guard. They're a bit big for shiphandling, but match up well with giant tankers, and they excel at ocean towing (in spite of an idiosyncratic corkscrewing motion reported by their crews in heavy seas).

The Invader class is being replaced with the Ocean class (see Controllable-Pitch Propulsion, page 46).

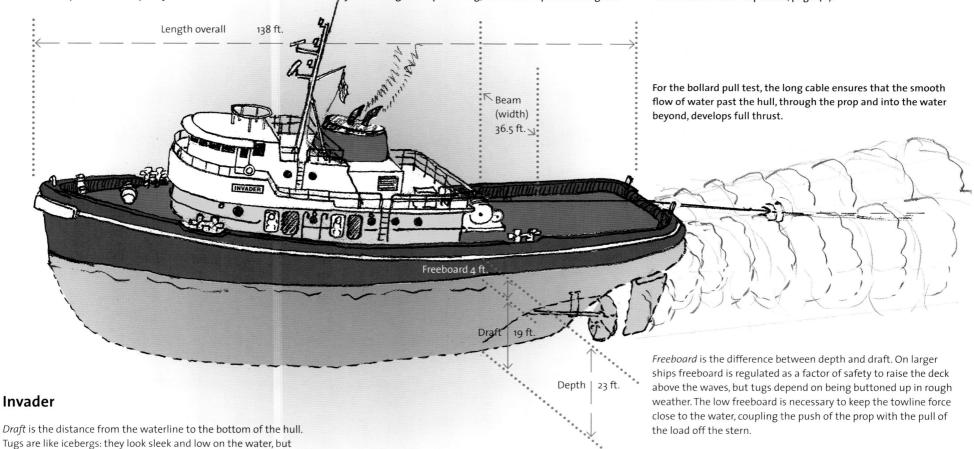

Length overall   138 ft.

Beam (width) 36.5 ft.

For the bollard pull test, the long cable ensures that the smooth flow of water past the hull, through the prop and into the water beyond, develops full thrust.

Freeboard 4 ft.

Draft   19 ft.

Depth   23 ft.

Invader

Draft is the distance from the waterline to the bottom of the hull. Tugs are like icebergs: they look sleek and low on the water, but have surprisingly deep hulls to carry their enormous engines.

Freeboard is the difference between depth and draft. On larger ships freeboard is regulated as a factor of safety to raise the deck above the waves, but tugs depend on being buttoned up in rough weather. The low freeboard is necessary to keep the towline force close to the water, coupling the push of the prop with the pull of the load off the stern.

Depth is the distance from the main deck to the bottom of the hull.

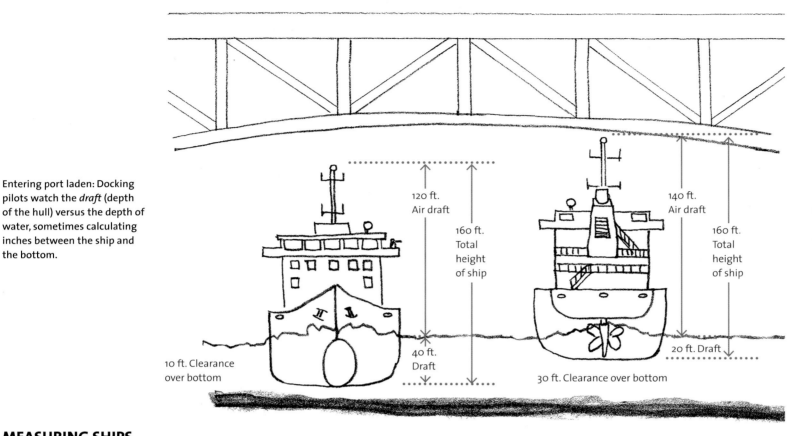

Entering port laden: Docking pilots watch the *draft* (depth of the hull) versus the depth of water, sometimes calculating inches between the ship and the bottom.

120 ft. Air draft

160 ft. Total height of ship

10 ft. Clearance over bottom

40 ft. Draft

140 ft. Air draft

160 ft. Total height of ship

30 ft. Clearance over bottom

20 ft. Draft

Departing light: Docking pilots watch the *air draft* (height of the ship above the waterline). Both drafts are affected by the tide and river currents and levels.

MEASURING SHIPS

Tug companies hired to dock approaching ships need to know what they're up against. They consult volumes published by classification societies, such as the famous Lloyd's Register, established in 1760, which lists the characteristics of every ship in the world insured by Lloyd's of London. If shipowners want insurance, they must build and operate their vessels to standards established by classification societies operated by insurers. The only variable a tug dispatcher needs for a full picture of a scheduled ship visit is draft — the depth of the hull below the water-line — which the ship must estimate as it approaches the port. Draft is affected by the load, the amount of fuel and water in the ship's tanks, and possibly the ship's trim (the stern may be set lower than the bow to improve handling, by pumping seawater into ballast tanks). Comparing the draft to the available depth of water determines whether the ship can be accommodated at a particular berth, and clear the bottom when entering and leaving port. The local shipping agent, representing the shipowner, contacts the ship to pass the draft and arrival time to the tug dispatchers. The size of ships is measured in several ways. *Displacement*, the true measure of the ship's weight at any moment (the weight of water it displaces as it settles in), is not relevant for vessels that constantly load and unload. *Gross registered tonnage* is the space available for cargo, a word descended from the number of eighteenth-century tuns (casks of wine) that a ship could carry. GRT is a useful indication of the general size of the ship. Length, beam, and draft (at the moment) are the most useful measurements. Car carriers, for example, have vast interior volume but don't carry much weight, and container ships carry much of their cargo above deck level.

The *Queen Elizabeth II* measures 963 feet long, beam 105 feet (Panamax: the maximum allowed through the Panama Canal before its widening scheduled for completion in 2016), depth 56 feet (main deck to waterline), and draft 32 feet. Her air draft is 178 feet. Liners usually maintain the same draft. As they use up fuel, fresh water, and stores, they ride higher in the water. They are then ballasted down with seawater pumped into tanks so they ride at their designed comfort level. Piling up public spaces and cabins above the waterline makes for a giant *sail area* (the surface presented to the wind). *QE II*'s is about 80,000 square feet. Many cruise ships call at out-of-the-way ports without tugs, so they are equipped with bow and stern thrusters to dock themselves, or they anchor and transfer passengers in small boats. Tugs win in the power-to-weight category. *QEII* moves her 52,000 tons with 130,000 hp: 800 pounds for each unit of horsepower. Tugs are truly floating engines, at about 200 pounds per unit of horsepower.

©John McGrail / MaritimePhotos.com

SHIP TYPES

Each ship type poses a different challenge to tug crews.

TANKERS carry liquid cargo: petroleum, chemicals, alcohol, even orange juice. Speed is less a factor than volume. Capacity is measured in deadweight tons (DWT): the actual weight, in long tons of 2,240 pounds, of cargo, fuel, and water that will bring an empty ship down to her allowable draft line. Very Large Crude Carriers (VLCCs) of over 200,000 DWT were built when war in the Middle East closed the Suez Canal. If ships weren't limited by the 52-foot depth of the canal, they might as well be giant. VLCCs were followed around the Cape of Good Hope by UL (Ultra Large) CCs over 1,000 feet long. Most ports don't see these giants, which shuttle from oilfields to refineries. Product tankers of 500 to 700 feet deliver refined products to consumer ports.

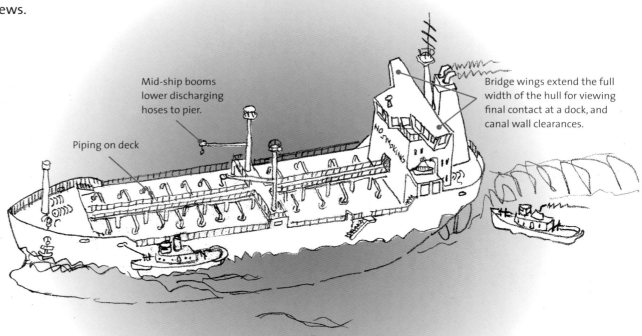

Mid-ship booms lower discharging hoses to pier.

Piping on deck

Bridge wings extend the full width of the hull for viewing final contact at a dock, and canal wall clearances.

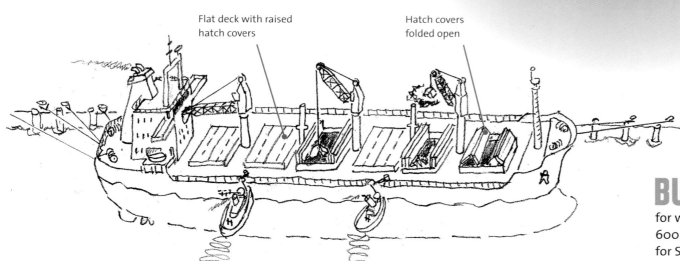

Flat deck with raised hatch covers

Hatch covers folded open

BULKERS carry ores, grain, coal, road salt, scrap metal: low-value products for which profit is in bulk. A small bulker may be 600 by 80 feet. The largest were named Capesize, for South Africa's wild Cape of Good Hope, which they needed to pass between the Atlantic and Indian oceans before the Suez Canal was enlarged. They shuttle coal and iron ore between a few deep-water ports. As with tankers, bulkers arrive at most developed ports full and depart empty and riding high, unless they're picking up scrap metal. Bulkers and container ships are "geared" if they carry their own unloading cranes, as this one does.

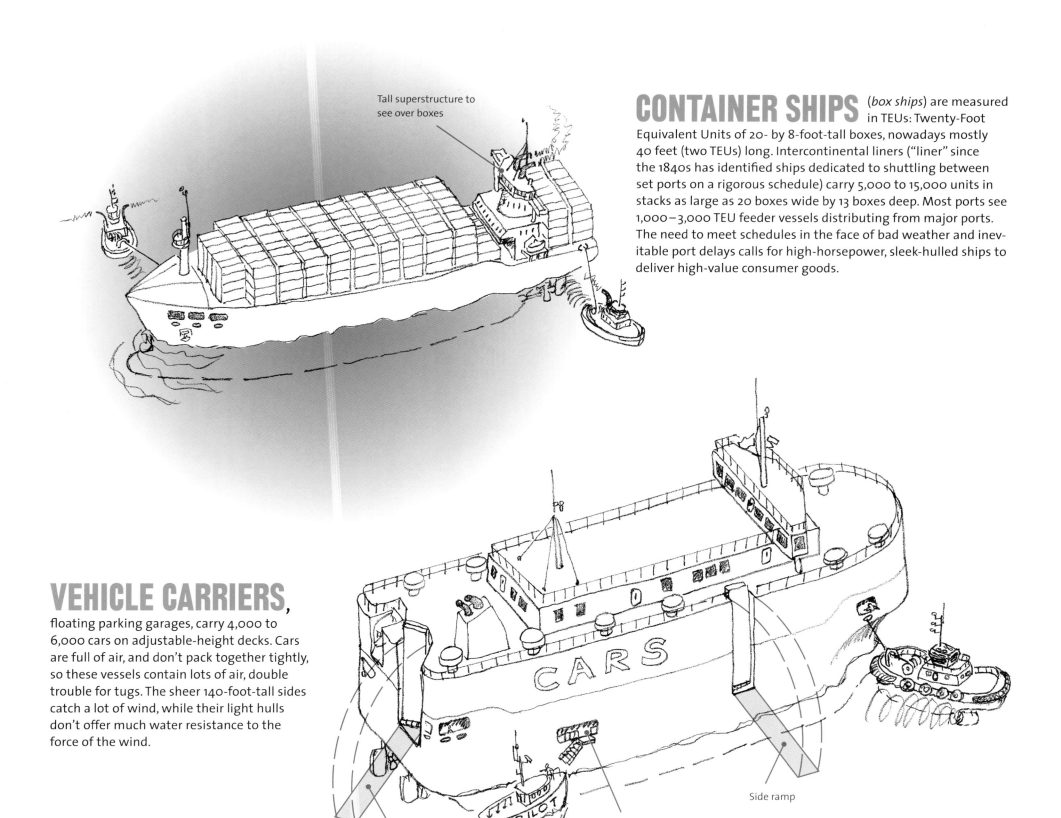

Tall superstructure to
see over boxes

CONTAINER SHIPS (*box ships*) are measured in TEUs: Twenty-Foot

Equivalent Units of 20- by 8-foot-tall boxes, nowadays mostly
40 feet (two TEUs) long. Intercontinental liners ("liner" since
the 1840s has identified ships dedicated to shuttling between
set ports on a rigorous schedule) carry 5,000 to 15,000 units in
stacks as large as 20 boxes wide by 13 boxes deep. Most ports see
1,000–3,000 TEU feeder vessels distributing from major ports.
The need to meet schedules in the face of bad weather and inev-
itable port delays calls for high-horsepower, sleek-hulled ships to
deliver high-value consumer goods.

VEHICLE CARRIERS,

floating parking garages, carry 4,000 to
6,000 cars on adjustable-height decks. Cars
are full of air, and don't pack together tightly,
so these vessels contain lots of air, double
trouble for tugs. The sheer 140-foot-tall sides
catch a lot of wind, while their light hulls
don't offer much water resistance to the
force of the wind.

CARS

PILOT

Stern ramp

Small galleries at tug level for
hawser handling, mooring, and
pilot transfer

Side ramp

McAllister's *Resolute* approaching tanker *Alpine Amalia* in the Kill Van Kull, Newark Bay. She is padded with rope fenders, formerly woven by master craftsmen from worn-out hawsers and surely a work of love by a crewmember, because rope hawsers haven't been fitted to tugs since the 1950s. They were replaced by old rubber tires hung on chains or cut into strips bolted together into pads. The angle of this photo exposes the beautiful three-dimensional swoop of a classic tug's hull.

Chocks, or *fairleads*, are connection points on the ship: these are openings with rounded edges at deck level through which the hawser is passed. A tug deckhand throws up a leader line to the ship's crew at the rail, who pass it in through the chock, then pull up the hawser and drop the eye over a deck bitt. Most are *Panama chocks*, closed all around so the hawser is enclosed even when being pulled upward when the ship is at the bottom of a canal lock. The docking pilot directs each tug to the chock he wants them at.

Anchors project from the bow of the ship (one is behind the tug's mast): in harbor, a ship crewmember with a sledge-hammer is assigned to stand by the bracket securing the anchor in place, ready to drop the anchor in an emergency. It's therefore a bad idea to position the tug under the anchor when working alongside.

Pat Folan

READING THE SHIP

Tug crews approaching a ship look for symbols and features they use to position the tug for the docking evolution, and to protect themselves from danger. Some are painted marks with information on hidden conditions, like draft, which tells how far under the surface the keel is. If you also know the depth of water, you can determine the clearance under the ship. The bulbous bow symbol is useful because the projection is hidden under the surface when the ship is loaded heavily. The symbol warns tugs and small boats of the presence of the underwater projection. Likewise, the bow thruster is a powerful propeller in a crosswise tunnel in the ship's hull, which can push a tug away at an inopportune moment, so it is marked on the hull above.

Other features are readily visible and set the locations where a tug needs to position itself. In the old days the ship's frames could be identified by rows of rivets as the strongest point to push against. With welded hulls, the frames are not so apparent and pushing between the frames can dent the steel plating, so they are marked on the hull.

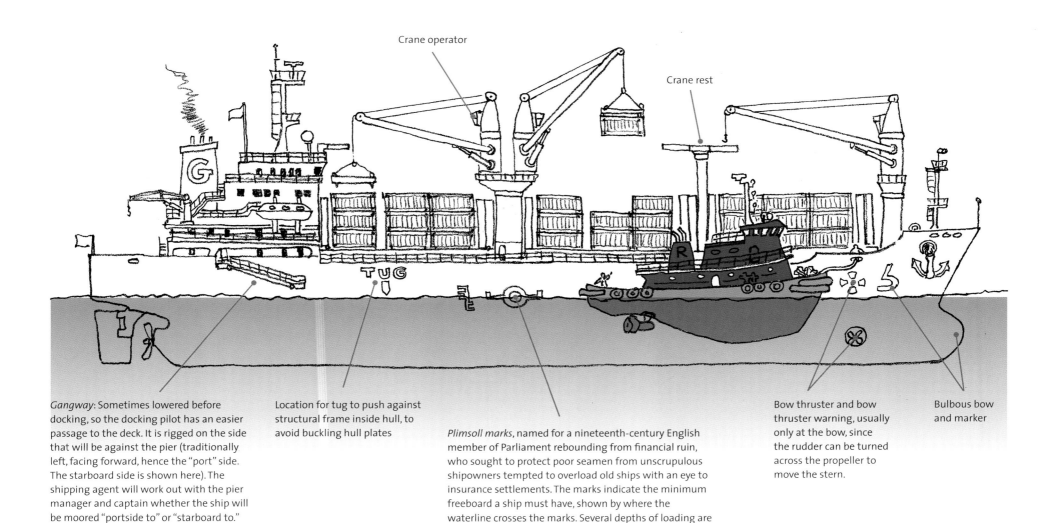

Crane operator

Crane rest

Gangway: Sometimes lowered before docking, so the docking pilot has an easier passage to the deck. It is rigged on the side that will be against the pier (traditionally left, facing forward, hence the "port" side. The starboard side is shown here). The shipping agent will work out with the pier manager and captain whether the ship will be moored "portside to" or "starboard to."

Location for tug to push against structural frame inside hull, to avoid buckling hull plates

Plimsoll marks, named for a nineteenth-century English member of Parliament rebounding from financial ruin, who sought to protect poor seamen from unscrupulous shipowners tempted to overload old ships with an eye to insurance settlements. The marks indicate the minimum freeboard a ship must have, shown by where the waterline crosses the marks. Several depths of loading are indicated, depending on how much of a factor of safety is required in different oceans and seasons.

Bow thruster and bow thruster warning, usually only at the bow, since the rudder can be turned across the propeller to move the stern.

Bulbous bow and marker

TF: Tropical freshwater (deeper loading because of operating in calmer waters)

T: Tropical (roughly aligns with F: Freshwater)

F: Freshwater

S: Summer salt water

W: Winter salt water

WNA: Winter North Atlantic, which recognizes the extreme wave heights of this ocean by increasing the freeboard (reducing the load so the ship rides higher) for smaller ships

Plimsoll Marks

The original Plimsoll line, a circle with a line through, matches the summer waterline.

The two-letter code is the classification society that registers the ship for insurance:

AB is the American Bureau of Shipping; other common classification societies are **LR** for Lloyd's Register, **DNV** for Det Norsk Veritas from Norway, **NK** for Nippon Kaiji Kyokai.

— *Courtesy NOAA*

In this picture taken from Captain Chuck Delory's pilothouse door at the Fore River tank farm in Quincy, Massachusetts, fellow Boston Towing and Transportation tug *H.J. Reinauer* is against the pier ahead of the tanker *Nor'Easter*, connecting a line. All three crew-members on the watch are visible: the skipper in the pilothouse, deckhand with hawser, and engineer helping out on the stern. Tugs are not small boats: *H.J. Reinauer* is 94 feet long and weighs about a million pounds (499 tons). Some of the graphic indicators that guide tug crews in shiphandling are visible on the tanker's hull:

Frame marks (in this case, FP 1, first frame from bow). Ships today are built of high-strength steel, stronger but thinner than iron ships, and with more widely spaced reinforcing frames. The thin plates can be dented or buckled by today's powerful tugs, so the frames are marked as locations tugs should push against.

The *bow thruster symbol* indicates a reversible propeller inside a tube crosswise through the hull, which is used to push the bow sideways when docking. If a tug is operating too near, the thruster's water flow can interfere with the tug's thrust, potentially reducing effectiveness at a critical point in docking.

Draft marks show depth of hull below the waterline, for bottom clearance. Docking pilots also need to consider *trim*, any difference in draft between bow and stern. Lightly loaded ships are trimmed down by the stern, to keep prop and rudder immersed as deeply as possible for effectiveness.

Captain Chuck Delory

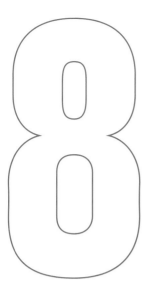

Who's Who

Captain Katrina Anderson sails the trailer carrier *Midnight Sun* (truck trailers are parked on a multilevel barge for delivery), on *Nordic Wind*, a twin-screw tug belonging to Cook Inlet Tug and Barge, founded by her great-grandfather and grandfather in 1924. She grew up on the family's tugs, where the kids scraped and painted and occasionally were allowed to steer for fun when in deep water, away from obstacles. (In an *Anchorage Daily News* profile she says her mother told her you haven't been sick until you are pregnant on a tugboat.) Her father convinced her that tugs were not just for men, so she started training seriously at eighteen, on the *Cosmic Wind*, their 52-foot twin-screw tug/workboat. She earned her captain's license in 2007. Since Cook Inlet was her home, she had no basis for comparison with other ports. In fact, her training took place in one of the most difficult harbors in the world. Cook Inlet has the second highest tides in North America, at over 50 feet in some areas, and 25 feet or more at the Anchorage piers. Tidal currents are 5 knots or more, complicated by trees carried into the Inlet by the tributary rivers, and winter ice packs pushed by the surging currents. Wide mud flats open up at low tide, limiting the times barges can be worked alongshore (and eliminating the appeal of Cook Inlet to cruise ships).

Bill Roth, Anchorage Daily News

A tug is vessel and crew operating like one organism. The crew serves the boat, and in return she extends their strength a thousandfold. The usual route to tug captain has been from the deck: through connections or luck land a deckhand's job, then pay attention to who's doing what and why. (As big tug and barge combinations have taken over from coastal tankers, merchant marine academy graduates are recruited to apprentice and work their way up to master on the complicated vessels.) Some deckhands may enjoy being outdoors on deck in all weathers, good and bad, but for the ambitious deckhand, a tug is small enough that there is lots of opportunity to ask, or learn by seeing cause and effect. Deckhands are welcome in the pilothouse, and can take a hand at the wheel between deck jobs. (Technically, the deckhand may take a test to become an apprentice mate/steersman and then can steer the boat as long as a licensed captain or mate is present.) Most mates and captains came up the same way, so there is no class gulf between deck and wheelhouse, as there might be on larger vessels.

DECKHANDS

Deckhands are more than just brute force: the success and safety of the evolution depend on their knowledge and skill. Hawsers on bitts must be overlapped evenly to spread the bite from thousands of tons of force transmitted from ship to tug without binding up, so that they can be tossed off quickly if necessary. Winches and capstans are dangerously powerful, as are lines strained to the breaking point. Deckhands work carefully and deliberately, alert to signs of trouble developing: engine noise increasing while their hands are still in the middle of building a hawser connection; ship and tug moving apart unexpectedly, threatening to put a strain on a slack line underfoot; or impending hard contact that could throw the deckhand down or over the low bulwarks. Climbing between tugs and barges puts the deckhands in utmost peril, because the two vessels are moving differently, and handholds are often makeshift or nonexistent.

Tug captain Pat Folan took this photo from his boat, the *Herbert Brake*, watching the *Sarah Ann*'s deckhand put a hawser up on a scrap-metal barge for alongside towing. The engineer is helping out on deck, tossing the stern line to the deckhand. The baby-blue boats of Donjon (also a well-known salvage company) shuttle barges from collection yards in Brooklyn, Queens, the Bronx, Eastchester, and Albany, New York, and Stamford, Connecticut, to the shipping port at Claremont Terminal in Newark, New Jersey, twenty-four hours a day. Folan estimated that he and his crew make 5,000 barge moves a year in their month-on/month-off schedule. The pilothouse-view videos on his website could be an online graduate-degree program in harbor barge work.

Pat Folan

ENGINEER

The engineer maintains all the tug's equipment: main engines, auxiliary engines generating electricity or pumping to fire monitors, hydraulic steering gear, fuel and water supplies, pumps, winches, electrical system, and even the plumbing. Day boats may not have an engineer on board, especially newer tugs with automated, reliable, low-maintenance engines. On bigger coastal or ocean tugs, or tugs with older engines, starting a tug and getting all the systems operating takes several hours, which means the engineer is the first on the boat and the last off, well after the captain calls "Finished with Engines." On steam tugs, the smooth, quiet operation of the engines was peaceful until interrupted by insistent gongs from the pilothouse ordering changes in speed or direction. Diesels allowed pilothouse control, leaving the engineer's hands free to cover his ears against the pounding combustion. Newer automated engines on large tugs are monitored from a soundproof station in the engine room. Since most tugs have only one engineer, there's no way to apprentice. Candidates may learn their trade in the company repair shop, or a deckhand with mechanical aptitude may learn enough from volunteering in the engine room between deck jobs.

Arlon Feurtado on the ASD tug *Gramma Lee T. Moran* stands in front of one of two General Motors EMD twelve-cylinder 2,500 hp diesels, which run at 900 rpm. Behind him, the quilting over the engine is heat insulation on the exhaust manifold.

Brian Gauvin

COOK

This happy photograph is from New York, about 1980, in the galley of a boat with two crews.

© John McGrail / MaritimePhotos.com

Until the 1980s tug meals were famous for their quantity and variety. Cost-cutting has eliminated the cook on most harbor tugs, where a deckhand is assigned to cook, or the crew takes turns. On coastal and ocean tugs, and on the Mississippi, however, where large crews are under way for months, cooking is taken seriously, and a good cook might be the key to keeping employees from jumping to another company. The cook has to lay in a month's provisions, of enough variety for interesting meals, and then prepare the food in a galley that rolls and pitches from morning to morning.

Essayist Edward Hoagland bummed rides on Moran tugs in the 1960s. In 1969 the *Village Voice* published "Knights and Squires," his account of a day on the *Teresa Moran*, in which he reminisced about the feasts on previous trips:

> We were told to wait awhile in the Gowanus Canal for an eight o'clock job. The cook fed us cube steak and beet salad. Years ago, when I was younger and hungrier, part of my pleasure was the feasts on a tugboat. The cooks buy their own food on an allowance of three dollars a day for each crew member, but the money went further then and the meals were baronial. A first course of herring in wine sauce, honeydew melon, shrimp cocktail, pickles and olives, soup and a choice of juices, all of them served simultaneously. A main course of roast beef, roast lamb, fillet of sole, macaroni and cheese and cold cuts, plus corn, squash, peas, lima beans, two salads, two kinds of potatoes. And there would be pies, rice pudding, a cake, ice cream, brownies, date bread, iced and hot drinks, Camembert cheese, and canned and new fruit. "Goes with the meal. Eat up. That's the best meat right next to the bone," the Norwegian cook used to say, bending over and pointing or pouring gravy, crushing an empty milk carton in his other hand.

MATE

The mate, second in command to the skipper, runs the boat when the captain is off watch. Mates understand connections from their time on deck, so the biggest jump in responsibility is boat handling: learning how the tug responds to the controls and the effect of proximity to a moving ship or currents when trying to stay "in shape" (correctly aligned) alongside. Boat handling is a learned skill, but requires natural hand-eye coordination and depth perception to know how to set the tug on a course that has it arrive in the correct place, accounting for the momentum of the tug and ship, tides and currents, and engine responsiveness. Tug handling is not for the clumsy or hesitant. There are a million ways to get a tug in the wrong place at the wrong time, with life-threatening consequences, not to mention embarrassment in front of experienced critics: the docking pilot, ship's crew, and other assist-tug captains. Mates take a Coast Guard exam to be licensed to pilot a tug.

The mate here is running the boat under the eye of the skipper, as Turecamo Coastal and Harbor Towing tugs move a historic sailing ship, the *Moshulu*, on the Delaware in Philadelphia. The mate is operating the hydraulic steering lever mounted next to the binnacle, a cabinet containing the compass, covered by a glass dome. (In older tugs—and possibly this one when built—the steering wheel was mounted vertically on the back of the binnacle.) One window has been dropped into the casement so the mate can call out directions to the deckhands. The tug beyond is firmly attached to the ship with spring, stern, and head lines so they move as one vessel, the tug becoming the ship's propeller.

© John McGrail / MaritimePhotos.com

The step from mate to captain (often called the skipper), involves the ability to make judgments about the safest and most efficient course of action, and calls for passing a Coast Guard exam to earn a master's license. When at sea, there's no other authority or appeal to more experience. In ship docking, the captain receives orders from the docking pilot, but even then he or she is responsible for refusing if the action may endanger tug or crew. Since most skippers have climbed from the deck, they're not brass-buttoned, isolated ship captains, but rather usually act like one of the crew so long as their authority is respected. Intelligence, steadiness under pressure, instinctive directional sense, and good hand-eye coordination are required for a tug captain.

Captain Elizabeth Bunch, on *Tiger 8*, is assisting a fuel barge and its ocean tug, departing from Kahului Harbor, Maui, on a route connecting the Hawaiian Islands. P&R Water Taxi built eleven *Tiger* tugs at its shipyard in Honolulu, to service all US Navy ships at Pearl Harbor and provide ship-assist work in major Hawaiian ports. The tugs have twin rudder propellers, and hawser winches on the bow and stern for ship work. Some of her sister tugs have a cable towing winch on the stern for occasional barge towing and cinching up against the rounded hulls of submarines. Bunch has her hands on controls for the corresponding rudder propellers below, rotating the control to steer, and pulling the lever on top to control the engine throttle. The radio is operated by foot pedals. The winch control is in the center of the console.

Captain Bunch grew up surfing on Maui and worked on tourist boats for a few years after high school, then decided to make a career on the sea. She graduated from the California Maritime Academy, got her mariner's license, and sailed on Chevron tankers until, wanting less travel but still to be involved in boat and shiphandling, she was hired as deckhand/engineer by P&R and, within a year, was a captain on her home island.

Philip Spalding

HARBOR AND DOCKING PILOTS

A pilot climbs down from the deck of a ship in a pilot transfer in San Francisco Bay as the ship and pilot boat move ahead smartly through the water. The pilot boat holds off from the ship slightly as the pilot climbs down. It's safer to fall in the water than onto the pilot boat deck until the pilot is almost down to the boat.

One pilot had spent six hours transiting the ship from an anchorage in the bay to the mouth of the San Joaquin River. Another pilot came up the ladder so they could exchange information before the relief pilot took the ship through channels in the river deltas to Stockton, another six-hour passage with as little as a foot of water under the ship. A pilot may board a strange ship in the middle of the night to meet a foreign crew speaking little English. Is the ship direct-drive diesel (shut down the engine to stop the prop, but will it start again?), or steam turbine (any level of power instantly available, but the prop can't be completely stopped)? The ship may turn more quickly than expected, or be sluggish to respond to the helm. The ship may be heavily laden, with slow response time and great momentum, or light and subject to crosswinds. Harbor pilots are the most confident and competent of seamen (just ask one!), taking charge of multimillion dollar ships in dangerous places without a moment to become familiar.

Alan Haig-Brown

Bringing a ship from the sea into port requires knowledge of local geography, tides, and water traffic, and of unique weather conditions like prevailing winds that can push a slow-moving ship off course. Harbor pilots based in the port (sometimes informally referred to as sea pilots to differentiate them from docking pilots, discussed below) are brought out to meet incoming ships. The pilot boats, built like fast Coast Guard rescue boats, are usually captained by a harbor pilot in training, who brings the boat alongside the ship so the pilot can climb onto a rope ladder and up to the deck. Since the pilot is to guide the ship into port, the exchange usually occurs in the open ocean, with the ship moving so it maintains steering (and schedule). Often, high seas toss the boat toward the ship, or force it away, while the pilot is trying to transfer. Modern pilots wear reflective float coats because of the danger of being flung into the sea, which happens several times a year around the globe. Up into the 1950s pilots wore formal overcoats, and were rowed to the ship in any weather in dories from fast-sailing pilot cutters. In Portland, Oregon, pilots are now lowered to the decks of ships from helicopters when seas are rough. The harbor pilot directs the ship's wheelhouse crew in course changes and engine speed, while the captain, for the purposes of liability still in charge, sweats in unaccustomed irrelevance.

In larger ports, when the ship nears its berth or enters the inner harbor, a *docking master* climbs the ladder from one of the escort tugs to take over the approach and docking itself. He or she is either a former tug captain who docks ships for a living, or an escort-tug captain who hands the tug over to the mate. The steps in docking a big vessel in tight quarters require a team leader familiar with the particular characteristics of each tug and crew. They develop a shorthand to communicate during the hectic maneuvering. (For pushing full ahead, one Boston docking pilot orders "Shake 'em up!") The tug answers in whistle peeps so the pilot can be sure he's been understood: one peep if going ahead or astern from stop or adding power, two peeps if switching direction. This way the tug captains don't tie up the radio in confirming orders while the pilot is talking to several tugs in critical second-by-second directions.

The Pivot Point

The pilot and docking master need at least an intuitive understanding of the location of what Henry H. Hoyer in his book, *Behaviour and Handling of Ships*, calls the peripatetic pivot point, an imaginary vertical axis through the center of water resistance of the ship.

When the ship is sitting dead in the water, the *pivot point* is directly in the center, since water resistance is equal in all directions. Under any force on the ship, it acts as if it were pinned into the water through the center.

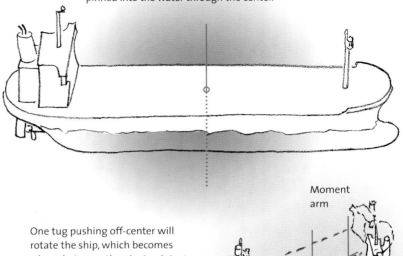

Two tugs (or one in the center) will move the ship bodily sideways.

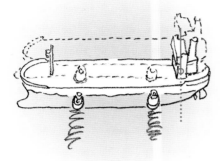

One tug pushing off-center will rotate the ship, which becomes a lever between the pivot point and the tug, increasing the tug's force, but rotating the ship around the "pin."

Moment arm

But the pivot point doesn't stay put! Since it's the center of water pressure resistance, if the ship moves forward or astern, it pushes water out of the way. This increases resistance to the ship's passage, and the pivot point moves toward the end pushing through the water. The ship captain and harbor pilot pay attention because the ship turns differently depending on where the pivot point is. For the docking pilot, moving the pivot point changes the effect of the tugs.

If the pier is alongside a river with current flowing out to sea, the docking master has the ship go ahead through the water at the same speed as the current is flowing past, to keep the ship aligned with the berth while it is being moved sideways to meet the pier. The ship's speed is zero "over the bottom," but several knots ahead through the water. Increased pressure at the bow moves the pivot point forward.

Two tugs are shown pushing the ship to the pier. Tug 1 pushes at the full center of water resistance (the pivot point). If Tug 2 pushes with the same force, the moment arm formed by the distance from the pivot point multiplies the effect. This could smash the ship's stern quarter into the pier, damaging both ship and pier, and possibly setting in motion a sequence that ends with the current pushing the bow sideways, putting the ship crosswise in the river, out of control. To dock the ship successfully, Tug 2 must reduce its thrust to stay aligned with Tug 1 as they push together.

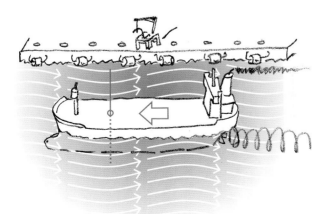

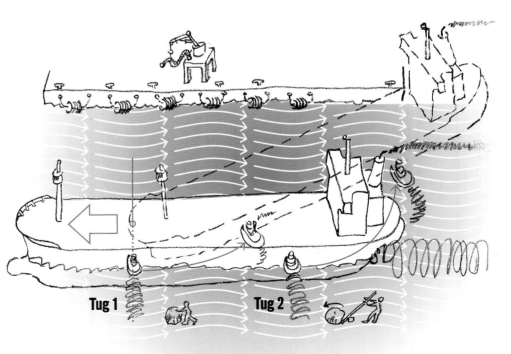

Tug 1   Tug 2

Effect of moment arm

THE DOCKYARD

Tug dockyards contain the best features of any boatyard, but scaled up. They are scattered with equipment and vessel parts. Boats of all ages and types bob at the piers, accompanied by a collection of salty crewmembers and maintenance workers. Some companies specialize in ship work, others in barge towing, but many specialize in survival: any work on the waterfront.

A *bunker barge* carries 50,000 gallons of fuel to bunker (refuel) visiting ships.

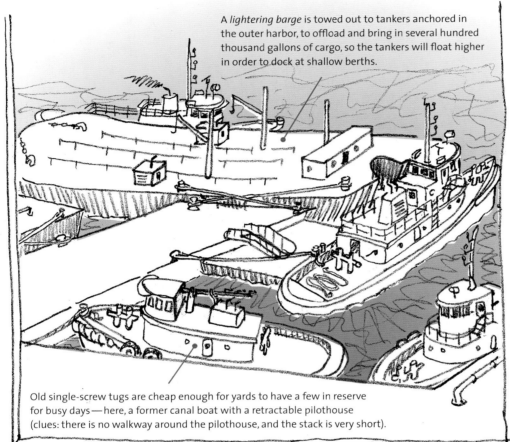

A *lightering barge* is towed out to tankers anchored in the outer harbor, to offload and bring in several hundred thousand gallons of cargo, so the tankers will float higher in order to dock at shallow berths.

Old single-screw tugs are cheap enough for yards to have a few in reserve for busy days—here, a former canal boat with a retractable pilothouse (clues: there is no walkway around the pilothouse, and the stack is very short).

One or two *on-call* boats have double crews living aboard for a week or two at a time, with auxiliary engines running, ready to head out on a few minutes' notice.

When tanks are down to a few thousand gallons, tugs are *bunkered* (the term is a holdover from coal bunkers on steamships) with 10,000 gallons. For a harbor tug, that will last a few weeks.

PORT CAPTAIN AND DISPATCHER

At tug companies of any size, a *port captain* manages the boats. Usually a tug captain with an interest in management or more regular hours, the port captain also needs a calm nature to put up with owners' foibles. The port captain is the link between the fun stuff (boats, crews, tides, and weather) and the management back-of-the-house (finance, personnel, unions, and contracts). While the owner is thinking deep thoughts, or hunting down new business, the port captain makes sure the boats are maintained and fueled, crews are fed and happy, and tugs make it to assignments on time and perform without embarrassment. The port captain is also involved in decisions about new building or buying and renovating equipment, often working closely with naval architects to make sure the boats suit the style of local tug work and the firm's maintenance practices.

The dispatch room of a ship-handling company operates around the clock, taking calls from local shipping agents who represent ship owners and hire the tug company, recording ship statistics, arrival and departure times, and draft (depth of loading). *Dispatchers* know the local berths, and on what state of the tide they can be worked. Dispatchers call in the tug crew next in rotation (the crews come in as needed, when they're next in line) or replace a boat whose crew would otherwise go onto union-mandated overtime pay.

As with all industries, dispatching has increasingly gone electronic. Crowley, for example, dispatches West Coast tugs remotely from Seattle, often communicating by cellphone while watching harbor charts as the tugs and ships are tracked by Global Positioning Systems (GPS).

A *marine railway* is a platform on railroad tracks that is rolled into the water until only the top walkways show. A vessel to be repaired is floated over the submerged platform. Straps running between the two walkways are passed under the hull and cranked up tight to the hull. Then the platform is winched out of the water along the rails. The tug (in this case) hangs on the straps until wood blocks are inserted underneath to support it and the straps can be removed.

Visiting coastal tugs tie up to take on fuel, water, and groceries.

A small marine construction workboat tows out a spud barge (corner poles can be dropped through the hull to pin the barge in place). An old crawler crane sits on wood sleepers that protect the barge deck.

Some yards keep repair crews busy building a new boat between other assignments.

A *honey barge* shuttles sewage pumped from visiting ships to a treatment plant.

The drawing is loosely based on the old Boston Towing and Transportation yard on New Street.

LLOYD'S REGISTER

SHIPS ANNUAL

TIDES

TUGS

Ship
MONTREAL EXP
Arrival
6 Sep 1412o
Berth
CHARLESTOWN #3
Draft
27
Tugs
. Cissy
. Fort Point
. Chelsea

TIME ON THE BOATS

Until the shipping revolution of the '60s and '70s, ships had gradually increased in size through the decades, but there was no call for supersized ships except crude oil tankers and industrial bulkers on certain routes. Numerous small ships filled the ports loading and unloading "break-bulk" cargo: boxes and crates of all sizes and shapes were winched into ships' holds by gangs of laborers and stacked on several decks. This was good for tug companies, whose boats were kept busy around the clock.

Today enormous ships carry thousands of identical containers between a few major ports, from which the containers move to bypassed ports and to the interior by truck. In smaller harbors, sturdy older tugs can do the jobs that are left: small product tankers, road salt and scrap bulkers, or auto carriers. A harbor that once might have kept three tug companies busy around the clock now probably can call on one dominant company and a few smaller competitors.

To be ready to respond to the vagaries of ship schedules set by weather or tides or loading complications, tug companies usually have at least one round-the-clock boat on duty, carrying two crews. They work for two weeks, then take two weeks off. Watches are six hours on, six off, with the captain and engineer usually taking the more desirable six-to-twelve shift (a.m. and p.m.), along with one deckhand. That leaves the mate and the other deckhand to stay up from midnight to six a.m., then get up again for the noon-to-six p.m. turn. It takes time to adjust to a schedule that crams getting ready for bed, turning in, getting up and dressed, eating, and going back to work, all in six hours.

Family men try to get onto the optimistically named "day boats." Crews are called in for ten-hour shifts when needed, day or night, with only a few hours' notice. It's a life more likely set by tide charts than clock time. They spend more of their time at home every day, but their schedules are less predictable.

This homey Philadelphia scene is aboard *Tug McGraw*, an old tug renamed in 1980 after Phillies pitcher Frank "Tug" McGraw got the final out, to give Philadelphia its first World Series pennant. Waiting, and plowing around the harbor from one job to another, take up most of the time on a harbor tug. There's an hour to fire up the tug, a half-hour run to the harbor entrance to meet the ship, waiting fifteen minutes for it to approach, then the work of wrestling with the hawser to connect alongside and powering up to dock the ship. Then there's more waiting, shoving slow ahead for fifteen minutes, pinning the ship to the pier as the mooring lines are set.

Tug McGraw is a tough old boat, matched by her captain in the pilothouse window. Part of its visor is torched off, probably after being torn loose under the overhanging hull of a ship, perhaps in the same incident that bent the rail. Wrought-iron hinges on the wood panel door date the tug to the early part of the twentieth century. She's painted in Turecamo Towing colors: all their boats sported this faux wood-grain pattern. The sixty-one-year-old Turecamo fleet succumbed to industry efficiencies in 1988 and merged with Moran Towing, founded in 1860.

© *John McGrail / MaritimePhotos.com*

Tides set the schedule for harbor tug crews. Ships and tugs at sea feel no effect from the slow rise and fall of water level, but when they approach ports at low tide, they are faced with shallower water at the harbor mouth, or narrower deep-water passages as tides recede. Tug crews are called out for ship handling that takes advantage of the tides, but tidal changes bear no relation to our daily solar rhythms. The tides operate on the moon's schedule. It is as if the tugboating clock has two sets of hands, one set moving at sun speed, and the other at moon speed, the pairs only randomly overlapping. Shiphandling depends on high tides for moving across shallows, or slack tides to avoid tidal currents, while marine construction usually benefits from the increased overhead bridge clearances that low tide offers. Harbor tug crews have the advantage of a seafaring life close to home, but in return they must work to tides whose continually shifting arrival disrupts normal sleep cycles and family routines.

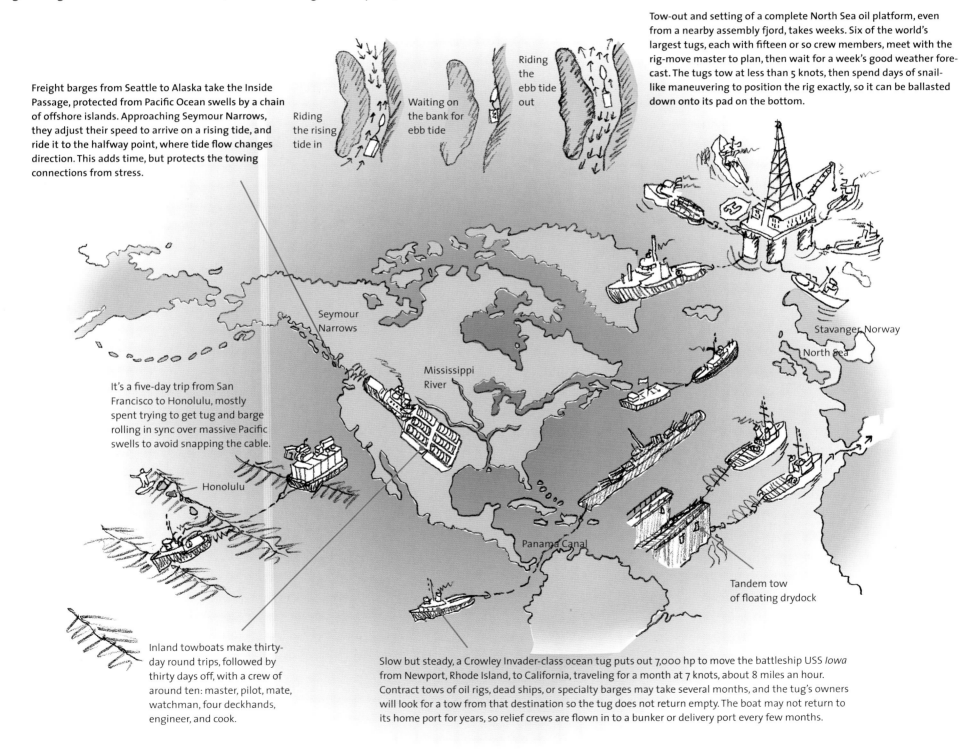

Freight barges from Seattle to Alaska take the Inside Passage, protected from Pacific Ocean swells by a chain of offshore islands. Approaching Seymour Narrows, they adjust their speed to arrive on a rising tide, and ride it to the halfway point, where tide flow changes direction. This adds time, but protects the **towing connections** from stress.

Riding the rising tide in

Waiting on the bank for ebb tide

Riding the ebb tide out

Tow-out and setting of a complete North Sea oil platform, even from a nearby assembly fjord, takes weeks. Six of the world's largest tugs, each with fifteen or so crew members, meet with the rig-move master to plan, then wait for a week's good weather forecast. The tugs tow at less than 5 knots, then spend days of snail-like maneuvering to position the rig exactly, so it can be ballasted down onto its pad on the bottom.

Seymour Narrows

Mississippi River

Stavanger, Norway

North Sea

It's a five-day trip from San Francisco to Honolulu, mostly spent trying to get tug and barge rolling in sync over massive Pacific swells to avoid snapping the cable.

Honolulu

Panama Canal

Tandem tow of floating drydock

Inland towboats make thirty-day round trips, followed by thirty days off, with a crew of around ten: master, pilot, mate, watchman, four deckhands, engineer, and cook.

Slow but steady, a Crowley Invader-class ocean tug puts out 7,000 hp to move the battleship USS *Iowa* from Newport, Rhode Island, to California, traveling for a month at 7 knots, about 8 miles an hour. Contract tows of oil rigs, dead ships, or specialty barges may take several months, and the tug's owners will look for a tow from that destination so the tug does not return empty. The boat may not return to its home port for years, so relief crews are flown in to a bunker or delivery port every few months.

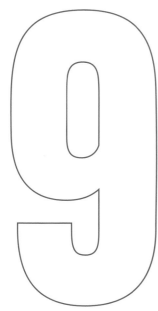

Modern Tug Design and Construction

That machines are extensions of people can't be made clearer than this. The operator on TugMalta's *Sea Salvor* is silhouetted in the center of the pilothouse, each hand on a joystick controlling a 2,250 hp rudder propeller. He looks to be at one with his tug: the central processor who can direct thousands of pounds of force with a twist of his wrist.

From ahead or astern, tugs and most vessels are as symmetrical as people, that is to say, almost. This is bilateral symmetry, and the axis of symmetry passes through the mast, the skipper, the greenhouse-like pilothouse, the deckhouse, the green synthetic line

wound on the winch, and the bulls-eye in the bow for leading a mooring line forward. The symmetry extends to the stacks flanking the pilothouse, the bitts set in notches on either side of the bow, and small mooring bulls-eyes. The discordant note is the set of fire monitors on the pilothouse roof. To regulate the force of water as it transitions from the engine room pump riser and through the pilothouse to the remote-operated swivel gun, the piping takes a horizontal loop. It makes manufacturing sense to construct the cannons identically, but the symmetry of the tug is disturbed, even though the vertical risers through the pilothouse roof are located symmetrically.

The symmetry ends at the tug's mission, which is to control the tanker looming to starboard. There is an asymmetry of power, of mass. Unlike a ship built to run free, a tug is intended to be up against a ship or barge. The skipper in this photo is applying uneven force as well: as the starboard drive pushes forward to stay alongside the onrushing tanker, his left hand is probably directing the port drive thirty feet below his feet to push toward the ship, counteracting the force of water flowing between the tanker's hull and the tug, which is trying to tear the tug away from the ship.

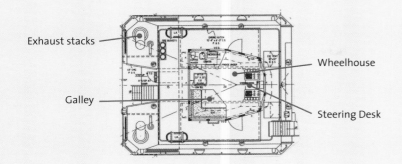

Exhaust stacks

Wheelhouse

Galley

Steering Desk

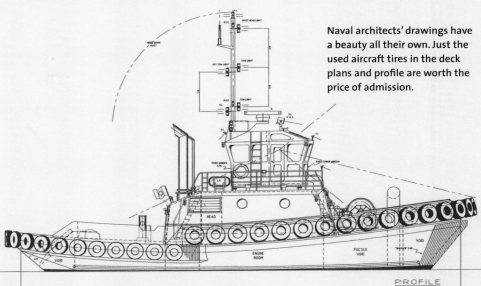

Naval architects' drawings have a beauty all their own. Just the used aircraft tires in the deck plans and profile are worth the price of admission.

PROFILE

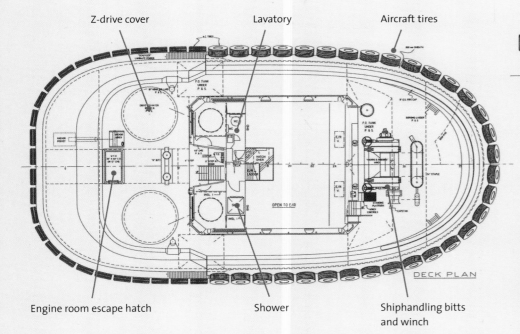

Z-drive cover

Lavatory

Aircraft tires

Engine room escape hatch

Shower

Shiphandling bitts and winch

DECK PLAN

Murray McLellan

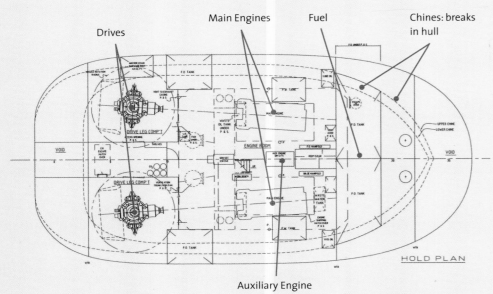

Drives

Main Engines

Fuel

Chines: breaks in hull

VOID

VOID

HOLD PLAN

Auxiliary Engine

Drawings A. G. McIlwain, Ltd.

DESIGN OF A SHIPDOCKING TUG FOR TIGHT QUARTERS

Vancouver's harbor was laid out with closely spaced piers that accommodated a sail-powered tall ship on each side of the slip, loading grain or coal. Today's larger ships barely fit, and leave little room for tugs to maneuver. Vancouver tug companies developed small tugs, sometimes requiring five or six to get sufficient horsepower for the task. The invention of tractor tugs and the development of compact, powerful diesels allowed a few smaller tugs to handle ships in the tight spaces. Naval architect A. G. McIlwain squeezed 5,400 hp into the 72-foot hull of *Tiger Sun* in a design that's as tight as a pocket watch. Most tugs of that horsepower would be 85 to 95 feet long. Such size limitations imposed compromises: fuel tanks hold only a three-day supply, accommodations are limited (none are even installed in *Tiger Sun*, which operates as a day boat), and there's no room for a barge-handling winch on the tiny stern deck. The boat is operated by a skipper and deckhand, and the pilothouse is located so that the skipper can see the deckhand wherever he is on deck as well as any part of the fendering that might be in contact with the ship's hull.

Don Wilson / Port of Seattle

DESIGN OF A COLUMBIA RIVER TANKER ESCORT TUG

In 1994, responding to increased environmental concerns, Foss Maritime and naval architects Glosten Associates designed the first high-horsepower dedicated tanker escort tug, to meet ships in the swells at the mouth of the Strait of Juan De Fuca, then shadow them in case of trouble on the 130-mile run up the Columbia River through scenic landscape and populated areas to Seattle, Washington. The 165-foot *Lindsey Foss* is stretched so that she can span two of the closely spaced swells that kick up over the Columbia River bar. A dedicated escort tug doesn't need a long stern deck to lay out barge shackles, so the pilothouse can move back to the center of the vessel for visibility. Her only function is towing ships over the stern, either bow or stern-first, and being fast enough to keep up with the ships she is escorting.

TUG HULL DESIGN: CHINES

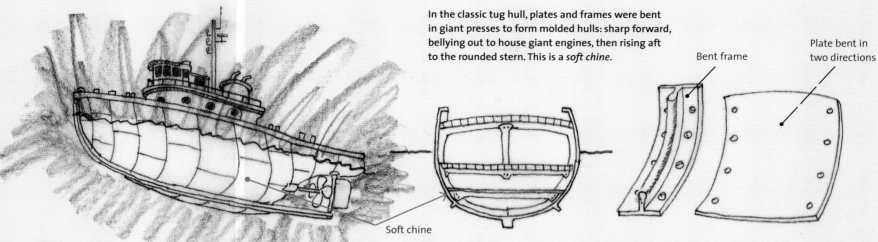

In the classic tug hull, plates and frames were bent in giant presses to form molded hulls: sharp forward, bellying out to house giant engines, then rising aft to the rounded stern. This is a *soft chine*.

Bent frame

Plate bent in two directions

Soft chine

Bent plates are expensive to produce. Tug designers searching for forms that took advantage of welded planar plate assembly adapted a wooden dory or skiff design: side and bottom planes meeting along a *hard chine*.

Hard chine

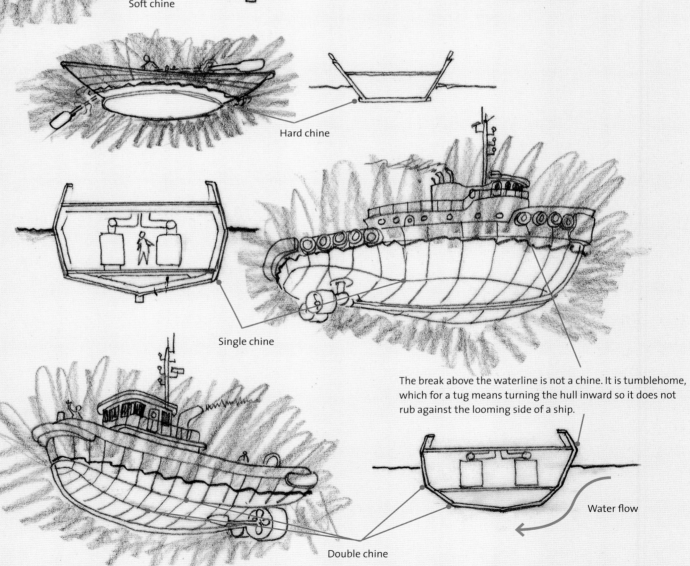

Ocean-going tugs are single chine: vertical sides meet at bottom plates along one chine, enclosing a deep hull that accommodates 100,000-gallon fuel tanks. The vertical sides also reduce the effect of crosswise waves and help the boat stay on course for long voyages.

Single chine

The break above the waterline is not a chine. It is tumblehome, which for a tug means turning the hull inward so it does not rub against the looming side of a ship.

Harbor tugs are double chine: an additional plane between the side and bottom planes softens the underwater lines, and makes swinging sideways easier during maneuvering for ship work. This compromise makes the tug less stable offshore.

Water flow

Double chine

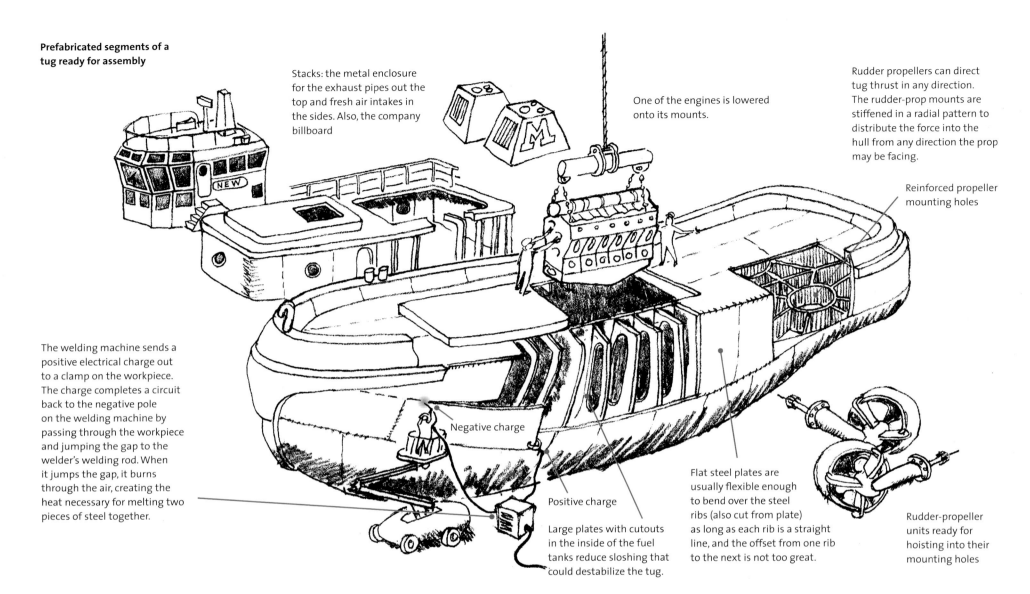

Prefabricated segments of a tug ready for assembly

Stacks: the metal enclosure for the exhaust pipes out the top and fresh air intakes in the sides. Also, the company billboard

One of the engines is lowered onto its mounts.

Rudder propellers can direct tug thrust in any direction. The rudder-prop mounts are stiffened in a radial pattern to distribute the force into the hull from any direction the prop may be facing.

Reinforced propeller mounting holes

The welding machine sends a positive electrical charge out to a clamp on the workpiece. The charge completes a circuit back to the negative pole on the welding machine by passing through the workpiece and jumping the gap to the welder's welding rod. When it jumps the gap, it burns through the air, creating the heat necessary for melting two pieces of steel together.

Negative charge

Positive charge

Large plates with cutouts in the inside of the fuel tanks reduce sloshing that could destabilize the tug.

Flat steel plates are usually flexible enough to bend over the steel ribs (also cut from plate) as long as each rib is a straight line, and the offset from one rib to the next is not too great.

Rudder-propeller units ready for hoisting into their mounting holes

NEWBUILDING: CONSTRUCTING A TUG

To replace ships sunk by U-boats early in World War II, American industrialist Henry J. Kaiser developed mass-production techniques, including welded steel plates and sectional prefabrication, to turn out 2,770 Liberty ships in four years. Welding replaced the labor-intensive hulls made by riveting together iron plates and frames shaped and punched in enormous presses. Without the need for expensive machinery, which had been centralized in a few world shipbuilding centers, ships could be built anywhere, as they had been in the age of wooden ships. After World War II, the economies and speed of welded steel construction filtered down to tugs, but the relatively small size and extreme shapes of tug hulls required a new design approach. Classic molded plates were squared off into planes that met at hard chines, lines where two flat plates meet.

Leftover wartime tugs, and steady building in the 1950s, provided a good inventory of tugs that were sufficient to serve the small ships that carried break-bulk cargoes around the globe into the 1960s. But with the introduction of containerized shipping and demand for oil from undeveloped parts of the world, ships grew larger and larger, and tugs had to follow suit. Tug companies competed to dominate ports by building large fleets of powerful tractor tugs. They distinguished the new construction from buying and modifying older tugs as "newbuilding" programs. Recent ecological concerns have required oil companies to pay high rates to companies that can provide the most powerful and best-equipped tug fleets for safe operations.

The hull plates are bent as necessary with clamps as they are seamed together to form the tug's skin. The white lines are discolorations where the hull plates have been welded to a skeleton of reinforcing plates inside the hull. A hull in construction before the skin is attached is the negative of the hull, drawn in spaced out flat plates. The round grill protects the bow thruster tunnel, which contains a centered propeller that can run in either direction to push the bow around. This is Crowley's *Ocean Wave*, whose stern is shown on page 47.

Brian Gauvin

Welding

Welding seams together thousands of separate steel plates into one object: a sturdy hollow vessel capable of floating and absorbing the tremendous punishment inflicted on tug hulls. Every line between two surfaces in this photo has been "drawn" painstakingly by the welder, peering through an obscure glass to gauge the distance between the electrode tip and the workpiece by the intensity of the light. After striking the tip of the electrode to the plates to start the current flow, the welder pulls the tip an inch or so away from the joint to be welded, forming a gap the electricity must arc across like a tiny bolt of lightning (thus "arc welding"). The electric current burns its way across the gap through the oxygen in the air, melting the steel at the edges of the plates together, and spitting some of the electrode across the gap to provide filler metal as well. A beautiful hand-welded joint is an even train of overlapping crescents like a reclining stack of dimes, combining metal from the two plates and the electrode into a single piece. Welding is a craft: the electrode must be advanced evenly along the joint, which isn't even visible through the glass, and the electrode must also be pushed toward the joint as it is shortened by sending metal across the gap to the joint. Because welding has also heat-treated the joint, the result is stronger than the original metal outside the joint.

A construction photo of *Curtis Reinauer*, being built for Reinauer Transportation of New York and Boston, at the Senesco shipyard on Narragansett Bay in Rhode Island. She is the tug portion of an articulated tug-barge (ATB) unit (see page 126). The pilothouse was fabricated in a shop, and loaded on a multiwheeled transporter to ferry it to the hull being assembled next to the water. Directly under the suspended pilothouse, the brown spot surrounded by white is the pin that will project to connect the tug and barge. It is set in a dark gray section which is the pre-fabricated module containing all the hydraulics for extending the pin. Long gone are the days of beautiful curved hulls. Economy dictates flat plates joining at facets. This style, called *facet tug*, was created by Massachusetts naval architect Robert Hill.

The pilothouse is tall for visibility over the barge, especially when the barge is light and riding high. It's made of aluminum to reduce the weight of the mass of metal swinging side to side in heavy seas (weight overhead is called *tophamper*).

*Rod Smith
(narragansettbay-shipping.com)*

YT (Yard Tug) 802 Valiant spreads her 3,620 hp over a rounded bow and set of cushioning rubber fenders to soften the contact when she pushes a ship hull, such as this aircraft carrier in Puget Sound, Bremerton, Washington. She is a product of the Pacific Northwest: designed by Robert Allen Ltd. of Vancouver, British Columbia, built by Martinac Shipbuilding of Tacoma, Washington, and operated by civilian crews through a contract with a local company. The fenders are extruded rubber, treated so they don't leave marks on the light gray naval hulls.

Brian Gauvin

Built for Contact!

"Tugboatin's a cawntac' spoat!" said a veteran New England tug captain and fleet owner, explaining the risks after one of his boats punctured the fuel tank of a tanker she was pushing against while mooring lines were released. A piece of the tug's rubber bow fender had come loose, exposing a steel bracket on the tug's bow, which punched through the fuel tank of the ship's single hull. (Double hulls are now standard. The outer hull protects the fuel tank wall several feet inboard.)

Safely bouncing off other vessels is the heart of tug work. The thousands of pounds of force that tugs produce must be spread across a ship's thin skin to avoid damage. Rubber or plastic fenders wrap tug hulls to cushion the force. The first fenders were disposable timbers hung off the rail, which could be pulled onboard out of the waves when not required. Traditional bow pudding, pads woven from old hawsers, gave the impression of a beard on the bow, below the "face" of the pilothouse. Later, woven pads replaced timbers alongside. In the 1950s, tug bulwarks were lined with discarded rubber tires, hung off the rail with chains. As tug horsepower increased the pressure on ship hulls, sliced-up tires were layered into heavy bow pads. European-style tugs had hardly any padding, since they didn't work alongside. That changed with the worldwide adoption of tractor tugs, whose spectacular maneuvering made pushing alongside at any angle very efficient. Now almost all ship-work tugs are fully fendered from bow to stern.

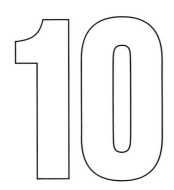

10

Tug master and photographer Pat Folan took this photo of the *Thomas J. Brown* (63 feet, 1,000 hp, built in 1963) passing down Brooklyn's Gowanus Canal with a ragged and beat up scrap barge, as Folan's tug waits to go upstream. The barge is on gate hawsers: a line from each horn of the H-bitts to one corner of the barge. The port hawser is taut as the tug turns to starboard. When the tug turns, the force is immediately transmitted to that corner, smartly pulling the barge's bow around. For this to work, the tug has to tow the barge dangerously close astern. The loops are tossed loosely over the barge bitts, so they can be flipped off by the deckhand without climbing onto the barge.

The *Thomas* is beautifully turned out, with her deep green bulkheads, red decks, and yellow rub rail punctuated by red deck peeking through the freeing ports. I like the red treads disappearing into the green as they rise. Painting the inside of the bulwark red to match the deck forms a tub in which the green deckhouse "sits." If only the boat-deck edge and rails were yellow instead of white (everyone's a critic!). She could be a model for the storybook *Little Toot* if not for the fact that she's twenty-three years younger. She seems too handsome to be on a waterway called Gowanus, which sounds as if it could be Brooklynese for something gross, and smells worse, but is actually named after local seventeenth-century Canarsee tribal chief Gouwane.

Thomas is named for the founder of Thomas J. Brown & Sons, New York, grandfather of current operators Jim and Tom Brown, who apply the gentle art of line handling, leverage, and perfect timing to make barges behave in extremely tight quarters. Tom told maritime writer/photographer Brian Gauvin about working on the boats on summer vacations from the age of eight and his mother's most effective threat to keep the boys in line: not working on the boats that day. Family-owned and -operated tugs are a tradition: a small barge-work tug is a good fit for a family: roomy decks, work that's not too onerous, bunk rooms and galleys, and lots of downtime cruising between assignments.

Pat Folan

Tugs and Barges

U nless they're adrift, barges go nowhere without tugs. Ship-docking companies do as much barge work as ship work. The word "barge" once described a type of English shallow-draft, round-ended, flat-bottomed coastal sailing craft, steered by a leeboard (oar-like rudder) hung over the side. They were slow freight carriers, meant to sit on the bottom at low tide for unloading. Old barges minus sails and rudder, used for storage or towed, became known as "dumb barges." Now "barge" refers to all unpowered towed vessels, although most tug crews would agree that "dumb barge" is still an accurate description for these lumbering, ornery, independent floating boxes.

The process of towing barges is one of constantly outsmarting the barge's powerful momentum and extreme sensitivity to wind and currents. Powered ships can work with tugs to counteract the forces of nature, but barges just go with the flow, for good or ill. It's awkward to connect to them, and the places the connections can break are numerous, increasing with heavy seas that also make reconnecting a broken line difficult and dangerous. Large tank and bulk barges are increasingly pushed by tugs pinned in notches in the barge's stern (see Articulated Tug-Barges, page 126), but a reliable attachment mechanism is too expensive for most applications, so most barges are still streamed out on the hawser at sea, and handled "on the hip" (tied alongside) in harbor.

The traditional rolling launch necessitated building ships on a launch cradle, or moving them onto a cradle to launch. Now large ships and complex floating utility barges, as in this illustration, can be built anywhere along the waterfront, transported to the pier, and gently lowered into the water by submersible barge.

1 First, the submersible barge is ballasted down by filling internal tanks with water to bring it down to match the pier height.

Power units send electricity to the bogies.

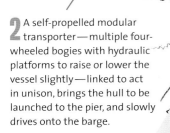
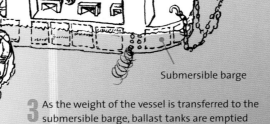
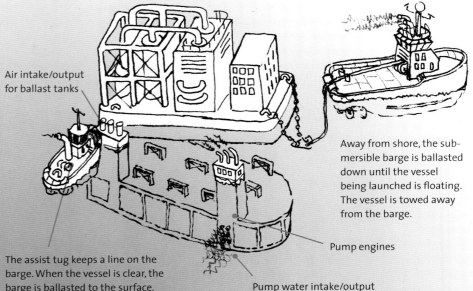

2 A self-propelled modular transporter—multiple four-wheeled bogies with hydraulic platforms to raise or lower the vessel slightly—linked to act in unison, brings the hull to be launched to the pier, and slowly drives onto the barge.

Submersible barge

3 As the weight of the vessel is transferred to the submersible barge, ballast tanks are emptied in sequence to maintain a level surface.

Air intake/output for ballast tanks

Away from shore, the submersible barge is ballasted down until the vessel being launched is floating. The vessel is towed away from the barge.

The assist tug keeps a line on the barge. When the vessel is clear, the barge is ballasted to the surface.

Pump engines

Pump water intake/output

4 Once on the submersible barge, the transporter's hydraulic pistons lower the vessel to be launched to sit on frames on deck, then continue to retract until the transporter can drive out from under.

Hopper barges carry their loads inside the barge, mostly below the waterline. This *dump hopper* has bottom trap doors to dump out dredged material in designated spoil areas.

Hoist to pass hoses

Tankerman's quarters

Pump house

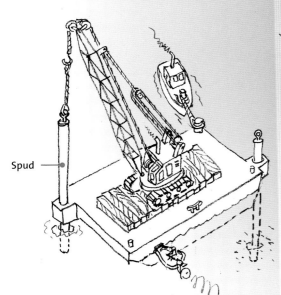
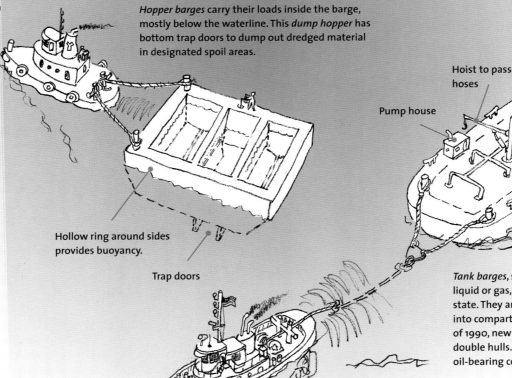

Spud

Hollow ring around sides provides buoyancy.

Trap doors

Pickup line in case hawser breaks

Deck barges just provide a flat surface to carry loads. Water can be pumped into the hull to raise or lower the barge to meet a dock height for loading vehicles and equipment. *Spud barges* used in construction have steel pins that can be lowered into the muck to hold the barge in place. The barge can rise and fall with the tides without losing its position.

Tank barges, such as this petroleum barge, carry liquid or gas, including asphalt heated to a liquid state. They are usually manned, and are divided into compartments. Since the Oil Pollution Act of 1990, new petroleum barges are made with double hulls. The outer hull is 5 feet from the inner, oil-bearing compartment.

On the Hip

On open water, tugs pull barges on wire or rope hawsers several thousand feet long. But in congested harbors, more control is necessary. Tugs pull in their hawsers and go alongside the barge to push, referred to as "on the hip." The tug with the green deck is pushing a barge stern first, a common practice called *head and tail*, which uses the skegs and the blunt stern to make the barge's course more predictable.

Movement is slower than if the barge were front first, but in a congested harbor control is more important than speed. But, if the tug were tied alongside parallel to the barge, the barge's water resistance would continually pull the combined unit in a circle.

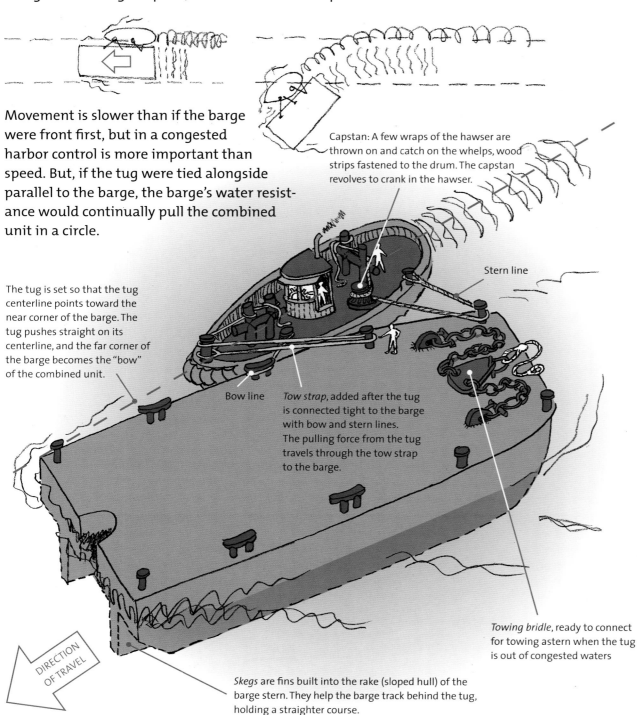

The tug is set so that the tug centerline points toward the near corner of the barge. The tug pushes straight on its centerline, and the far corner of the barge becomes the "bow" of the combined unit.

Capstan: A few wraps of the hawser are thrown on and catch on the whelps, wood strips fastened to the drum. The capstan revolves to crank in the hawser.

Stern line

Bow line

Tow strap, added after the tug is connected tight to the barge with bow and stern lines. The pulling force from the tug travels through the tow strap to the barge.

Towing bridle, ready to connect for towing astern when the tug is out of congested waters

Skegs are fins built into the rake (sloped hull) of the barge stern. They help the barge track behind the tug, holding a straighter course.

DIRECTION OF TRAVEL

In Praise of Complex Shapes

The classic rounded tug hull—the peapod shape—was a traditional boatbuilding design that rode the water easily. As we have seen, the hull shape proved useful when American tugs started going alongside to move ships, because the rounded tug could pivot toward and away from the ship's hull without getting pinned to the ship by suction of the passing water. In developing methods of towing barges from alongside, tugmen found another use for their hull's shape, as a fulcrum against a barge hull to tighten the lines.

The goal is to have the tug end up tightly connected facing the corner of the barge.

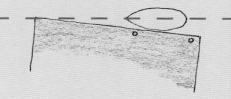

The first step is to put up a bow line at a length that holds the tug at an angle.

Then a stern line is run from the tug bitt, around the barge cleat, and back to the capstan next to the stern bitts. The capstan is cranked to pull the stern around to achieve the desired angle, which rotates the tug and stretches the bow line so both ends of the tug are connected tightly to the barge.

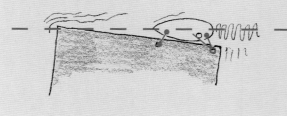

The *Carol Moran* has two barges on the hip and one doubled up in front, as she backs away on a bow line from a Department of Sanitation pier in Brooklyn, New York, for a trip to the Fresh Kills landfill on Staten Island. The hawsers are wrapped on the tug's stemhead chock and H-bitts. The barge in front will act as the bow for the flotilla, with its front corner aligned on the tug's centerline. One deckhand is walking the narrow ledge of the barge to adjust lines. Working between tug and barge is one of the greatest dangers of tug work.

At the landfill, crane buckets will unload the barges. Earlier practice was to take barges to sea, where the tug crew shoveled the garbage overboard.

The *Carol* is in a typically tight space for maneuvering. The barges behind her are car floats for railroad cars, although they are all empty. The white "tombstones" at the front stop railcars from falling off the end of the barge into the harbor during loading. The right-hand rail barge appears to be for small deliveries in which two

railcars are barged to a pier and unloaded by hand over the center platform onto the pier. When rail cars are loaded, the barge would be ballasted to match the rails, which would be at pier level at the railhead.

© John McGrail / MaritimePhotos.com

MUD BOATS: TUGS FOR CONSTRUCTION WORK

rews of marine construction tugs and
workboats spend their working lives in
hard hats and beat-up life vests, churning
around an assemblage of barges pinned to the
bottom, as workers build bridges, tunnels, piers,
and pipelines, or dredge navigation channels.
Everything needed for the work is piled on the
barges: offices, storage containers, portable
toilets, and diving equipment, usually presided
over by a large crane on tracks, rolling over a bed
of timbers that protect the barge's steel deck.

Since most barges are unpowered, they depend
on tugs or small workboats for relocation.
Because they usually work in sheltered waters,
construction tugs, or "mud boats," can be
smaller than their shiphandling cousins. Small
size and draft are an advantage at constricted
sites near shore. The farthest out a mud boat
may go (other than when relocating to another
port, with one eye on the weather) is a few
miles to a dumping ground for dredged material. Their engine power is likewise lower, sav-
ing on fuel costs.

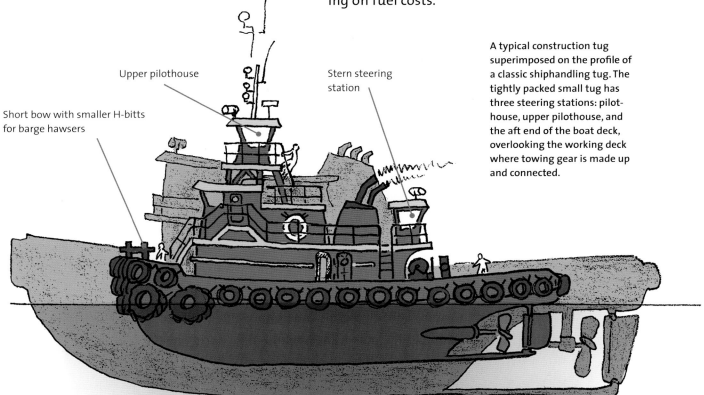

Upper pilothouse

Stern steering
station

Short bow with smaller H-bits
for barge hawsers

A typical construction tug
superimposed on the profile of
a classic shiphandling tug. The
tightly packed small tug has
three steering stations: pilothouse, upper pilothouse, and
the aft end of the boat deck,
overlooking the working deck
where towing gear is made up
and connected.

In 2010, tugs *F. Dawson* and *Elizabeth*
relocate barges used to deliver the
replacement Willis Avenue swing bridge
that spans the Harlem River between
the Bronx and Manhattan Island (the tan
bridge). The bridge's turntable is a drum
on railroad wheels (behind the truss that
extends down), which rests on a circular
track in the base. The new bridge was
delivered sitting on the grid of steel pads
on the linked barges in the foreground,
with the bridge hanging over the sides. It
was lifted off the barges shown here, on
pontoons placed under the overhanging
ends. The bridge was barged into position
over the turntable at high tide, and the
falling tide lowered the pontoons until
the bridge was sitting on its circular track.
The new bridge was built next to the
old (the blue bridge beyond), so passage
was not interrupted, and the new base
was staggered from the old bridge base
so the old bridge could operate without
hitting the base under construction.

After the new bridge was completed, the narrower 1901 swing bridge (left-hand blue span behind the new bridge) was lifted onto a single barge, the new span was swung open, and tugs pushed the old bridge to the Hudson River scrapyards in Bayonne, New Jersey, to be dismantled. The old blue fixed span (to the right)

followed it to the wrecker. The red and white *Elizabeth* has push straps from her stern to the barges, and a head line at the bow, to keep her lined up behind the barge. She is off center, to avoid pushing at the gap between the barges. The starboard hawser is wrapped on the side bitts, while the port strap runs to the stern, around a

fairlead, and up to the winch, where it is snugged tight. The small stern working deck is typical for construction tugs. *F. Dawson,* the yellow tug, may be steering the barges side to side. Her shortness is paying off as her stern barely slides past the channel marker. Both tugs have dropped their masts to clear bridges, at least at low tide.

The white box at the back of *Elizabeth*'s boat (second) deck is a stern steering station from which the tug can be run as the skipper overlooks activity on the stern deck and astern. It is located to the side of the boat deck to give some visibility ahead. Short hawsers are coiled anywhere there is room on any deck.

CANAL TOWING

Most canal crossings are at or near grade level, so canal tugs are necessarily short to pass under low bridges. Each canal system builds to a specified clearance, and the boats used on that system are designed accordingly. Canal tugs are either short or have retracting pilothouses mounted on hydraulic rams, and masts for navigation lights and radar/radio equipment that can be swung down onto cradles to obtain clearance.

Natural waterways offered an easy way to transport heavy loads, and human settlement followed rivers. As societies developed more order and more demand for exchanging excess production, they applied intelligence, will, and labor resources to digging their own channels of buoyancy: canals dug through dry land to connect resources to cities, or heavy stones to monument sites. Egyptians built canals 6,000 years ago. The Tigris and Euphrates rivers in Mesopotamia were connected by a canal in 2200 BC. In 600 BC China connected major cities by canal. At the same time, the Roman Empire's system was operating: one of Rome's canals, built in occupied Britain, was rediscovered and reopened a thousand years later, in 1211, by King Henry I. In the Renaissance, canals became the focus of a new profession, engineering, and captured the imagination of society as symbols of technology and progress. The bulk of the projects were simple ditches, suited to the available labor force, while skilled craftsmen concentrated on locks, and aqueducts over valleys. Canal towing suited the available towing power of man and animal, and the simple boatbuilding skills of local craftsmen.

The high point of canal development was the early to mid-1800s, when populations were increasing. Trade became two-way: not only from farms to cities, usually downstream on rivers, but also manufactured goods moving from cities to farm areas. Before the advent of steamboats that could power their way against the current, this upstream trade required canals. Manufacturing also called for reliable supplies of coal and iron, not limited by rivers' extremes of floods and droughts. The canals that survived the development of railroads twenty or so years after the big canal boom were those in heavy use, like the Erie Canal, or those delivering bulk materials like coal, for which canal boats provided cheaper service than railroads.

waves when the tug pulled petroleum barges offshore while the canal was closed by ice for the winter. *Margaret Matton*'s bow has an impressive array of bitts squeezed onto the truncated foredeck. Tugs on older canals are compact to fit with their barges into the old locks.

The barge, *Petroleum No. 7*, has a shallow notch in the stern to receive the tug's bow, which is heavily padded with bow pudding woven from old hawsers. The deckhouse across the barge's stern covers cargo pumps and the barge crew's quarters.

Collection of Brent Dibner

The *Margaret Matton* passes through a lock on the Erie Canal. At low bridges the masts were leaned back out of the way, giving her a maximum clearance of 17 feet above the waterline. The pilothouse, stack, and her rowboat are at about the same level; the boat davits are also low.

The skipper has the front windows down for communication with deckhands and canal workers, and to ring the bell hanging off the visor. The circles below the windows are portlights mounted in steel plates that can be slid up to protect the pilothouse windows. Portlights were small windows of heavy glass that could withstand crashing

The crew loads a mule onto the boat at shift change, in Fultonville, New York, late nineteenth century. The animal is refusing to go, so they are moving it with a block and tackle on the barge, pulled by another, more cooperative, mule at right. The ramp is a miniature version of the change bridge truss (see opposite page). A hatch in the stable roof has been slid over so the mules can enter. Giant lanterns on the bow of the front barge light the canal and the towpath, where the team is at the end of a 250-foot towline. The length reduces the angle of the towline between the barge and bank, minimizing the amount of steering required. Cleats for securing the tow rope line the rail, reducing the pull of the towline toward the bank. If the towing cleat were in the bow, the boat would be continually pulled toward the bank.

Cargo is carried under the hatch covers in the center. The family quarters are in the stern cabin, but it was so small that most family life took place on deck. Originally barges were steered by a tiller in the stern, but when barges were doubled up for economy, a system of pulleys transferred the steering force from the wheel visible in front of the cabin, to pull the rear barge off center, so it acted as a giant rudder.

Courtesy of Jean Keplinger, Perinton Historic Archives

Towing on the Erie Canal

The Erie Canal spans 400 miles from Buffalo on Lake Ontario to near Albany on the Hudson River, operating May through September. Barges were originally pulled through the canal by mules to the terminus at Albany, then floated down the Hudson by the current to New York City. Later they were rafted together at Albany and pulled to New York by tugs. The canal was conceived and constructed before engines were readily available, so it was built for animal power, and continued thus from its completion in 1825 until the early twentieth century, even as the world became motorized around it. The advantages of powered barges seem obvious, but other factors made animal power the choice during this period.

The steam engine was initially seen as a powerful boon to canal barge work, eliminating the complications of mules, drovers, ropes, and towpaths. The British canal tugboat *Charlotte Dundas* was the first practical steam tug, but was only used once on the canal it was designed for. Conservative canal owners in Europe and North America tried and abandoned steam tugs in favor of retaining animal power. Steam power was much more quickly and profitably applied to railroads, where long-distance travel using animal power was uncomfortable and inefficient because it lacked the canal's benefits of buoyancy to overcome friction and smooth the ride. (Railroads benefited from the creative engineering of the canal surveyors. Rail lines often followed the paths of canals, which followed rivers as a source of water.) Later, when screw propellers and smoother control of the power train were perfected, and canals were enlarged with reinforced banks, tugs and powered barges took

over. Canal culture shifted with the passing of animal power. When there were animals to care for, and hoggees (drovers) to feed, it made sense for a barge owner to travel the canal with his family during the May-to-December season so the wife could cook and older children tend the animals or guide the teams. Many reminiscences of nineteenth-century life on the canal paint a bucolic picture of slowly passing towns and scenery and playing on the barge and the banks as the boat traveled at a leisurely three to four miles an hour. Another reward was the tow to New York City, where country kids could wander its streets and markets.

Boats Meeting on the Erie Canal

At some points in the canal, an obstruction tight to the canal, such as a rock formation or building, made it necessary to shift the towpath to the other side of the canal. Change bridges were erected to allow the team to cross the canal without unhitching. The bridge and its connecting paths are precursors to modern highway cloverleafs.

With one towpath serving both directions of travel, the meeting of vessels needed to be carefully choreographed.

The teams for boats headed both east and west had to share one towpath. The team pulling the boat on the bank opposite the towpath (Eastbound, trimmed in green) stops pulling and steps to the side of the shared towpath.

The westbound red boat's team steps over the green boat's towline and keeps pulling. The green boat's line drops to the bottom, allowing the red boat to float over it.

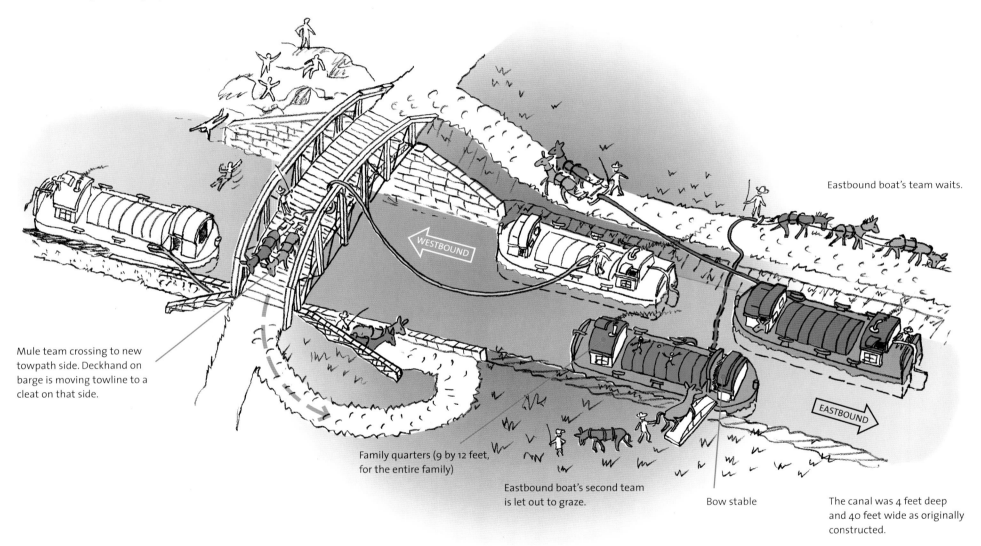

Eastbound boat's team waits.

Mule team crossing to new towpath side. Deckhand on barge is moving towline to a cleat on that side.

Family quarters (9 by 12 feet, for the entire family)

Eastbound boat's second team is let out to graze.

Bow stable

The canal was 4 feet deep and 40 feet wide as originally constructed.

Each boat had two teams of mules, two or three mules to a team. One team and its hoggee pulled for six hours while the other team rested in the bow stable on the boat. To switch teams, a ramp was dropped onto the bank. (If this boat were actually switching teams, it would be on the towpath side.) The hoggee sometimes held the tail of the mule while it boarded to establish that he was there and in control of the animal. Mules were considered stronger, smarter, and more willing to work than horses. They were also less fond of water, and thus less likely to jump in the canal on a hot day.

Three Pacific Northwest river tugs on the Upper Columbia River in 2009 deliver a turbine destined for a hydroelectric plant in Revelstoke, British Columbia. The 188-ton stainless steel turbine was manufactured in Brazil (coincidentally by Voith Hydro, sister company to the cycloidal propulsion maker), shipped up the Columbia River to Vancouver, Washington, towed up the Columbia by Foss Maritime to Pasco, Washington, then transferred 117 miles by a 148-wheeled custom trailer to Coulee City. The barge was disassembled into three 23-foot sections and hauled overland to Coulee City.

There the barge was reassembled and the turbine was returned to the Columbia for a record 368-mile, eleven-day upriver trip into Canada's Columbia Mountains, west of the Rocky Mountain Trench. At Shelter Bay it was taken off the barge and continued overland for thirty miles to the dam, where a 300-foot rock tunnel had to be widened to get the turbine to its raceway. The tug captains had scouted the river for four years to determine the route and timing. They were guided by a tug captain in a jet speedboat, and the barge was equipped with two 300 hp azimuthing thrusters (framed in blue in the front corners of the barge, with exhaust pipes sticking up) controlled by a tug captain on the barge to guide the bow and add pulling power.

The tugs were former Foss tugs *Cougar* and *Pine Cat* and the *River Chief*. The trip was made possible by BC Hydro, which released water from three dams along the route to raise river levels. At Tin Cup Rapids the only option was to release water from a dam behind the flotilla, so that a perpendicular rush of water would act as a dam itself, making a temporary pool for the barge to float over rocky rapids. And an adventure such as this would not be complete without a passage named Deadman's Eddy.

Note the axes on *Pine Cat*'s engine room roof, for cutting a hawser in an emergency.

Courtesy of BC Hydro

RIVER TOWING

Rivers flow to the sea. The one-way current presents challenges to two-way navigation. Going downstream with the flow, power is useful to keep the towboat moving faster than the current, so water is passing the rudder, and can be deflected to turn the boat. Downstream stopping power is necessary also to hold the tow back against the current while positioning to turn, or stop for locks, or wait for operable bridges to open.

Going upstream, against the flow, power is required just to stay in one place in the moving water relative to the bank, or "over the bottom." More power is required to go fast enough to make progress ahead over the bottom. The earliest shipping on the Mississippi was one way: timber barges carried cargo downriver on the current, then the barges were broken up and sold as lumber. Movement upriver was very difficult before the steam engine.

River Crossings

New Haven Railroad's *Transfer No. 10* is moving two car floats of boxcars across the East River in New York City, between railheads on opposite sides of the river where no bridge connects. By definition, river crossings are perpendicular to the river's current, requiring the best boat handlers and most responsive tugs to align with the railhead while the tug and barge are being pushed sideways downriver.

Her hull is the classic peapod shape: from a sharp stem, the sides curve continuously to the rounded stern. Ahead, out of the picture, the barges' front corners meet. The tug is held rigidly in place by the hawsers, which begin and end on the tug so the deckhands don't need to climb onto the barges. At the bow, hawsers are looped over the bow bitt, then over cleats on the barge, and back to the H-bitts, so the tug can reverse to slow the tow. Spring lines run from side bitts on the tug (just ahead of the house) back to the barges, then forward to the bitts again, transmitting the tug's forward motion. At the stern, hawsers are looped over the single bitt off-center in the stern, run around bitts on the barges, then back to the bitt, where they turn forward to the capstan which cranks them tight (concealed by the boat deck in this view).

Where the barges contact the tug bulwarks, the rails are hung with easily replaced sapling trunks to protect both hulls. *No. 10*'s triple expansion steam engine required the tall stack to build up a draft of rising hot exhaust that would suck fresh air into the front of the boiler. Since she worked close to freshwater sources along the shoreline, the white plume of steam was vented to the atmosphere instead of being condensed for reuse.

In the years before electronics, these minimalist boats had almost nothing on the pilothouse roof — just (as here) a searchlight and the two navigation lights. The long rectangular boxes on the stern deck running from the house to the stern are covering rudder cables fastened to the steering quadrant that turns the rudder and is protected by the semi-circular wooden cover across the stern. The cables are directed up to the boat deck and then forward through a tube sitting on brackets, to the giant wheel in the pilothouse, large to provide leverage to move the rudder against the pressure of passing water.

Collection of Brent Dibner

Chain Steamers

Chain boat and barges on the River Neckar before 1885. The Neckar is a winding river in southwestern Germany, which drops about 2,000 feet in 228 miles to where it joins the Rhine. It is now tamed by dams and locks for motorized barges, but before the dams and a railroad along the bank, a 96-mile chain was laid for chain steamers (*kettenschiff* in German) pulling barges upstream against the rapid flow. The chain is in tension as it comes over the bow, pulling the boat forward. At the stern the slack chain drops vertically back to the bottom. The first barge is connected on crossed hawsers for control, and eight more follow the winding course.

Early barge towing on rivers was constrained by the inability of the low-powered engines then available to overcome the current when going upstream. Between the 1830s and the end of the nineteenth century, chains were laid on the bottom along rapidly flowing rivers (mostly in Europe), and steamers pulled themselves upstream along the chain with chain winches. Since the chains were lifted at the bow, and redeposited at the stern by each steamer, their position on the bottom was not fixed.

Chain steamers were effective in moving upstream under low power because the weight of the chain sitting on the bottom acted like an anchor holding the boat in place against the current, with no power from the boat. All the available power was used to pull the steamer upstream along the chain. A paddle or propeller boat would expend force just to stay in place in the current flowing downstream, and more force to move upstream. Heading downstream, hauling the chain slowed the tug to the point that the barges, floating freely in the current, would overtake the tug. The barges either floated free downstream, or propellers on the chain steamer allowed towing downstream off the chain. Higher-powered propeller tugs and the addition of dams and locks bypassing rapids made the cumbersome chain steamer obsolete. On the already-developed European rivers, tugs and barges were replaced with self-propelled barges, which are more compact and therefore easier to move through small locks. In the United States simple-to-build railroad lines beside smaller rivers took over the freight routes, less expensive than improving the wild waterways. Tugs with barges became the US standard for shipping on larger rivers.

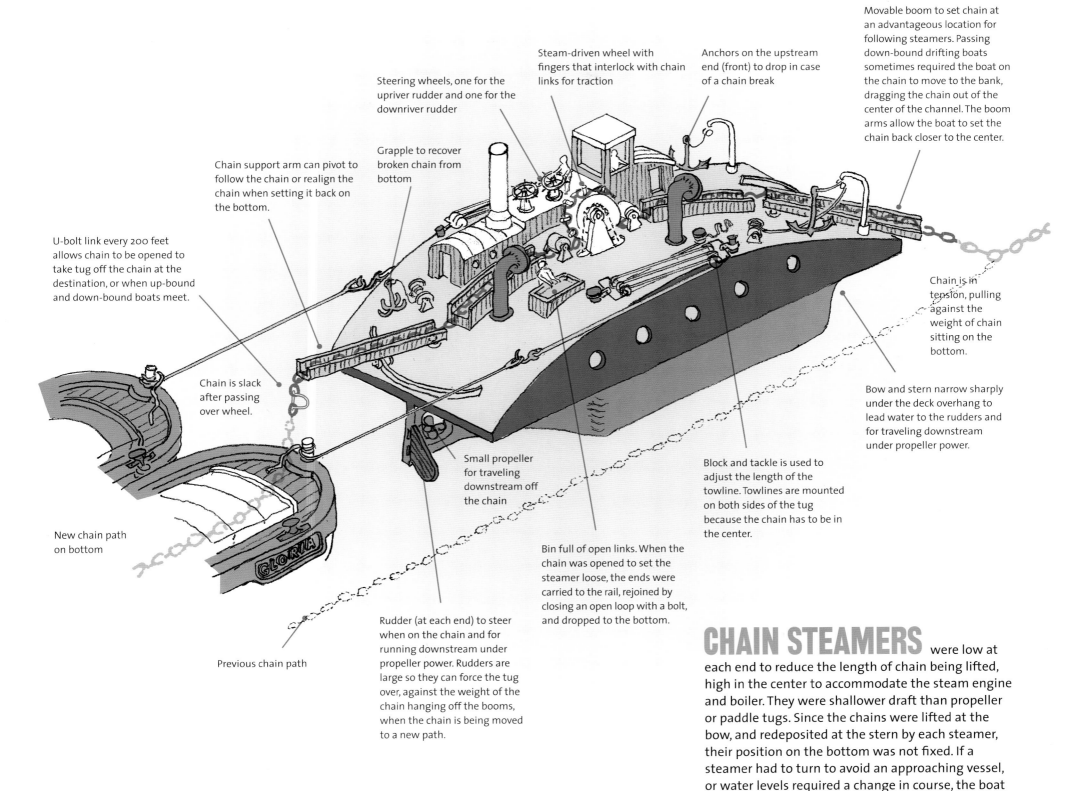

Movable boom to set chain at an advantageous location for following steamers. Passing down-bound drifting boats sometimes required the boat on the chain to move to the bank, dragging the chain out of the center of the channel. The boom arms allow the boat to set the chain back closer to the center.

Steam-driven wheel with fingers that interlock with chain links for traction

Anchors on the upstream end (front) to drop in case of a chain break

Steering wheels, one for the upriver rudder and one for the downriver rudder

Chain support arm can pivot to follow the chain or realign the chain when setting it back on the bottom.

Grapple to recover broken chain from bottom

U-bolt link every 200 feet allows chain to be opened to take tug off the chain at the destination, or when up-bound and down-bound boats meet.

Chain is in tension, pulling against the weight of chain sitting on the bottom.

Chain is slack after passing over wheel.

Bow and stern narrow sharply under the deck overhang to lead water to the rudders and for traveling downstream under propeller power.

New chain path on bottom

Small propeller for traveling downstream off the chain

Block and tackle is used to adjust the length of the towline. Towlines are mounted on both sides of the tug because the chain has to be in the center.

Bin full of open links. When the chain was opened to set the steamer loose, the ends were carried to the rail, rejoined by closing an open loop with a bolt, and dropped to the bottom.

Previous chain path

Rudder (at each end) to steer when on the chain and for running downstream under propeller power. Rudders are large so they can force the tug over, against the weight of the chain hanging off the booms, when the chain is being moved to a new path.

CHAIN STEAMERS were low at each end to reduce the length of chain being lifted, high in the center to accommodate the steam engine and boiler. They were shallower draft than propeller or paddle tugs. Since the chains were lifted at the bow, and redeposited at the stern by each steamer, their position on the bottom was not fixed. If a steamer had to turn to avoid an approaching vessel, or water levels required a change in course, the boat laid the chain in a different place. Each river only had one chain, because two chains would eventually find themselves overlaid and tangled.

Mississippi River Towboats

The characteristic that distinguishes tugs from inland-waterway towboats is how the hull is shaped to meet the water. Tugs In the Mississippi River system are called towboats, but the century-old name is misleading, since they never tow but always push their barges. They are founded on barge-shaped hulls, without raised bows or bulwarks. The low hulls are suited for flat rivers and canals, and the calm intracoastal waterways protected behind coastal barrier islands. One inland exception is the Great Lakes, whose vast water surface can build ocean-sized, wind-driven waves requiring ocean- and coastal-rated tugs, usually towing on the hawser or pushing in the notch of a dedicated barge.

Without waves to disrupt them, vast assemblages of barges can be lashed together and pushed by multiengined boats on the wide rivers of the midwestern United States. Ocean-going tugs are almost never as long as 200 feet, but river towboats of 180 to 200 feet are common, churning steadily for weeks without stopping as experienced pilots follow the twisting river. Crews are changed by local supply boats, so the towboat never stops until it reaches its turnaround point.

The enormous size of the tows requires three or four engines, spread over large shallow hulls that leave plenty of room for big galleys and staterooms. The necessity for a tall wheelhouse to see the head of the quarter-mile-long tow requires setting the pilothouse height-of-eye at 50 feet off the water, on a stack of decks. Above the deckhouse protecting the engines and steering gear, the galley and crew quarters are on the second deck, a third deck has more sleeping rooms or sometimes an owner's stateroom, topped by a communications and air-conditioning space under the pilothouse.

Push knees in the front of the towboat (with flags) transfer force to the barges, and incorporate steps to reach the barge decks when the barges are empty and riding high.

Barge-to-barge connections are tightened with hand winches welded to the barge decks. The yellow and blue lines are synthetic fiber hawsers led back to deck cleats, or fairleads, that direct the lines to winches on deck.

Alan Haig-Brown

Fighting the current, either pushing upstream against a six-mile-per-hour flow or reversing to slow down-bound tows for a bend in the river, takes horsepower and turning force. *Line haul* towboats (long-distance pushers) carry two, three, or four 4,000 hp engines, each turning a 9-foot-diameter propeller. For steering, each prop has a rudder astern plus two flanking rudders ahead of the prop. The bottom of the hull is raked up to keep everything above the 12-foot depth of channel. Towboat hulls are often the same width as a standard barge, so they face up neatly.

The vast scale of the Mississippi and the operations on it are apparent in this dramatic view. The tow is seven barges wide and varies from four to five barges long. These covered barges carry bulk products like corn, grain, or soybeans. In the distance two smaller switching tugs are holding the tow in place against other barges fleeted up along the bank. Deckhands roam over the flotilla of barges, which can cover nine acres at maximum size, tightening connections and checking for leaks.

At the end of the last Ice Age, 10,000 years ago, a deluge of water poured from the glaciers of North America, toward the Gulf of Mexico. The melt water and the rocks it carried dug a deep channel from the center of the continent to the Gulf. As the glaciers disappeared, the reduced downflow didn't fill the channel, so regular floods filled it up with silt, which became the fertile soil of the Mississippi Valley. The diminished river doesn't have the power to cut a straight channel, so it meanders across the silt in broad turns, changing its course as it finds a route with weaker soil. As it nears the Gulf, it slows and drops sediment to form deltas, each surrounding a branch of the river. Currently six branches split the river's flow. The point where the main branches used for navigation meet is called Head of Passes. The Gulf and Lower River pilots maintain a stilt village there, to exchange pilots from in- and outbound ships, which have deep water as far as Baton Rouge, Louisiana, 230 miles above Head of Passes. The Mississippi flows without dams from St. Louis to the Gulf. Mileage is measured from Head of Passes upriver 953 miles along a minimum 12-foot-deep channel to where the Ohio meets the Upper Mississippi at Cairo, Illinois. There mileage starts upriver again at zero to mile 850, the head of a 9-foot-deep navigation channel at Coon Rapids, Minnesota.

Photo Alan Haig-Brown

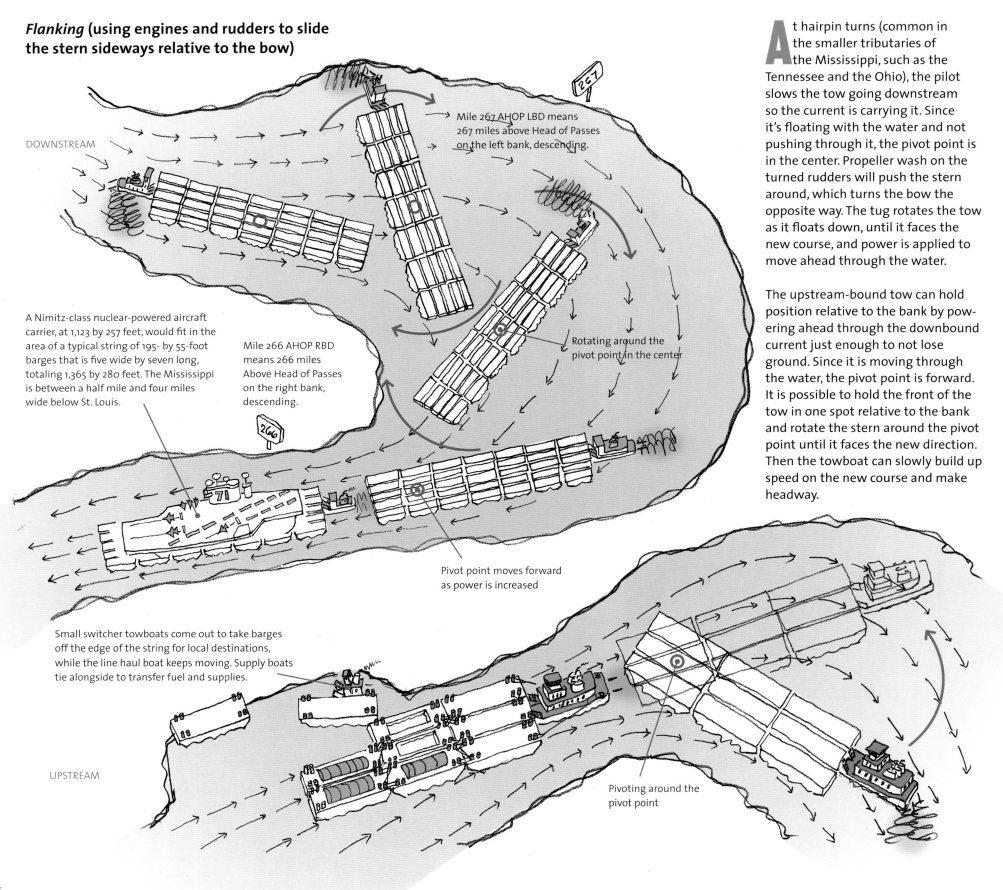

Flanking (using engines and rudders to slide the stern sideways relative to the bow)

DOWNSTREAM

Mile 267 AHOP LBD means 267 miles above Head of Passes on the left bank, descending.

A Nimitz-class nuclear-powered aircraft carrier, at 1,123 by 257 feet, would fit in the area of a typical string of 195- by 55-foot barges that is five wide by seven long, totaling 1,365 by 280 feet. The Mississippi is between a half mile and four miles wide below St. Louis.

Mile 266 AHOP RBD means 266 miles Above Head of Passes on the right bank, descending.

Rotating around the pivot point in the center

Pivot point moves forward as power is increased

Small switcher towboats come out to take barges off the edge of the string for local destinations, while the line haul boat keeps moving. Supply boats tie alongside to transfer fuel and supplies.

UPSTREAM

Pivoting around the pivot point

At hairpin turns (common in the smaller tributaries of the Mississippi, such as the Tennessee and the Ohio), the pilot slows the tow going downstream so the current is carrying it. Since it's floating with the water and not pushing through it, the pivot point is in the center. Propeller wash on the turned rudders will push the stern around, which turns the bow the opposite way. The tug rotates the tow as it floats down, until it faces the new course, and power is applied to move ahead through the water.

The upstream-bound tow can hold position relative to the bank by powering ahead through the downbound current just enough to not lose ground. Since it is moving through the water, the pivot point is forward. It is possible to hold the front of the tow in one spot relative to the bank and rotate the stern around the pivot point until it faces the new direction. Then the towboat can slowly build up speed on the new course and make headway.

Coastal and Ocean Towing

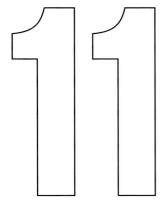

11

Erie Railroad tug *Albert J. Stone* tows three empty schooner barges (old sailing schooners with reduced masts, converted to barges) through the Cape Cod Canal, returning from delivering Pennsylvania coal to the Northeast. Another tug astern of the last barge keeps the flotilla in line in the narrow waterway. Yacht-like coastal tugs had more freeboard than harbor tugs, to limit green water coming over the side. (Green water means flowing liquid, as opposed to spray, which looks impressive but doesn't have the destabilizing weight of a wave filling the deck to the bulwarks.) The pronounced sheer of a harbor tug, sweeping from a tall bow to a low stern deck for alongside work, was not necessary to a coastal tug. Once the hawser was set, she steamed steadily for several days, if all went well. The clean lines were unencumbered by rope fendering, since these elegant tugs seldom went alongside their barges. Wood saplings hang over the rail on ropes to act as fenders. Here they sit on the rub rail so they are not banging in the waves, ready to be hung down when needed. Once in open water the barges would be spaced out a few thousand feet apart by hawsers

between the hulks. Unlike present-day barges, these still had their rudders from sailing days, so the barge crew could steer to stay in line, as well as hoist sails when the wind was advantageous.

The Erie Railroad owned the tug and barges, completing the transportation chain that started with trains shuttling from the bituminous coalfields of Pennsylvania to Baltimore, where the barges were loaded. *Albert J. Stone* is burning the company's product. If it were burning harder anthracite coal, the smoke would be cleaner.

Tugboat Photos + Research
Steven Lang Collection

GOING OUTSIDE: COASTAL TOWING ON THE HAWSER

"Going outside" means leaving the safety of working in port to tow barges along the coast. The homonyms "weather" and "whether" are central to coastal towing. Unlike towing on the open ocean, where gear is sized expecting the worst, coastal towing is often undertaken by large (and sometimes not so large) harbor or construction tugs. If sea conditions are threatening, the tows can wait in port for better weather, or head to shelter if at sea. Most large fuel-delivery fleets use ocean-rated tugs and barges because the liability for a spill is so great, but almost any tug could be sent outside, if only for short tows between nearby ports, towing deck barges loaded with construction equipment or dead vessels headed for repair.

In the tight confines of old European ports, large seagoing tugs towing barges would have been unwieldy. Instead of tugs and barges, motor coasters shuttled bulk cargo between coastal ports, often continuing far inland on a river and canal system that was well developed before the advent of railroads. Since the United States industrialized later, railroads developed simultaneously with the coastal towing business, and most connections from ocean ports to the interior were by rail, not water. Large tugs and tows connected major ports, then cargo was transferred to railcars to continue inland. The biggest coastal shipping business was Appalachian coal, brought to railheads in Norfolk and Baltimore on endless lines of coal cars and transferred to barges for shipping to the Northeast. Often the coal mines, railroads, and tugs were owned by the same conglomerate. Tugs gradually supplanted the enormous fleet of schooners that had been the bulk haulers along the East Coast, ranging as far north as Prince Edward Island and as far south as the Caribbean, carrying ice, coal, lumber, building stone, salt fish, rum, and fresh fruit. A big tug with two licensed officers and a crew of ten could tow up to five old sailing hulls with reduced sailing rig, crewed by low-paid sailors. (Hawser breaks in rough weather often sent these unfortunates to their deaths, as the tugs struggled to save themselves.)

In contrast to today's complicated string of connectors, nineteenth-century tugs had three components: a massive hawser of multiple hemp ropes twisted together, iron H-bitts, and a steam-powered capstan. On a trip delivering a dredge from New York for construction of the Panama Canal, the deck crew of the *M. E. Luckenbach* is probably lengthening the tow by feeding their hawser out of belowdeck storage through the hatch, and loosening the turns around the massive bitts by having the tug slow to take strain off. They would have a thousand feet or more of hemp hawser to slowly work over the stern as the tow was streamed out to full length. The length of towline allowed the tow to track behind the tug better and acted as a damper, evening out the jerks between tug and barge as one or the other was pitched up or slowed by a wave.

To shorten the towline, the tug slowed to slack it and crew took it off the bitts, giving it a few turns around the capstan (in the center of the picture). The vertical bars are *whelps*, which helped grip the hawser. When the saturated hawser ground slowly around the capstan, lots of seawater would be wrung out, but the hawser still had to be draped all over the decks to dry before being fed belowdeck. Deckhands would be finding footing on the pitching deck on top of the bags of coal that augmented the coal bunkers, and the snow and ice covering the deck. Manhandling the large, heavy line required deck crews of six or more. (The hawser here looks brand-new, perhaps because this was a publicity photo for Samson Cordage, which still produces hemp rope as well as modern composite lines.)

Tugboat Photos + Research
Steven Lang Collection

CABLE AND CHAIN

Hemp hawser lines were used for two centuries in towing, and similar polyester hawsers are still used by most tugs handling barges in harbors. They are flexible, so they can be secured by the friction between multiple loops tossed around towing bitts. The bends around the big steel tubes of the bitts do not overly stress the fibers. Rope and polyester hawsers are not strong enough for the power of tractor tugs, so they are equipped with towropes made of synthetic fiber braided into high-strength hawsers. These are bulky and expensive, and run off a winch instead of being wrapped on bitts. Their cost limits them to the 500 feet or less used in ship work, harbor barge work on short lines, and escorting. Hemp hawsers are occasionally still used for barge towing, but they degrade in salt water, their waterlogged weight slows the tow, and hauling them in and storing them around the deck is unwieldy. For offshore towing, where a barge may be a mile behind the tug, steel wire cable is used instead. Wire rope, or cable, was available from the middle of the nineteenth century, but there was no way to handle it or store it on deck until towing winches were developed in the late 1880s. Winches were expensive, and most tug owners stayed with labor-intensive natural-fiber hawsers into the 1950s. Then almost all towing companies adopted cable because it lasts longer, is more compact (so winches are a reasonable size), and has less drag in the water. One deckhand, or the skipper in the pilothouse, can manage the winch.

Seamen on the Heerema Marine Construction tug *Retriever* disconnect the barge pendant (on the left), leading off the stern here, from the tug's towing shackle (on the right, leading to the winch). *Retriever* and her sister tug *Husky* had been connected to the giant crane barge *Thialf* for five weeks, traveling 6,070 nautical miles (7,000 land miles) from the Gulf of Mexico to Malabo, Equatorial Guinea. The barge pendant cable is contained between two tow pins that rise hydraulically from the deck (at left, with plates on top turned to face each other after the cable is between them, to contain it). In this photo, the shark jaw (a two-pronged fork) has been raised to capture the cable socket, which is too big to pass through the gap. The strain of the cable leading off the stern is picked up by the fork. Forward of the fork, the cable to the tug's winch is slack, so the deckhand can punch out the pin of the towing shackle, disconnecting the tug from the barge. After the deckhands disconnect the barge cable and retreat, the wire stopper is lowered by the winch operator in the pilothouse, and the barge pendant slides off the deck into the sea, to be stored by the barge until the lifting job is over. The tug's gear includes the shackle having its pin poked out, then a pear-shaped link that is lashed to the shackle with rope to keep them aligned, and the loop at the end of the tow cable (at right), with a metal collar inside to protect the wires in the loop, and a heavy woven sleeve on the outside.

© *Jan Berghuis, Terschelling, The Netherlands*

Tug Towing a Barge on 3,000 Feet of 2-inch Cable

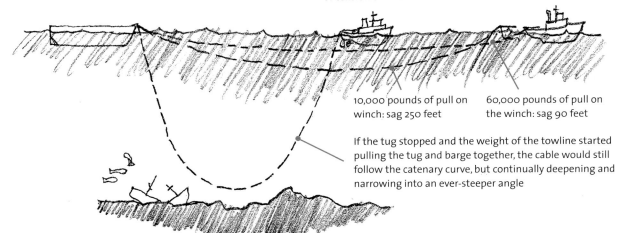

Catenary at different towing speeds, showing different amounts of tension on the winch

10,000 pounds of pull on winch: sag 250 feet

60,000 pounds of pull on the winch: sag 90 feet

If the tug stopped and the weight of the towline started pulling the tug and barge together, the cable would still follow the catenary curve, but continually deepening and narrowing into an ever-steeper angle

Architects and engineers reversed catenary curves determined by hanging chains to build efficient and beautiful masonry arches. The catenary is almost identical for any length of chain and distance between supports, but shorter chains or longer distances between anchor points use only segments of the curve, and the curve scales up or down to fit the unique measurements.

The cumulative weight of the chain pulls it down into a sharp U shape.

Most towing uses only this part of the catenary curve.

The Catenary and the Cable

In towing nomenclature, *catenary* describes the droop in the towline due to the weight of the cable, as the tug tows the barge. In mathematics, the catenary curve is the shape taken by a hanging chain or rope under the force of gravity alone. (*Catena* is Latin for chain.) "Catenary" in towing is actually a misnomer, since towing by definition puts forces other than gravity into the line. As soon as the tug starts to pull, the catenary shape is distorted.

The catenary droop in towing is beneficial, because the weight of the extra cable, together with the weight of water over the cable, acts as a shock absorber, damping the sharp jerks as swells toss the vessels apart. The underwater catenary is always changing as the relative speeds of the connected vessels change, putting more or less strain on the cable. The crew must constantly visualize its depth so the line doesn't touch bottom, especially as they enter shallow water. Tug crews can consult tables, or on-screen readouts on newer winches, to determine the depth of sag in the towline, given the length of cable out, the tension on the winch, and distance to the barge. They must haul in cable to lift it off the seabed, which also reels the barge in, whether desired or not. The cable could be damaged by dragging on the bottom, or snag on a wreck or a rock, which would stop the tug but maybe not the barge.

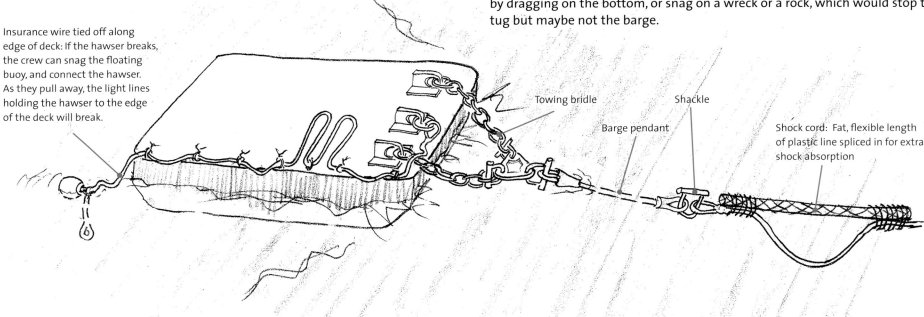

Insurance wire tied off along edge of deck: If the hawser breaks, the crew can snag the floating buoy, and connect the hawser. As they pull away, the light lines holding the hawser to the edge of the deck will break.

Towing bridle

Shackle

Barge pendant

Shock cord: Fat, flexible length of plastic line spliced in for extra shock absorption

On Western Towboat's *Ocean Navigator*, the skipper (partially visible at far right) can run the tug from the stern steering station. The tug is often at a standstill or moving very slowly when paying out or retrieving the wire. If going ahead, a crewmember on the bow or in the pilothouse radios directions to the skipper.

The winch consists of a steel drum wound with 2,800 feet of 2-inch-diameter wire cable. Winches may be turned by an electric motor, hydraulics, or a dedicated diesel engine (a "donkey engine"). The grooved horizontal bars between the spool and the H-bits support the *level winder*, projecting up with the cable feeding through. The center bar is grooved so that when it is rotated by a gear from the spool, it draws the level winder back and forth across the winch drum, evenly distributing the turns of cable as it spools in. This is essential because the enormous tension on the cable is applied to the rows below. If the cable is pulled into a loose space

between those rows, it can jam. If wires cross, the pressure there can damage the strands.

Rope hawsers are loosely draped from the H-bits, hanging over the tug's bulwarks and connected to the corners of the barge. In the narrow locks of Seattle's waterfront, the barge will be towed on these twin nylon "gate" hawsers, with the towline sitting loose on the stern deck. The end of the towing cable is a metal socket, here attached to the barge's chain bridle, in front of the kneeling crewman. Behind the other deckhand, the yellow-sided box built into the stern contains hydraulics to raise or retract the *Norman pins* rising out of the counter surrounding the stern deck (shown raised with the chain passing through), which will keep the towline leading from the center of the stern. Numerous wide-open freeing ports line the bulwark to quickly drain waves that crash onto the stern deck on the rough Seattle-to-Alaska passage.

Photo Alan Haig-Brown

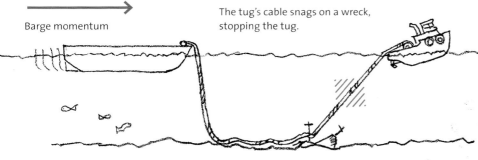

Barge momentum →

The tug's cable snags on a wreck, stopping the tug.

Tug Overrun by Barge

If the cable catches on a sea-floor obstruction it may stop the tug but not the barge, whose momentum will carry it toward and possibly over the tug, unless the tug can use its propeller and rudder to swing sideways on the cable.

¼- to 1-mile tow cable

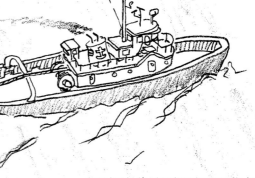

A saying in the towing community indicates the importance of managing the wire:

"You tow the cable, the cable tows the barge."

The tow cable is a wire rope. The one illustrated is 8 x 25: twenty-five wires twisted into a *strand*, eight strands twisted together to form the rope. Another popular towing cable is 6 x 37: thirty-seven wires in each of six strands. A cable may last a year in regular use, more if turned end-for-end part way through its life, so the worn end is put on the inside of the winch drum, where it gets less use.

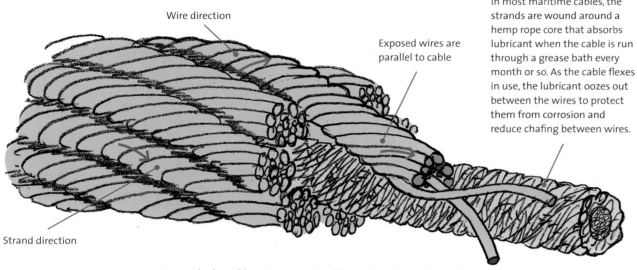

Wire direction

Exposed wires are parallel to cable

Strand direction

In most maritime cables, the strands are wound around a hemp rope core that absorbs lubricant when the cable is run through a grease bath every month or so. As the cable flexes in use, the lubricant oozes out between the wires to protect them from corrosion and reduce chafing between wires.

Section of a Strand

(1) Core wire or rope

(8) Wires in inner row. For strength and to distribute the strain, wires should be in maximum contact. Each inner wire is touching six other wires.

(8) Small filler wires in the second row keep the inner and outer rows in a compact bunch so they share the strain equally, and so each outer wire is supported by contact with three inner wires.

(8) Wires in outer row

In *regular lay* cable, wires are twisted in one direction and strands in the opposite direction. The result puts the individual wires parallel to the cable direction, so they ride more smoothly over bulwarks and other metal fittings they rub against in the rough use on tugs and barges. Shown is *regular lay right lay*: the strands turn toward the right when looking at the cable from above.

Splicing a Loop

Strands are unwound at the end and wires fanned out to tie into the open wires at the splice.

Cable strands are opened and the wires are picked apart to allow wrapping of the wire ends into the splice.

Each end wire is wrapped around one of the picked-apart wires to lock the loop.

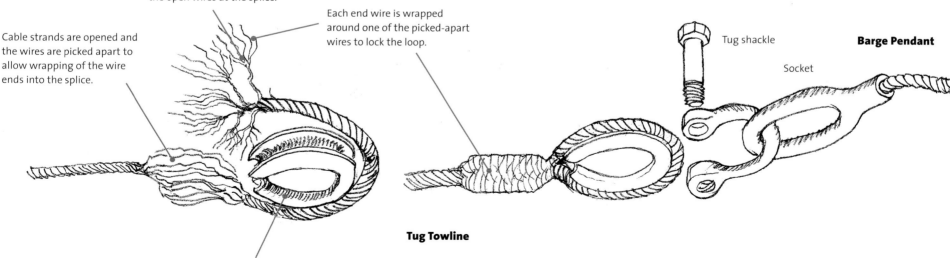

Tug shackle

Socket

Barge Pendant

Tug Towline

Here the eye incorporates a steel thimble to protect the end of the loop.

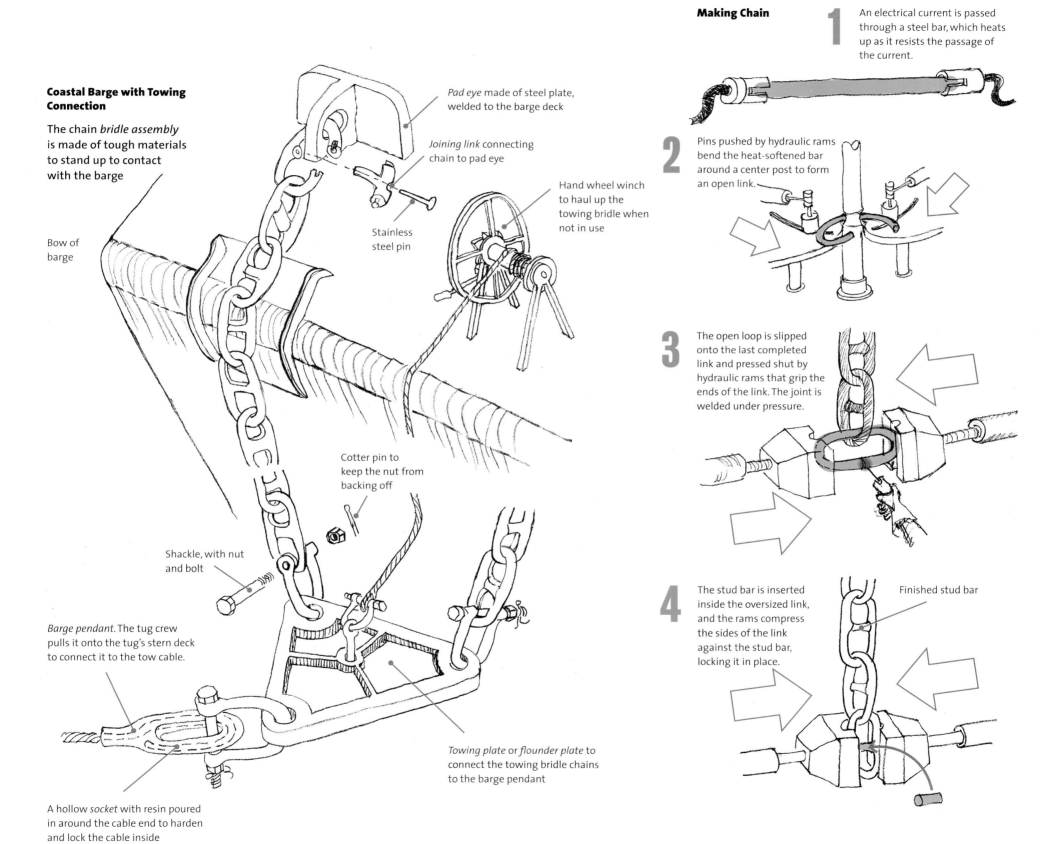

Coastal Barge with Towing Connection

The chain *bridle assembly* is made of tough materials to stand up to contact with the barge

Pad eye made of steel plate, welded to the barge deck

Joining link connecting chain to pad eye

Hand wheel winch to haul up the towing bridle when not in use

Stainless steel pin

Bow of barge

Cotter pin to keep the nut from backing off

Shackle, with nut and bolt

Barge pendant. The tug crew pulls it onto the tug's stern deck to connect it to the tow cable.

Towing plate or *flounder plate* to connect the towing bridle chains to the barge pendant

A hollow *socket* with resin poured in around the cable end to harden and lock the cable inside

Making Chain

1 An electrical current is passed through a steel bar, which heats up as it resists the passage of the current.

2 Pins pushed by hydraulic rams bend the heat-softened bar around a center post to form an open link.

3 The open loop is slipped onto the last completed link and pressed shut by hydraulic rams that grip the ends of the link. The joint is welded under pressure.

4 The stud bar is inserted inside the oversized link, and the rams compress the sides of the link against the stud bar, locking it in place.

Finished stud bar

OCEAN TOWING

Smitwijs Singapore, operated by a joint venture of two famous Dutch towing companies, Smit Tak and Wijsmuller (later joined by South African and Chinese ocean towing companies to form Global Towing Alliance), enters Rotterdam New Waterway after towing the pontoon barge *Sainty 1* from Shanghai piled with twenty inland-waterway vessel hulls to be fitted out in Holland. The towering load sheered from side to side behind the tug for the 110-day tow, requiring stops for adjustments to the over-stressed tow gear in Singapore and Cape Town, South Africa.

Smitwijs Singapore's hull shape is dramatic evidence that she may be a ship at the bow, but astern she still must respect the essential nature of a tug: getting the towline down as close as possible to the propellers' line of force.

If the towline is high, energy is wasted as the load tries to tip the vessel backwards, and stability is threatened if the tow load pulls to the side. The tall bow cuts waves taken ahead, but waves astern are free to wash over the only place the crew really needs to go outside: the stern working deck. The last step-down of the hull includes an inward curve designed to catch the towline before it can hit the superstructure if the towline is pulled around by a wildly shearing tow. The tug-ship has no rubber fendering because she doesn't work alongside: support tugs at the beginning and end of the voyage guide the load and ferry lines between tug and tow. The foremast shows a vertical row of three lights, indicating a tug with a tow.

Courtesy Smitwijs

The Atlantic, Pacific, and Indian oceans; Cape Horn and the Cape of Good Hope; the Strait of Malacca; the Panama and Suez canals: ocean tugs wander for years among these great waterways, crews flown in and out every few months from the nearest port. Most of the big ocean tugs are collected into a few towing syndicates that assign them worldwide, since the few jobs for these specialized vessels won't support competing companies. A true ocean tug is capable in any weather or sea, with fuel, water, and provisions to stay at sea for months. In ocean storms and wind-driven swells that build over thousands of miles into endless rows of 70-foot monsters, size does matter. Power also, to keep the tug moving in front of an enormous tow such as an obsolete supertanker headed to the ship-breakers of

India or Turkey. An ocean tug may be three times as long as a harbor tug, ten times as heavy, with ten times the horsepower. Free-running speed matters, too, over the vast oceanic distances tugs must travel between assignments, or when racing to find and rescue a vessel adrift or ashore. The legendary Crowley Invader-class tugs are at the small end: 125 feet long, 7,200 hp. The biggest are a pair of 300-foot Russian monsters built during the Soviet era to show the world the self-sufficiency of their maritime fleet.

Ocean tugs carry a master, first and second officers, mates, deckhands, engineers, and a cook, totaling between ten and fifteen crew, plus accommodations for an additional ten, either a salvage crew or other specialists.

A small crew may be put aboard the towed vessel to monitor conditions or adjust the tow connection, an unenviable assignment, since dead vessels wallowing at the end of a towline are not as steady or comfortable as a vessel under power, and usually lack of power means no heat or electricity.

Demand for true ocean tugs has been cut by the availability of big oil-rig anchor-handling tugs, just as powerful, and sometimes free to take towing assignments during slow times in the oil patches of the world. Some of the handsomest tugs in the world are being lost to obsolescence: sleek ocean-rated ships, with towering cutter bows, massive twin stacks, and as big as freighters.

Ocean Tug

The pilothouse is centered in the tug-ship, with equal controls and view ahead to the course and astern to monitor the tow. Vessels under tow, especially heavily laden ones, don't readily follow the tug, but want to pick their own direction. Long narrow ship hulls are hard to haul back on line after they sheer off course, unlike relatively shallow barges with bluff or rounded bows, which can be pivoted in the water. In the open ocean, aided by radar to see ahead, most minute-to-minute attention goes astern, watching how the tow is tracking behind the boat, and the condition of the towline. TV cameras monitor the winches and drums belowdecks. A clear view of the stern working deck is essential, and winch controls are often at the pilothouse stern steering station.

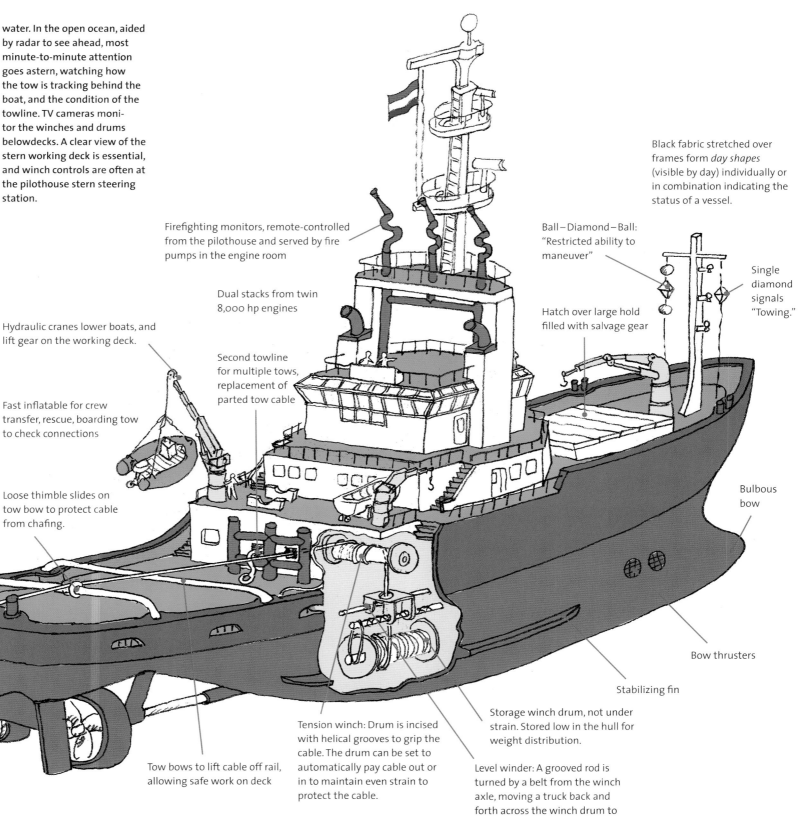

Firefighting monitors, remote-controlled from the pilothouse and served by fire pumps in the engine room

Black fabric stretched over frames form *day shapes* (visible by day) individually or in combination indicating the status of a vessel.

Ball–Diamond–Ball: "Restricted ability to maneuver"

Single diamond signals "Towing."

Dual stacks from twin 8,000 hp engines

Hatch over large hold filled with salvage gear

Hydraulic cranes lower boats, and lift gear on the working deck.

Second towline for multiple tows, replacement of parted tow cable

Fast inflatable for crew transfer, rescue, boarding tow to check connections

Retractable Norman pins (tow pins set in the counter) that keep cable leading off stern when raised

Loose thimble slides on tow bow to protect cable from chafing.

Bulbous bow

Bow thrusters

Stabilizing fin

Tow bows to lift cable off rail, allowing safe work on deck

Tension winch: Drum is incised with helical grooves to grip the cable. The drum can be set to automatically pay cable out or in to maintain even strain to protect the cable.

Storage winch drum, not under strain. Stored low in the hull for weight distribution.

Level winder: A grooved rod is turned by a belt from the winch axle, moving a truck back and forth across the winch drum to distribute the cable evenly.

SEA CONDITIONS: PITCHING AND ROLLING

The depths of the sea are unfathomable and invisible, and better left unimagined by those bobbing in vessels on the surface. Even the largest supertankers are slivers suspended by buoyancy above an average of two and a half miles of water. But the top 50- to 100-foot layer is constantly roiled by waves tossed up by wind, and by wind-driven currents circling the ocean basins.

Ships are designed with waterproof hulls and sufficient freeboard to keep most waves off the deck. The hull is topped by a lighter construction that keeps out rain and occasional high seas. Submarines, on the other hand, are fully enclosed in a watertight hull, and tugs are built more like submarines than like surface ships. A tug's low stern working deck exposes it to the wash of waves. The drag from thousands of pounds of cable drooping in a catenary astern presses down on the counter, which prevents the stern from rising above waves overtaking the slow-moving tug from astern. Heavy deck and bulkhead hatches are dogged watertight by levered handles, and all surfaces are reinforced against crashing walls of water. The pilothouse is higher and needs less protection, but still has waterproof hatches for doors, and reinforced windows.

Tug crews have no escape from the continually rolling and tossing world when at sea. Even experienced sailors after years of healthy sailing may develop bouts of seasickness that can affect them for many trips before disappearing as mysteriously as they arrived.

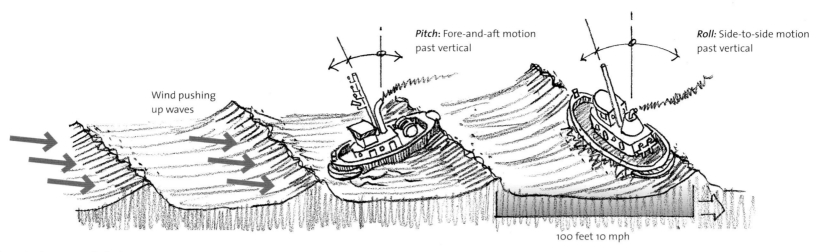

Pitch: Fore-and-aft motion past vertical

Roll: Side-to-side motion past vertical

Wind pushing up waves

100 feet 10 mph

Young wind waves push up ripples, some of which grow to sweep up others and become waves at regular spacing. Cold air drops as it blows, pushing up bigger waves than warm wind.

Barges move differently than tugs because their length spans several waves, whereas a tug is tossed on each wave. If tug and barge were connected directly instead of through the heavy towline, they would bang together violently. The heavy cable acts as a shock absorber, taking up the difference in motion. A taut cable is liable to break.

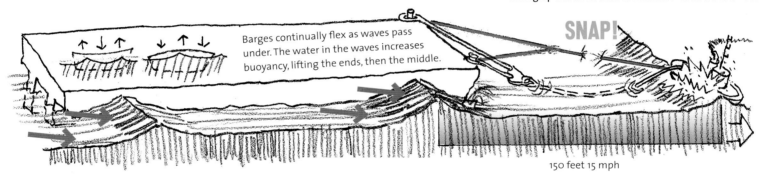

Barges continually flex as waves pass under. The water in the waves increases buoyancy, lifting the ends, then the middle.

SNAP!

150 feet 15 mph

Older waves still being pushed by wind spread out and gain speed. They are not as steep or uncomfortable as young waves.

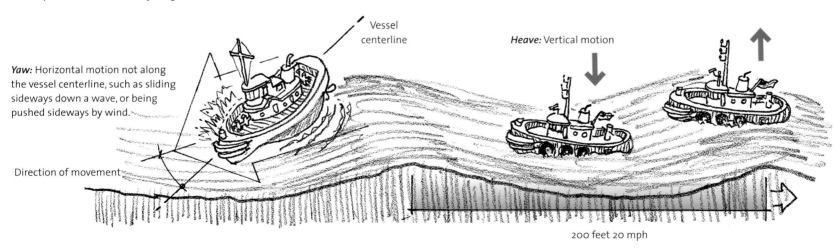

Vessel centerline

Heave: Vertical motion

Yaw: Horizontal motion not along the vessel centerline, such as sliding sideways down a wave, or being pushed sideways by wind.

Direction of movement

200 feet 20 mph

Swell: Waves that have continued after the wind dies down become wide rolling ridges of water that may lift a small vessel without pitching or rolling.

Pacific Reliance was built for Crowley Maritime, to be mated with a 650,000-barrel petroleum barge. Here she is fresh from the builders, entering the barge notch for the first time. The helmet (outlined in white) that will engage into the toothed ladder on the barge is retracted, in the hull below the crewman at the rail. (The toothed ladder on the barge is not visible in this photo.) Near the center of the barge notch, step holds (marked by a vertical white stripe) are set into the barge hull, for access to the barge deck.

These dedicated pusher tugs have only one pilothouse, mounted high over the barge for visibility in all states of loading.

Brian Gauvin

The traditional method of ocean towing — a barge at the end of a long cable — sounds simple but is complicated in practice, with numerous points of failure and a low degree of safety. Steering is the art of pointing the tug and hoping the barge, thousands of feet behind, eventually gets the message. There is no stopping except by letting the barge slowly lose momentum, and if the tug stops or is stopped ahead, the barge may overrun her. As barges and tugs get bigger, matching winches and cables for towing astern would be enormous and unwieldy.

Many ideas for replacing cable with a direct connection were imagined or tried, but successful solutions had to await the miniaturization of systems and computer controls that permit simple, reliable, robust connection assemblies. Early designs had shelves projecting from the back of the barge that the tug unit slid onto, then complicated brackets tied the tug to the barge. The resulting strangely shaped tug was hardly seaworthy by itself, and the only real benefit was that the vessel met Coast Guard manning requirements for tugs, which were about a third of comparable ship-manning crews.

Successful articulated tug-barge (ATB) designs connect the tug directly astern of the barge through hydraulic pins that extend sideways from the tug into recesses in the barge notch. With the two units joined, the tug's oversized props and rudders directly control the barge's direction and speed, and reversing the engines provides reliable stopping power. In waves, the tug and barge move together in heave, roll, and yaw. In pitch the tug can rotate on the pin to keep the propeller underwater.

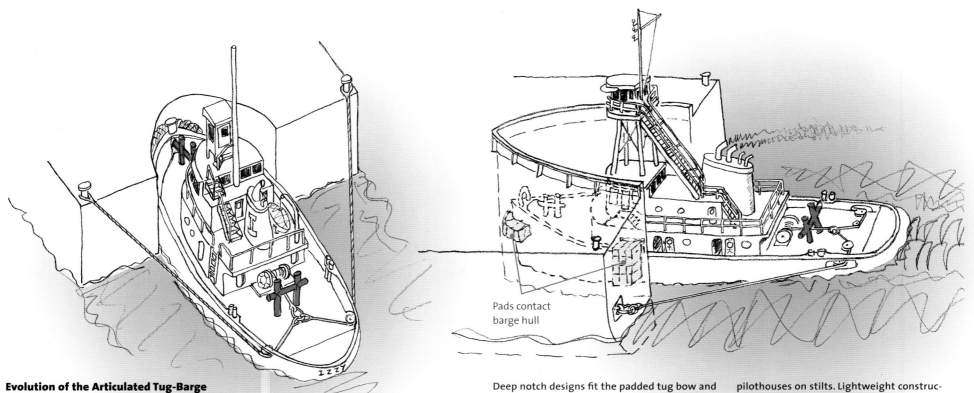

Evolution of the Articulated Tug-Barge

A shallow notch in the barge stern kept the tug in place, pushing with bow pads until seas of 6 to 8 feet caused the tug to grind in the notch. When the tug had to switch from pushing to towing, a rope hawser was run from the H-bitts to the bow of the barge. These connections were not suitable for long ocean voyages, and the difficulty of going on the hawser as seas were rising meant that if there was any doubt about the weather, the tug would start the voyage on the hawser.

Small pilothouses with minimal electronic steering and throttle controls were added to raise the height of eye over the barge. Before electronics, a second steering station was too expensive for most tugs.

In the *Artubar* system, hydraulic rams project pins into sockets in the barge hull. When the barge is full and riding low in the water, the tug connects to the upper sockets. When the barge is light and riding high, the tug uses the lower sockets. To precisely hit the sockets, the tug must be ballasted up or down by pumping water into tanks in its hull. Bulk dry products such as cement and grain are usually delivered as full loads, a good match for this system. The pins are shown projecting in this view. In reality, they would be retracted into recesses in the hull until the tug is inside the notch and the pins align with the holes. Then they would be extended to connect tug and barge.

Pads contact barge hull

Deep notch designs fit the padded tug bow and bulwarks exactly into a long notch. Some tugs have pads extended hydraulically from the sides to keep the tug and barge traveling together. Empty barges ride so high that push tugs added pilothouses on stilts. Lightweight construction of these add-ons was required to reduce top-hamper — weight mounted high in the vessel that acts as a pendulum, increasing pitch and roll (and skipper discomfort, since the upper pilothouse moves through a wider arc than the tug).

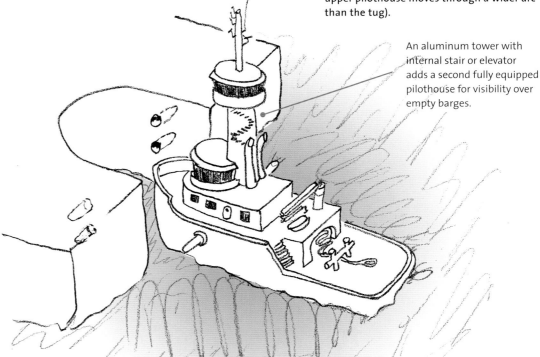

An aluminum tower with internal stair or elevator adds a second fully equipped pilothouse for visibility over empty barges.

Intercon Linkage

Port and starboard prefabricated modules contain rams that project out when the tug settles in the notch, forcing serrated helmets into the prefab ladder sections at any draft of the barge. A ball-and-socket joint allows the helmet to rotate on the end of the ram while engaged in the ladder, so the tug can pitch independent of the barge. The relatively simple machinery allows easy disconnection, important because the tug has to pull out while the barge discharges or loads, then reconnect at the new draft. The tugs are expensive investments, usually designed for their barge, or swapped among identical barges. ATB tugs carry hawsers, loosely connected to their barges, in case they have to leave the notch in extreme seas or emergencies. In reality, a connected ATB can stay out in a sea state that would drive a wire boat (tug towing on a cable) to seek shelter to protect its towing gear.

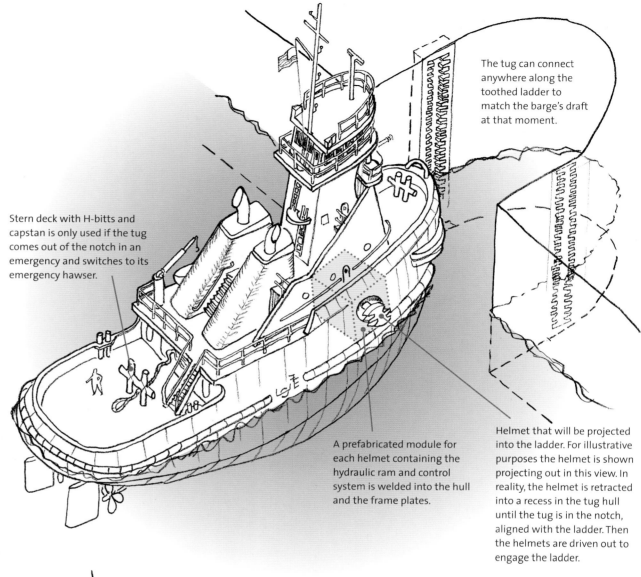

The tug can connect anywhere along the toothed ladder to match the barge's draft at that moment.

Stern deck with H-bitts and capstan is only used if the tug comes out of the notch in an emergency and switches to its emergency hawser.

A prefabricated module for each helmet containing the hydraulic ram and control system is welded into the hull and the frame plates.

Helmet that will be projected into the ladder. For illustrative purposes the helmet is shown projecting out in this view. In reality, the helmet is retracted into a recess in the tug hull until the tug is in the notch, aligned with the ladder. Then the helmets are driven out to engage the ladder.

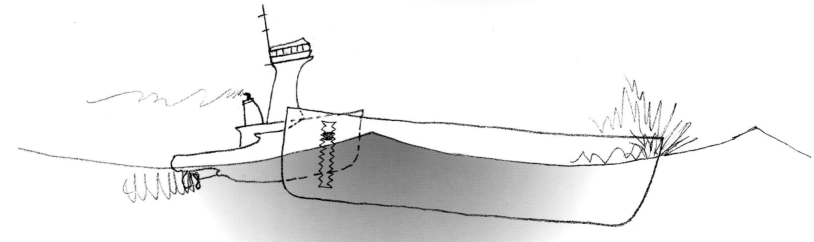

The tug rotates on the pin so the weight of the tug's engines, drive train, and rudder can force the stern down, keeping the props under water for maximum thrust. If the tug and barge were locked together in pitch, the long barge would lift the tug's stern out of the water as it pitched forward.

Ebb Tide was the first purpose-built oil field supply vessel, and the prototype for AHTS vessels. After Gulf of Mexico entrepreneur Alden "Doc" Laborde designed and built *Mr. Charlie*, the first semi-submersible drilling rig (see page 132), he realized that his invention called for another invention, the oil rig supply boat. He and nine partners cut down a fishing boat hull behind the bow to form a low stern deck lined by steel guardrails. An old bootheel tugboat wheelhouse was dropped on the bow for good visibility all around. Engines below the working deck exhausted through low stacks halfway to the stern. Minimal crew quarters were behind the portholes below the wheelhouse. The long deck with no obstructions at the stern was a good platform for towing as well as delivering supplies. Gooseneck vent pipes, protected by being placed outside the rails, vent the fuel delivery tanks under the supply deck. Tug-type half-pipe rub rails run along the sides of the hull for protection when alongside a rig leg. Anchor handlers and supply boats look very similar to each other, and some are used both ways.

Courtesy of Tidewater Inc.

Anchor-Handling Tug/Supply Vessels for Offshore Oil Exploration

A temporary semi-submersible ocean oil exploration rig spends several months drilling a test hole at a promising site identified by oil geologists. The drill string (a series of pipe sections screwed together with the drill bit at the bottom) has to be lowered through thousands of feet of water just to reach the sea floor, then bore through several miles of rock. If an exploration well finds a working hole, the exploratory rig caps it and is towed off. A permanent production platform is then constructed on the seabed, and accommodations, engine rooms, and derrick are barged to the site and piled on the platform, which drills a series of wells angled over a wide area.

The semi-submersible rigs used for oil exploration are platforms built on pylons over floating pontoons that can be filled with water. For drilling, the pontoons are ballasted down to float a hundred feet below the surface, where waves won't affect them, and held in location by eight to sixteen anchors radiating from the rig. Enormous specialized anchor-handling tug/supply (AHTS) vessels and crews set and raise the anchors, and tow the rigs between explorations. While the rig is drilling, they use the long stern anchor-handling deck to deliver equipment and supplies, well casing, and drill pipe, and carry underdeck tanks for fuel, cement, drilling mud, and water that are pumped up to the rig's tanks. AHTS vessels incorporate advanced position-holding systems such as tunnel thrusters and auxiliary rudder propellers, and GPS to hold steady over an anchor location or alongside a rig when transferring supplies. These are the largest tugs built today: 200 to 300 feet long; 8,000 to 25,000 hp.

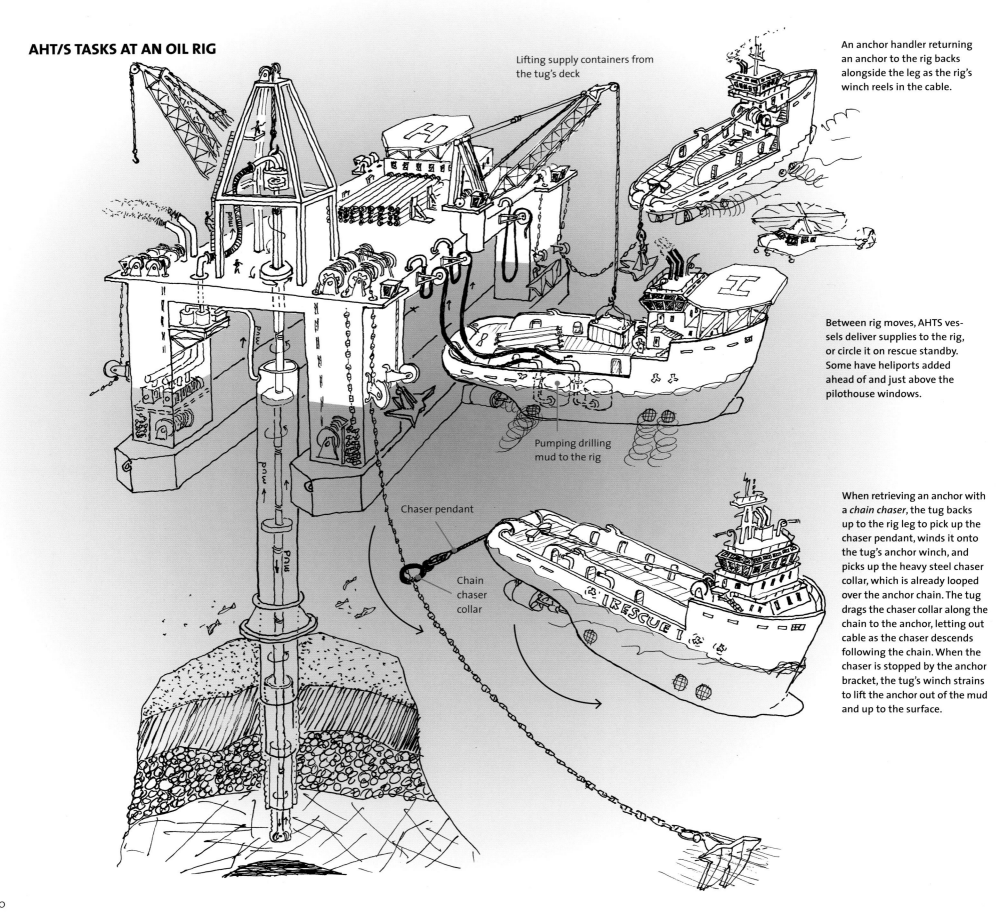

AHT/S TASKS AT AN OIL RIG

Lifting supply containers from the tug's deck

An anchor handler returning an anchor to the rig backs alongside the leg as the rig's winch reels in the cable.

Pumping drilling mud to the rig

Between rig moves, AHTS vessels deliver supplies to the rig, or circle it on rescue standby. Some have heliports added ahead of and just above the pilothouse windows.

Chaser pendant

Chain chaser collar

When retrieving an anchor with a *chain chaser*, the tug backs up to the rig leg to pick up the chaser pendant, winds it onto the tug's anchor winch, and picks up the heavy steel chaser collar, which is already looped over the anchor chain. The tug drags the chaser collar along the chain to the anchor, letting out cable as the chaser descends following the chain. When the chaser is stopped by the anchor bracket, the tug's winch strains to lift the anchor out of the mud and up to the surface.

AHTS *Normand Prosper*, in the distance, is backing toward the oil exploration rig *Borland Dolphin* to connect the tug's tow cable to one of the floating rig's towing pendants. Rigs this large may be towed by two tugs on separate towlines connected to separate corners. The advantage is redundancy, and less strain on the gear. Towing with a single tug means there is no safety factor if the tug malfunctions (but on the other hand no worry about keeping a safe distance from the other tug alongside). *Normand Prosper* has a heliport built over the bow, above the pilothouse windows. The silver-colored roll-up door in the

side of the superstructure is for launching the submersible remotely operated vehicle (ROV) to work at the sea floor and inspect the rig underwater. Cranes are mounted on rails over the crash rails along the sides of the working deck, one of which is also visible on the anchor handler *KL Sandefjord* in the foreground, with some of the deck crew gathered under the hook, in a photo taken by Norwegian Chief Officer Christian Romberg. Norway's long coast faces the North Sea oil fields, and many oil exploration support companies are home-based in the fjords. When the rig is at the drill site, the tug will pick up one

of eight anchors stored aboard the rig and pull it one to two miles from the rig as the rig lets out anchor chain. At the required distance, the tug feeds a cable through one of the yellow buoys on deck, attaches the loose end to the anchor, and uses the cable to lower the anchor to the sea floor. The buoy stays on the surface, holding the top of the cable so the tug can find it and use it to lift the anchor when the drilling is finished.

The *KL Sandefjord* has both sets of towing pins raised, one containing a cable running to the rig, the other a chain running to the anchor. When

lifting an anchor on board, the pins are retracted into the deck, out of the way. Anchor handlers are always open across the stern, exposing the deck crew to green water breaking over the stern and washing the deck (and them) with a foot or more of icy salt water. These sister anchor handlers are about 310 feet long and 78 feet wide. Berths for seventy house the crew of eighteen plus occasionally technicians operating oil exploration equipment or submersibles temporarily installed on the vast deck.

Christian Romberg

ORIGIN OF THE SEMI-SUBMERSIBLE EXPLORATORY DRILLING RIG

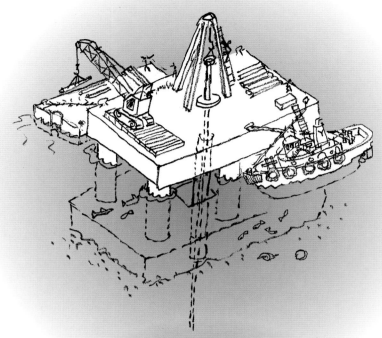

1 Double barges were built for drilling in shallow water. The lower barge was ballasted down to the sea floor, leaving the upper barge and drill deck above the surface.

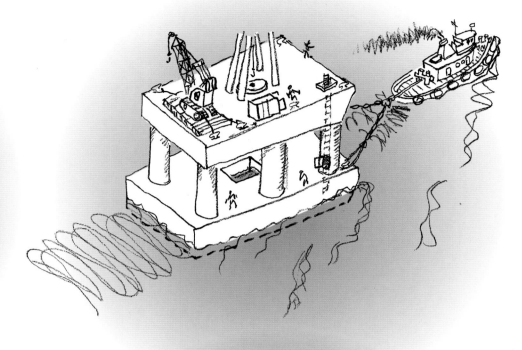

2 When exploratory drilling was complete, the lower barge was pumped out, and the rig was towed to a new assignment.

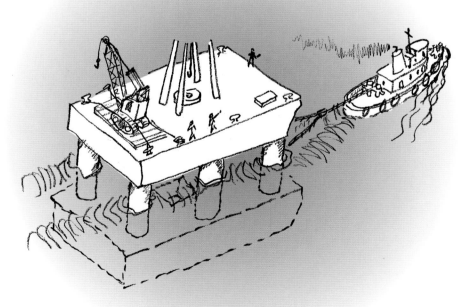

3 To save time, the lower barge was sometimes partly pumped out just enough to clear the seabed when it was towed. Crews noted how steady the barge rode, even under tow. They started anchoring and drilling from the partly submerged barge.

4 Next, enormous semi-submersible drill rigs were designed to float on ballasted pontoons held in position by numerous anchors set by specialized anchor-handling tugs.

Heerema crane barge *Hermod* lowering Mumbai High North N 20 Jacket by night. Operations continue day and night: unending rounds of six-hour shifts for a month, followed by a month off. In the foreground is Heerema tug *Retriever* photographed from sister tug *Husky*. They have towed the enormous crane barge to the Indian Ocean, and now are setting and moving anchors as the barge assembles a fixed platform on the coastal shelf. That Dutch AHTS officer Jan Berghuis recognized the drama of this scene shows tug crews are conscious of their world of technological marvels and the majestic fury of nature, all set to a metronome of transcendent sunrises and sunsets. For this they trade lost days with family, and endure floors that never stop moving. To be at a scene like this is to participate in a true spectacle.

This platform replaced the original Mumbai High North platform, destroyed by fire in 2005 when a diving support vessel came alongside in a storm that had grounded helicopters, to transfer to the rig a cook with cut fingers. The rig crane on the leeward side (protected from the wind by the rig) was out of service, so the vessel approached with the wind forcing it toward the platform. The vessel's azimuthing thrusters malfunctioned, so it backed toward the rig on manual control in the stormy waters. After the rig crane had lifted the injured crewman, the vessel was slammed into the side of the rig, breaking one of the riser pipes that collect petroleum product from adjacent wells. The subsequent fire destroyed the seven-story platform in two hours, and set the dive support vessel on fire. Twenty-two people died on the rig, including the cook, who never got out of the basket. As usual, a catastrophe consists of a string of mishaps. Subtract any one, and it would not have happened: no cut fingers, or no storm, or no leeward crane out of service, or no thruster malfunction.

© Jan Berghuis, Terschelling, The Netherlands

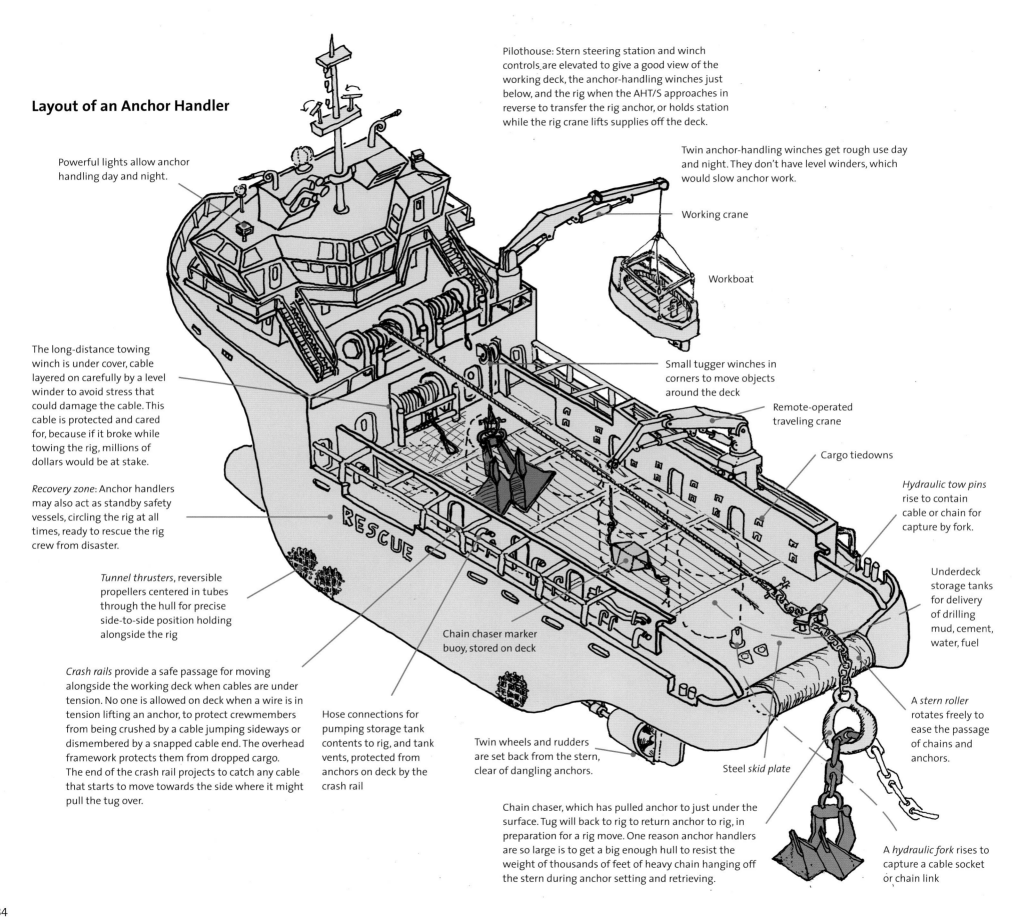

Layout of an Anchor Handler

Pilothouse: Stern steering station and winch controls are elevated to give a good view of the working deck, the anchor-handling winches just below, and the rig when the AHT/S approaches in reverse to transfer the rig anchor, or holds station while the rig crane lifts supplies off the deck.

Powerful lights allow anchor handling day and night.

Twin anchor-handling winches get rough use day and night. They don't have level winders, which would slow anchor work.

Working crane

Workboat

The long-distance towing winch is under cover, cable layered on carefully by a level winder to avoid stress that could damage the cable. This cable is protected and cared for, because if it broke while towing the rig, millions of dollars would be at stake.

Small tugger winches in corners to move objects around the deck

Remote-operated traveling crane

Cargo tiedowns

Recovery zone: Anchor handlers may also act as standby safety vessels, circling the rig at all times, ready to rescue the rig crew from disaster.

Hydraulic tow pins rise to contain cable or chain for capture by fork.

RESCUE

Tunnel thrusters, reversible propellers centered in tubes through the hull for precise side-to-side position holding alongside the rig

Underdeck storage tanks for delivery of drilling mud, cement, water, fuel

Chain chaser marker buoy, stored on deck

A *stern roller* rotates freely to ease the passage of chains and anchors.

Crash rails provide a safe passage for moving alongside the working deck when cables are under tension. No one is allowed on deck when a wire is in tension lifting an anchor, to protect crewmembers from being crushed by a cable jumping sideways or dismembered by a snapped cable end. The overhead framework protects them from dropped cargo. The end of the crash rail projects to catch any cable that starts to move towards the side where it might pull the tug over.

Hose connections for pumping storage tank contents to rig, and tank vents, protected from anchors on deck by the crash rail

Twin wheels and rudders are set back from the stern, clear of dangling anchors.

Steel *skid plate*

Chain chaser, which has pulled anchor to just under the surface. Tug will back to rig to return anchor to rig, in preparation for a rig move. One reason anchor handlers are so large is to get a big enough hull to resist the weight of thousands of feet of heavy chain hanging off the stern during anchor setting and retrieving.

A *hydraulic fork* rises to capture a cable socket or chain link

ANCHOR-HANDLING DECKS AND WINCHES

This photo is taken from Level 3, the main deck of *KL Sandefjord*, using her cranes to sort out chains from anchor handling. (Levels 1 and 2 inside the hull give access to the tops of the mud and liquid delivery tanks.) In the center are two vertical reels that lead to two *chain lifters*—vertical wheels that have grooves that fit chain links (like winches for chain). The chain lifters and main cable winches themselves are inside the superstructure. Above the reels are small angled chain lifters to feed chain to underdeck storage lockers. A "J" hook for fishing up cables is lying in the center of the deck with chain connected to a cable running over a (rust-colored) roller and to a winch inside the superstructure, on Level 4. Above on Level 5, two side-by-side rollers lead

to two more winches. One winch is loaded with chain fed over the roller and under the level winder that distributes the chain evenly across the reel. The other winch on Level 5 holds only the working cable feeding over its roller, connected to chain in the foreground. Levels 6 and 7 are support spaces. Officers operate the winches from behind the dark canted windows on Level 8, the Bridge Deck, from which they can see the whole stern deck, and the sea astern. Above that is the Sky Lobby, an open steering station. The main engine and auxiliary engine exhausts spill out above that, flanked by ventilation intake louvers ducted to the engine rooms, then a stack of platforms for radars and communications equipment.

The cranes run on top of the crash rails, which are lined with openings to passages along the rail that let the crew move fore and aft when cables and chains on the main deck are under tension. Each crane boom has two arms. The one folded back here ends in two yellow articulating hands: the one on the left grips chain links or cables between two plates like a duck's bill. The one on the right forms a tube around a cable to grip it, or to hold it loosely when the strain is taken off, while the cable that has been stretched under load untwists itself. If not contained, it would whip wildly around the deck. The other arm is a conventional crane boom shown lifting a connector plate and chains. The yellow box against the starboard rail is a buoy that will hold

the pendant cable to an anchor on the seabed. The articulating arms are also used to set a lasso around the floating buoy, which is led to the work winch to haul the buoy out of the water, pull it on deck, and connect the tug's working cable to the buoy's anchor pendant to jerk the anchor out of the mud and lift it to the surface.

Christian Romberg

135

ANCHORS AND CHAINS

Above: This oil rig anchor has been pulled onto the anchor handler's deck by the chain chaser (looped around the anchor chain where it connects to the anchor). The hydraulic fork at the stern was raised from below the deck to capture the chain, after it was centered over the fork by the tow pins farther aft. The weight of the chain leading back to the rig has been picked up by the fork, so it is safe to work around the anchor. The anchor has been recovered neatly, upside down so it can be dragged around the deck by tugger winches, and with the chain centered between the tines (projecting points). The deckhands are connecting a crane cable to lift the chain pendant belonging to the chaser, to clear the way for finding and opening the removable link in the anchor chain so the chaser can be removed and returned to the rig along with the anchor chain, while the anchor stays on the tug until the rig is redeployed in a new location. The chain to another anchor is coming out of the water in the distance on the right, rising to the rig.

Right: Both sets of pins are up, the starboard set (on the left in this photo, which faces the stern) having contained the chain over the fork, which was then raised to engage with a link and pick up the weight of the chain between the tug and rig. The port-side pins are fully lifted, and brackets extended to contain the cable. The hole forward of these pins is the retracted port fork. Chain and cable lead off the stern over the roller. The rusty steel casting on the anchor chain is a chain stopper, which will stop the chain chaser at a selected point to bring up a connecting link that can be opened. The crewman in red pants is holding the crane remote, as they look for the removable link, which will be opened with his colleague's heavy hammer.

Photos Christian Romberg

BOURBON ORCA, winner of the 2005 Norwegian Engineering Feat of the Year, was built by naval architects/ship builders Ulstein Design. Hull, deck, and engine room innovations increase crew safety and comfort, and reduce energy use.

The flat vertical planes of a conventional bow smash into waves, jolting the vessel and crew every minute for days, and throwing heavy gouts of water against the pilothouse windows. With every wave impact, the bow also lifts as the passing wave increases buoyancy.

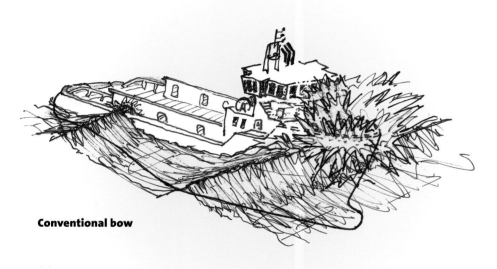

Inward-sloping bow

Remotely operating cranes lasso the yellow anchor buoy, lift it on deck to disconnect buoy, capture anchor pendant (*sequence continues bottom left*).

1

Waves flowing over *Bourbon Orca*'s inward-sloping bow press it down, reducing the lift from buoyancy as large waves pass around the bow. The reduced pitching and slamming makes work on the stern less dangerous, and living conditions more comfortable. Accommodations are pushed forward into the expanded hull at the bow, leaving more of the tug's length for the working deck.

Diesel-electric drive allows the six engine-generators and large batteries to be forward under the house, connected by power cables to the propulsion pods: two astern, and one drop-down unit in the bow. Elimination of propeller shafts between engines and props leaves more space for under-deck supply tanks. While *Bourbon Orca* is idling, waiting for connections to be made up, several engines can be shut down to reduce energy use.

Conventional bow

Robot arms on the two traveling cranes spread a lasso to catch an anchor buoy and pull it on deck, where automated deck equipment rises to clamp the anchor pendant attached under the buoy (as shown in drawing above right). Crewmen only go on deck to unshackle the buoy, and attach the tug's pendant, which is held at the ready by one of the cranes.

2

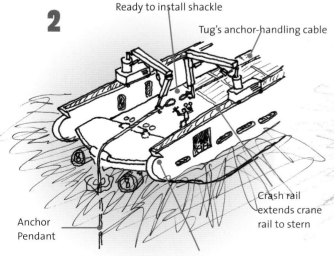

Ready to install shackle

Tug's anchor-handling cable

Anchor Pendant

Crash rail extends crane rail to stern

Notch catches errant cables

3

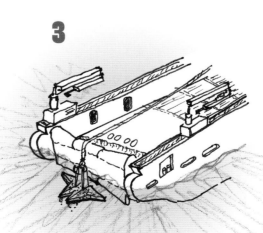

Small stern rollers are built into a platform that tilts and slides down to receive the anchor

4

Platform rotates back to bring the anchor up to deck level.

Rescue and Salvage

13

Ocean towing and salvage tug *Tempest* is shown assisting the bulk freighter *Western*, whose engine failed in the North Sea. *Western* was drifting amidst several offshore oil platforms in heavy seas. The rigs were evacuated by helicopter in case the ship drifted into one. *Tempest* fought through 20-foot waves to the ship, connected just before dark, and towed the ship away from the platforms and into Ijmuiden, where harbor tugs brought her and her cargo on to Amsterdam. The aptly named *Tempest* brings to mind the best name ever for a salvage tug: HMS *Turmoil*, famous for her WWII service on the icy "Murmansk Run" delivering war material to Russia through U-boat packs operating off Norway.

Don Elsman, Courtesy of Tschumi Offshore

Since the start of reliable motorized tugboating, large specialized salvage tugs (and tug-ships) have been built and maintained on station along busy or dangerous ocean shipping lanes. From 125 to 250 feet long, they have tall bows and bulwarks for heavy weather. Tall masts with cargo booms overhang bow and stern hatches with access to cargo holds filled with pumps, air compressors, cables, block and tackle sets, anchors, patching cement, and wood and steel to fashion covers over collision-damaged hulls. Heavy workboats are mounted for quick deployment in high seas, as well as seaworthy dories (now replaced by inflated zodiacs) to put men aboard the casualty.

Recently, larger and more reliable ships have replaced the enormous fleet of small, low-powered merchant ships that previously supplied abundant work for salvage tugs. Classification societies that rate the design of ships and inspect their condition on a regular basis for insurance companies have also done their part to weed out unsafe ships, so few new dedicated salvage tugs have been built recently.

At the same time, the worldwide search for undersea oil has produced hundreds of big, powerful anchor-handling tugs, spread through ports and backwaters around the globe. Intense competition for exploration efficiency leaves many capable older, rough-weather anchor handlers sitting idle. Their large open decks can be stocked with flown-in salvage gear, and the powerful winches are ideal for towing damaged ships or setting anchors for ground tackle. Salvage companies may have dedicated vessels, usually giant floating cranes for clearing wrecks, but mostly they maintain equipment warehouses near major airports. Salvage masters fly out immediately to a casualty, and call back for equipment to be flown in, while tugs, barges, and workboats are hired locally. Most equipment can be ferried by helicopter to boats at the scene.

The art of salvage, especially of a ship in immediate peril, is doing the almost impossible with almost nothing but tenacity and ingenuity, when each minute that passes can make the situation exponentially worse. Salvage crews bring experience, determination, and the stomach to get wet, oil-soaked, dirty, and exhausted, and stay that way for days without sleep as they crawl over and through dark, powerless, strange ships that could sink at any moment.

Why do it? Successful salvage is well rewarded, usually under the terms of Lloyd's Open Form (LOF), an agreement between the shipowner and salvage company that the salvage reward will be arbitrated later by Lloyd's of London, an insurance underwriting clearinghouse. Getting agreement to the LOF is often the first stressful hurdle for salvagers, as the shipowner on shore tries to determine how much danger its ship is in, while conditions on the vessel deteriorate. Often the captain is desperate to take the tug's line before things get worse, but managers safe on shore take their time to decide. The first line of the LOF is "NO CURE, NO PAY": if the ship is not saved, the salvage company gets nothing. Recent revisions reward the salvagers for pollution avoided in the effort, even if the ship sinks.

A New Zealand Air Force helicopter lowers a salvage master to the container ship *Rena* in October 2011 as anchor handler *Go Canopus* stands by. *Rena* had run into the charted and partially visible Astrolabe Reef fourteen miles off the coast of Tauranga, New Zealand. Her bow was driven over rocks barely under water, and she stopped with her stern hanging over deep water. Listing in the exposed ocean, waves soon toppled containers, and started to slowly tear the ship apart. The unsupported stern flexed in the waves, and cracks developed on both sides. Salvage firm Svitser marshaled teams and equipment from Holland and Singapore and hired local crane barges, small tankers and tugs, and a firm specializing in recovering floating and submerged containers (aided by the detection gear on New Zealand Navy mine hunters). Remotely operated subs hooked cables to sunken containers to eliminate the possibility of future pollution. Eventually almost a thousand of the 1,368 boxes were recovered. *Go Canopus* set anchors for the crane barges and received some of the *Rena*'s fuel into fuel cells lashed on her open stern deck. Salvors fabricated and welded level platforms on the sloping deck for portable generators and pumps, and a level copter pad on the bow. The ship's pumps were powered up to transfer fuel in tanks around the ship to stern tanks, where the fuel was pumped into a small tanker through heavy hoses dragged into the listing wreck. A large crane barge from Singapore lifted the toppled containers off in stacks of six.

Three months after the grounding, the stern separated completely and sank out of sight. Almost a year later, salvors were still cutting the bow into pieces, some small enough to be removed by helicopter. Several thousand birds were oiled, including a few penguins; the local population of an endangered species was quickly rounded up for safekeeping. The *Rena*'s captain and chief officer went to jail for seven months for "operating a ship in a dangerous manner, and attempting to subvert the course of justice by altering records afterward." They had taken an unauthorized shortcut to get to port before the tide changed.

New Zealand Defence Force

Salvage Chief was converted from a World War II Landing Ship Tank that had served in the Pacific, by dive master Fred Devine who bought her after the war and dropped in three salvaged LST electric mooring winches at the stern and three at the bow operated by five diesels running a generator. The salvage ship herself is propelled by two diesels. To pull a ship off the beach she attaches the stern winches to pad eyes welded to the ship's deck, and connects her bow winches to anchors dropped ahead. The winches crank, and the props add their thrust also. *Salvage Chief* has worked the Pacific Coast since 1948, from the *Exxon Valdez* wreck to the Panama Canal.

Local tugs rafted together to help with the pull

Cranes unloading cargo to lighten the load

Salvage Chief

The ship's fuel tanks being pumped out to lighten the load and reduce the risk of pollution if the ship breaks apart

Ballast tanks

Dredges and earthmoving equipment clearing sand and silt from around the hull

SALVAGING A SHIP ON THE BEACH

ALLISION is the term for a one-ship accident, which by definition involves something fixed: an anchored vessel, the beach, a rocky coast, bridge, pier, or riverbank. At sea the goal is to stabilize the vessel so it doesn't sink, then tow it to a repair facility. In groundings, the ship may not sink, but might be pounded to pieces against the shore by the surf. Salvors must overcome the friction of enormous weight never meant to bear on solid earth. Like a grounded whale whose weight crushes its internal organs, a grounded ship's hull is stressed in ways never designed for. It takes days to prepare a dry dock, using builder's plans, so a ship can sit safely on carefully spaced blocks. When such an enormous bulk is haphazardly tossed on shore, afloat at the stern, aground at the bow, quick action by salvors must pump ballast around (in a ship that may have no power, miles from any port) to stabilize the hull, and pump out the fuel tanks onto barges to avoid pollution if the ship breaks up. When a ship goes aground, local harbor tugs are usually the closest, so all tug crews have to have knowledge of salvage operations. After stabilizing the ship, the process of refloating may take months, or the ship might come off on the next high tide with a couple of tugs pulling. The tough cases involve repairing the hull to make it watertight, then pulling with a combination of tugs, anchors attached to pulleys on the ship (beach gear), and barges hired locally and fitted with hydraulic pulling gear flown in for the operation. Pulls are scheduled for the highest tide of the month.

The ship's ballast tanks and pumps, normally used to level the ship as cargo is discharged, are pressed into service in a grounding. When the ship first grounds, they may be pumped full of seawater to hold the hull on the bottom so waves don't lift and drop the ship, which could break it apart. As the ship is pulled free, ballast may be shifted to the buoyant area of the hull, lifting the pressure on the end that is hard aground. If waves drive the ship sideways on a beach, the first task may be to dig or dredge enough sand to rotate her so one end faces the sea.

GROUND TACKLE, made up of blocks of sheaves in opposition,

is used to increase the pulling force of the ship's own winches. When salvors arrive on scene, they have to improvise with whatever is at hand. If the ship can still provide power, the various winches scattered around the deck, for pulling mooring lines or loading cargo, are pressed into use to pull the ship off the beach. Many sets of ground tackle can be deployed, each attached to a different winch. Older ships had cargo winches at each hatch, so multiple tackle sets could be led off to rock ledges or anchors, or even to tugs anchored nearby.

The fixed block is attached to bollards on deck, and, in the example depicted, the traveling block is connected to an anchor offshore. The running cable (yellow) is connected firmly to the fixed block, then passes over eight sheaves on the way to the mooring winch. Each pass over a sheave takes some of the pulling force. As the traveling block is pulled toward the fixed block, each sheave feels a ton of force, for a total of eight tons. The mooring winch is pulling at one ton, but pulls eight feet of cable for each foot the blocks are pulled together. This is the mechanical advantage: greater length at low power equals higher power over a shorter distance. If the anchor is firmly set, the only movable object is the ship.

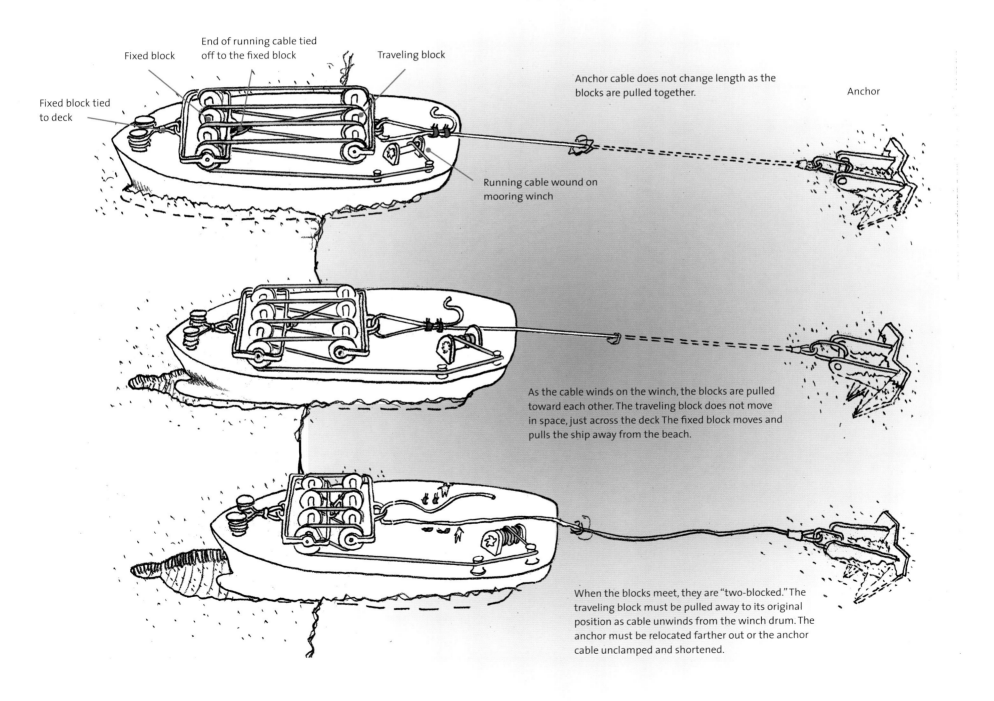

Fixed block tied to deck

Fixed block

End of running cable tied off to the fixed block

Traveling block

Anchor cable does not change length as the blocks are pulled together.

Anchor

Running cable wound on mooring winch

As the cable winds on the winch, the blocks are pulled toward each other. The traveling block does not move in space, just across the deck The fixed block moves and pulls the ship away from the beach.

When the blocks meet, they are "two-blocked." The traveling block must be pulled away to its original position as cable unwinds from the winch drum. The anchor must be relocated farther out or the anchor cable unclamped and shortened.

FIREFIGHTING

In 1991, the ultra-large crude-oil carrier (ULCC) *Haven* was unloading part of her one-million-barrel cargo at an offshore platform near Genoa, Italy. *Haven* had been hit by an Iranian missile in 1987 during the Iran-Iraq war, and had spent years neglected and then in dry dock. She was on her first voyage after being rebuilt. Her master reported a fire around noon, and a Genoa pilot boat rushed out the seven miles to her mooring. As the pilot boat arrived about fifteen minutes later, they were on the radio with the master when the ship exploded near the bow. The radio went dead, and nothing was ever heard or seen of the master again. Burning oil spread around the ship, and the pilots headed to the stern, where there were fewer flames on the ship or the water. They dragged eighteen oil-coated crewmen from the burning water, almost swamping the small pilot boat. The tug *Istria*, of the Genoa towing company Rimorchiatori Riuniti (*rimorchiatori* is Italian for tugboats), picked up two more of the crew. Eventually eight of their tugs spread floating booms and sprayed water on the burning tanker and the surrounding oil before authorities decided that the oil should be left to burn. On the second day, the harbormaster ordered the tugs to tow the burning hulk closer to the coast, where cleanup would be easier.

The bow had broken off, and the forward end of the remaining hull sank low in the water, raising the stern to expose the rudder and propeller. One tug and a fireboat approached through flaming oil, and a messenger line was passed from the tug around the rudder to the fireboat, and back to the tug. The messenger line was followed by a steel cable, and several tugs began towing the hulk toward the designated flat-bottomed spot, about five miles toward the coast. Smoke and flames filled the sky from the tanker as it was towed across the Mediterranean for six hours. It exploded and sank as they towed, in 328 feet of water, and leaked oil for the next twelve years, even after the cargo was pumped out.

Associated Press

Tugs are usually the first responders to fires on the water. They are available, since they have a lot of downtime between assignments, and crews are experienced in improvisation and working around other vessels. Most tugs are equipped for firefighting, and some have contracts with petroleum terminals that specify the level of firefighting ability of the tugs. Most tugs have a fire monitor connected to a fire pump. Tugs specifically rated for firefighting ability meet classification-society standards. Most new harbor tugs are built to meet FiFi 1, which requires two monitors capable of throwing water 120 meters (394 feet), a deluge sprinkler system that sprays water over the tug to protect it from the fire's heat, and ability to fight a fire for twenty-four hours. FiFi 2 is the standard for anchor handlers and other large ocean tugs requiring two monitors capable of throwing 180 meters (590 feet), or three or more monitors throwing 150 meters (492 feet). No deluge system is required because of the standoff distance allowed by the long water stream.

Tugs are uniquely capable as firefighters. Their maneuverability allows them to move slowly around the casualty and use their drives to counteract the backward force that the water jets impose on the spraying vessel. Tug engines are sized to push giant ships, so when idling at a fire there is plenty of power available for the takeoffs that spin the pumps. Some tugs have telescoping masts that lift fire monitors to spray down on deck or into the hold. Dedicated fireboats are often based on tug designs, since their requirements are so similar. Smaller cities may contract with a tug company for harbor fire response instead of paying for a dedicated fireboat.

ART OF SALVAGE

Marek Sarba recreates maritime tug scenes based on researching events and the vessels involved. He is also, not incidentally, a former officer on Polish salvage tugs, which adds immediacy to his depictions of weather and seas. *Drifting East* is based on an episode in Farley Mowat's book *The Grey Seas Under*, as *Foundation Franklin* maneuvers in a gale to connect a towline to the drifting *Empire Abbey* in mid-ocean. The ex–Liberty ship had left Bristol, England, empty and therefore riding high, to pick up postwar food relief in New Brunswick, then fought heavy weather for sixteen days trying to cross the Atlantic. Each time the ship was tossed up by a wave, her prop came out of the water to run free, then suddenly was jolted as it plunged back in the water and came under load again. Finally the 16-inch-thick propeller shaft snapped and the crew sent out an SOS. Continuing gales pushed *Empire Abbey* 120 miles back east in the two days it took *Franklin* to fight 500 miles to her side. Finding her without radar took educated guesses from the tug crew, based on years of sailing the stormy North Atlantic, aided by primitive radio-direction-finding equipment. The towing connection was made in another gale, followed by two broken towlines and eight days of fighting to the west (at one point tug and ship were forced 50 miles backward). *Franklin*'s engineers shut and opened the steam valve to the engine on every big wave to protect their own shaft. Early on the eighth day of the tow, *Franklin* received a Morse code message from *Empire Abbey*: OUR CAPTAIN HAS JUST DIED HE HAD NOT SLEPT FOR 13 DAYS. Eventually the *Empire Abbey* was towed to Halifax. *Franklin* looks like a short tug with a tall pilothouse, but only because her afterdeck is buried in the sea in this view. Built in 1918 as the naval salvage and rescue tug HMS *Frisky*, she was rescued from depression-era neglect in Germany by a seasoned Canadian captain who recognized a classic Clyde-built vessel that would be perfect as the backbone of a new Canadian salvage company.

Drifting East,
by Marek Sarba,
oil, 16 x 20 in.

Conclusion

This image by renowned photographer David Plowden was included in his 1976 book *Tugboat*, marketed as "juvenile" but really for all ages. He threaded the narrative of a day in the life of the *Julia C. Moran* in New York Harbor among photographs recorded over a year. This view of undocking and sailing the *Mormaccape* from Brooklyn's Gowanus Canal captures the essence of tugboating: deckhand Ollie Woodcock adjusts the hawser as mate Russ Syvertsen stands high above, between the wheel and the open pilot-house window, to talk with Ollie. Probably few words are necessary between these two after years of dockings and undockings together. Two men on their capable boat, a looping hawser, the swoops of the hull of a ship looming over, and the roiled liquidity of the water in the foreground kicked up by the tug's propeller as they back away, all captured in an everlasting fraction of a second from their daily lives.

David Plowden

I know a number of architects like myself who are interested in tugs. They are creative people who design every day. Why do such workmanlike objects appeal to them as they do to me? Perhaps that is a window to tugs' appeal to everyone else. As architects, we are usually starting with a structure meant to be concealed, then cladding it to "express" the structural and functional forces that went into the design.

Tugs are designed, certainly, but the extreme and punishing environment they work in guides most of the design decisions. The distinctive curves and steps, pronounced pilot-house, and air of sturdiness are all defined by the requirements of towing and shiphandling. There's not much about a tug that's the result of a purely aesthetic decision, and yet they have an undeniable character that transcends their utilitarian function. Of course, talented naval architects can take the already-interesting program for a tug, and then make it grand, or dramatic, or beautiful.

Many people are attracted to the sleek, the new, the glamorous: Jaguars, executive jets, swoopy fiberglass-hulled pleasure yachts. Those of us with more proletarian tastes enjoy an affection for the sturdy, the robust: a beautifully detailed Kenwood or Peterbilt semi-tractor, or a fat stubby C-130 Hercules transport plane — or almost any tug.

Satisfaction is a state of pleasure, of contentment. Looking at *Saturn*, here passing up Boston's Chelsea Creek in the colors of Eastern Towboat Company, it's a pleasure to experience her "rightness": homely, handsome, noble, forthright.

Saturn was built in 1907 as a steam tug, to service ocean ships that came up the Delaware to Philadelphia. In 1947 her steam engine was replaced by a diesel taken out of a World War II Landing Ship Tank. She later became the *Muriel McAllister*, then went to Boston, then to Maine Maritime Academy. She is now under restoration by the Friends of *Saturn*, in Winterport, Maine.

James Giammatteo

Acknowledgments

After I sent a rough set of pages out to publishers in 1996, I was shocked when our architectural office manager told me W. W. Norton had called. When I returned the call, Editorial Vice President Susan Barrows Munro told me that when she brought a stack of submissions home to review, she'd had to fight her husband over whose bedtime reading *The Life of Tugs* (as it was then named) would be. So she took a leap and signed me up. Neither of us knew it would take me twenty more years to complete. People say they've never seen a book like it, and now I can tell you why. Third editor extraordinaire Jim Mairs bravely defended the book when an editorial board, ten years in, asked him why Norton was publishing "a book like this." Maybe more to the point, not like "that." It's more an enthusiast's scrapbook than a linear narrative. Thanks also to first editor John Barstow and W. W. Norton itself, for having such a great team, and the longevity to match my procrastination, and to final editor Elisabeth Kerr who quickly and gently put an end to it. And at the end, copy editor Nancy Green was the best reader the book will ever have, with recommendations on connectivity and comprehension far beyond what I expected of copy editing. Book designer John Bernstein provided a playful touch that matches the book's tone, presented complex ideas simply and clearly, managed the varying quality of one-hundred amateur and professional photos spanning three centuries, and added dynamic color to my drawings up to the last possible second before printing.

I am grateful for the support and indulgence of my friends and colleagues Dan Dyer, Myron Miller, and Will Spears, whose architectural office and copiers got lots of off-hours use in assembling all the complicated pieces of this book over the years.

Thanks to my critical readers through the years, who told me what they read, as a corrective to what I thought I wrote: my brothers Rob, Pete, and John Pat; coworkers Maria Barral, Marrikka Trotter, Sherri Rullen, Donna Harris, David Anderson, and Roberto Illanes. And to steady boosters and early readers Rick Shea, Mike McGowan, and David Eppstein. And to Walker Shields, a patient guide for many years.

Tug enthusiast and author Steven Lang's definitive *On the Hawser* was a fountain of information and the example of a book that takes months of intermittent study, with time off for digestion, and that you can pick up with satisfaction year after year. I am grateful for all the images from his collection that appear here.

Tug enthusiast and naval architect Brent Dibner was generous with his advice and photo collection, including what might be the best photo in the book: the 1930s view of the tug *Ned Moran* being towed alongside a tanker.

I thank Brian Gauvin and Alan Haig-Brown, professional photographers and vagabonds I got to know online through *Professional Mariner* magazine, for their patience, and for sending so many images I could choose among. As our shipping fleet declines, tugs are one of the few opportunities outside the navy for Americans to make a life on the water, so *Professional Mariner* covers tugs extensively. Publisher Alex Agnew and editor John Gormley put out an essential and fun magazine that suits both the industry and enthusiasts, and is the source of much of the background information assembled in this book. Photographer John McGrail has waited since 1998 for me to use his classic, beautifully composed tug-life photos from the 1970s and '80s.

Some incredibly talented tug crewmember–photographers have contributed images of tugs and crews at work, among them Pat Folan of everywhere there's enough water to float a tug on the East Coast; Christian Romberg, North Sea anchor-handler skipper of Norway; and Captain Jan Berghuis of Holland and the rest of the globe. For all the industry administrative professionals who tracked down company photos for the book, I'll thank one to stand for all: Cori McPherson of BC Hydro, who spent six months patiently tracking down the right person to ask for permission to publish the river towing shot of three little tugs pushing a delivery barge upstream against a mountain river's current.

Boston-area tug operators and characters Russell Tripp of Bay State Towing and Skip Lee and Arthur Suprenant of Boston Towing and Transportation let me experience a little of tug life on the water. The Boston/New England Chapter of the World Ship Society gave me companionship, and an introduction to the Boston Harbor Tug Muster I helped to organize for several years, which gave me once-a-year access to Boston Harbor's tug fleet and community. Doug Dellaporta allowed me onto my first tug, *Saturn* (which also ends this book), at a Tug Muster after I incoherently waved a few rough pages of an idea for a book on tugs. And Conrad Roy and family always welcomed me and my wife on their boats.

My family has put up with my absence as the book took most of my free time: my lovely wife Gloria, children Alejandro, Yliana, and Hernan, and friend of the family and honorary grandchild Izzy. The pleasures of writing this book remind me of an episode with Izzy: a four-year-old sitting in my lap at my tiny drawing board on the top-floor landing under the skylight, as we sketched a progression together: egg to tadpole to frog. When we finished, he rushed downstairs waving our drawing: "Look, Mommy, we got the 'structions for frogs!"

Thanks to Mary Jane Brazet for years of dedicated tutoring that allowed Alejandro to read this book.

Maurice Smith tried to teach me architecture at MIT, but what I learned from him instead was to look for the essences of things, the meaning/resonance/particularity of forms and materials. What is *this*, how is it different from *that*, and how can the difference be accentuated to make being alive more awesome. And that architects could love words as well as forms. And a nod to architecture as a vocation. It trains you in many useful skills: analysis, synthesis, communication, understanding systems from built assemblies to social organizations, and how to recognize and exploit the surprising connections between the two.

And spending part of each day solving three-dimensional puzzles by idly scribbling on tracing paper is pleasant mental exercise.

Gaston Bachelard's *The Poetics of Space*, originally read in the context of architecture, gave me license to explore the emotional resonance of objects like tugs, and the beauty available to tug crews in their everyday lives. *On Growth and Form* by D'Arcy Thompson informed my appreciation of scale as it relates to the limits of materials and shapes.

I have learned to appreciate photography in an age of video. It freezes an instant for examination, while in a video one is distracted by action, the story line, the sound. Photographs capture time by pulling out an instant that represents continuing time. A video comes to a conclusion, action ends, but a photograph always hangs on the edge between the previous moment and the one following, incomplete and full of potential. See Pat Folan's shot from his pilothouse window as a tug deckhand tosses a hawser across the gap to another on a barge, the rope forever hanging in space between them: thrown in the previous moment, to be caught in a future moment.

Ah, the drawings. It took ten years of rough sketching intended to guide a mythical illustrator who would intuit just the right feel and content, until I realized my limited talents were enough. I think the breakthrough was the series of tug hull chines viewed from underwater. The drawings owe more to *Mad* magazine's marginal Spy vs Spy cartoons and Richard Scarry's patient and charming drawings than to the world of art.

So, readers, thank you for making it possible to send this assemblage of ideas, conjectures, facts, fiction, doodles, and snapshots out of my head, and making it necessary to organize it into what I hope is a fun and rewarding immersion in this small but fascinating slice of Life on Earth.

Pat Folan